Teachers, Pupils and the Internet

**Una Cunningham
and Staffan Andersson**

STANLEY THORNES (Publishers) LTD

First published 1999 by
Stanley Thornes (Publishers) Ltd
Ellenborough House
Wellington Street
Cheltenham
GL50 1YW
UK

ISBN 0 7487 4307 3

99 00 01 02 03/ 10 9 8 7 6 5 4 3 2 1

Typeset by The Florence Group, Stoodleigh, Devon
Printed and bound in Great Britain by TJ International Ltd, Padstow,
Cornwall

Contents

About the authors

Una Cunningham has been a keen computer user with no technical interest for some 20 years. She is, however, a a keen Internet enthusiast. Her background includes teaching and lecturing in English, as well as research into language acquisition.

Staffan Andersson has been a teacher of computing and electronics since 1978. His experience of the Internet ranges from web design to the installation of LINUX-based web servers.

Together, the authors have written exclusively about the Internet and its uses in, and implications for, education.

Acknowledgements

The authors and publishers would like to thank the following people and organisations for permission to reproduce material:

Bible Gateway, Bill Arnett, City of York Council, Classroom Connect, Computer Industry Almanac Inc, JPL/NASA/Caltech, Network Wizards, NicoMak Computing Inc, Redacción El Diario, Volcano World; Netscape: Portions Copyright Netscape Communications Corporation, 1998. All Rights Reserved. Netscape. Netscape, Navigator and the Netscape N Logo are registered trademarks of Netscape in the United States and other countries; the British Educational Communications and Technology Agency (BECTa) for permission to reproduce the picture of the National Grid for Learning (NGfl) home page which is shown on page 68. Copyright in this work is the property of BECTa and further reproduction of it is not permitted under the terms of this permission.

Every effort has been made to contact copyright holders and we apologise if any have been overlooked.

Preface

The Internet has come to stay. In the space of a couple of years it has progressed from being exclusive to being commonplace. Political and commercial factors have combined to make Internet access cheaper and more widely available, for example in libraries and other centres as well as at home.

Nonetheless, not everybody has found the way to the Internet. There is concern that our society will be divided into those who can use the new technologies and those who cannot – a division every bit as devastating as any socioeconomical index. Schools have an important role in giving all pupils access to the tools they need to participate in the information society. An ability to read and write has always been important. Knowledge about computers and the Internet has now become another prerequisite for those who are to be full participants in society.

Many of those who have jumped onto the Internet bandwagon are younger, while many of those who have not are older. Teachers are, in this respect, no different from anyone else. Some teachers found the Internet intuitively attractive and immediately set about learning how to use it and devising ways to share its benefits with their colleagues and pupils. Other teachers were unfamiliar with computers and unsure whether their pupils would benefit from the Internet. They were unlikely to invest the time and energy necessary to learn about the Internet. Now the decision whether or not to learn about the Internet has, in many schools, been taken out of teachers' hands. There is no longer a choice. Schools are at the centre of our society and reflect changes in it. There is considerable political certainty about the benefits of the use of the Internet for information and communication in schools.

This book is intended for all teachers. Those who know little about the Internet will find an account of what the Internet is and instructions about how to use it for information and communication.

Those who know how to navigate the Web and use e-mail will find a discussion about how the Internet can be useful for teachers, both in their own preparation and with pupils in class. We present many educational web sites and other Internet resources.

Those who have been using the Internet for a while will find tips and ideas for using the Internet in specific school subjects. We suggest various kinds of activities, including collaborative projects which show pupils that their classroom is not isolated, but rather part of a world-wide community.

Those who are proficient Internet users will find ideas for developing web material of their own and a collection of useful links to others' web sites as well as suggestions for setting up their own collaborative projects.

The Internet is shaped by its users. It is what we make it. Traditionally, the Internet has been a very generous place, where knowledge and information are shared freely. The more of us who participate actively by taking part in discussions and creating web material, the better a place the Internet will become.

Visit the book's web pages (*http://www.thornes.co.uk/internet_add*) for updated links and don't hesitate to get in touch with your questions and comments.

Una Cunningham and Staffan Andersson 1999

liljansberg@starmail.com

What is the **Internet**?

The Internet – from Whitehall to the neighbour's eight-year-old, people are talking about it as though it had always been a part of their lives. Parents, pupils and the education authorities are urging that the Internet be incorporated into education. But just what is it? The World Wide Web is often described in the media, with colourful pictures and text on a computer screen, but the Internet has more to offer than that.

This chapter will let you get acquainted with the Internet with a brief introduction to some of the services it offers.

The Internet and other computer networks

History

The Internet's origins in the dark ages of cold-war military intelligence are well known by now – the US authorities wanted to develop a bombproof way to communicate. In 1969 an embryo network, ARPANET, was set up with just four computers at the University of California at Los Angeles (UCLA). Since computer time was extremely expensive in those days the idea was that scientists could communicate with each other using electronic post and share computer resources. Their text-based messages and data were the only traffic for many years.

In 1973, the first non-American connections to ARPANET were established, including one to University College in London. Many other countries followed suit and now the Internet is truly global. Computers and entire existing networks were added to ARPANET throughout the 1970s and 1980s and the network came to be known as the Internet (or the *Net*).

E-mail is messages sent from one computer to another.

It was not until 1990 that the World Wide Web (often known as the Web) came to exist. At first, only text could be transmitted on web pages. In 1993 the program Mosaic, a forerunner of modern web browsers, was developed which meant that the World Wide Web could also involve pictures. That allowed the Web to become a global noticeboard. By 1995, the Web had become the most popular Internet service, overtaking **e-mail**, data transmission and other services. At around this time it became possible for private persons to engage the services of an Internet Service Provider (ISP) and get themselves online via a **modem** and a personal computer.

A **modem** is a device which allows computers to communicate via the telephone system.

The Internet today

The number of Internet users is impossible to estimate. Since there is no central registration required, no one can really hope to keep track of how many individuals currently have access to the Internet. People can use public connections, such as those in public libraries and Internet cafés, even if they do not have their own **account** with an ISP.

An Internet **account** is an arrangement whereby subscribers pay an ISP for access to the Internet.

Attempts have nonetheless been made to keep track of the Internet's exponential development. The number of computers which are connected to the Internet rose from about six million in 1995 to almost thirteen million by the middle of 1996. Many of these connected computers may in turn have provided Internet access to dozens, hundreds or even thousands of individuals via school or company networks or via modem connections to ISPs. Estimates of the number of individuals throughout the world who have access to the Internet vary, but figures from August 1998 suggest that over 130 million people around the world are online, and the Internet's expansion shows no signs of slowing down. In the UK, over seven million adults had tried the Internet by the end of 1997, almost 60 per cent up on the year before. As many as 35 per cent of all current users access the Web from home, and the overall frequency of usage has increased to over five times per week.

The Web

The best-known Internet service is the World Wide Web. Often when people talk about things they have found on the Internet, they are referring to information they have seen on a web page somewhere. But there is more to the Internet than the Web. There are several more-or-less separate Internet services existing side by side. E-*mail* is one such service. Others offer you the possibility of joining in ongoing discussions on any of thousands of predetermined topics. Some of these discussions are in real time as written or spoken communication with other people. This is known as *chatting*, and you can chat either by arrangement with people you know or just with anyone who happens to be around in the virtual world sometimes known as **cyberspace**. Fantastic make-believe worlds have been set up in cyberspace and all comers are invited in to pass the time of day in a virtual pub or to play dungeons-and-dragons-like games with others elsewhere. The main

Cyberspace is the imaginary (virtual) place where Internet activity happens.

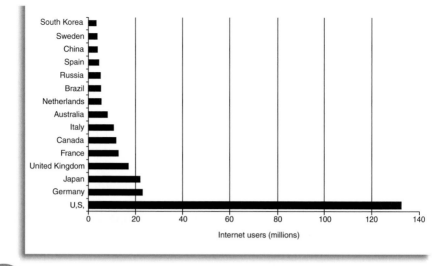

1.1 *Predicted world distribution of Internet users in 2000*

Copyright © 1998, Computer Industry Almanac Inc., Arlington Heights IL, USA (www.c-i-a.com)

difference between the Internet services available is that some of them, such as chatting and games, are real time, that is your message gets through instantly and you can get an immediate response; the assumption is that both parties are present at the same time. Other services, such as the Web and e-mail, do not require the person receiving the message to be online at the same time as the person sending it. A web page is available to anyone who knows its address until it is removed; an e-mail will lie in the recipient's mailbox until she has time to open it.

Information, contact and sharing

The Internet services all have in common the sending of information from one computer to one or more others. What started off as a way for scientists to share expensive computer facilities has developed into something much more useful for the rest of the population. As more individuals are gaining access to the Internet at school, at work and at home, the Internet's usefulness is increasing, just as the newly invented telephones did not become really useful until enough people had one. The uses of the Internet fall into three main functions:

❑   the transfer of information from a sender to one or many receivers

❑   direct contact between two or more individuals who are, thanks to the Internet, able to communicate with each other easily, quickly and cheaply

❑ the means for people to share their work or their knowledge with other users.

When the Internet is discussed in connection with education, the assumption is often made that it is most interesting as a source of information. The Web's apparently endless procession of colourful pages where all sorts of topics are presented for the entertainment and/or education of any one who is interested may seem to be a teacher's dream come true. At last, teachers and pupils have access to an up-to-date source of facts and figures and can compare different points of view. They can simply follow a series of links and surf their way from one page to the next. Searching for information about a particular topic couldn't be easier: just by typing in a key word in a search engine's window you can get thousands of tips about where to look for information about your subject.

In fact, as we shall see, things aren't always quite that simple. Information from the Internet needs to be scrutinised meticulously, especially if it is to be used by pupils: Where does it come from? Who wrote it for whom and why? When was it written? Is the information correct? There is no central organisation or standards committee who sees to it that everything is done professionally and correctly. The Internet is a free-for-all. But you are free to join in to make the Internet a better place.

You can contribute

The passive reception of information from the Web is only one side of the coin. Everything that's out there has been put there by someone. Thousands if not millions of people around the world are each looking after their own corner of the Web. Why not let others use those lesson plans that you spent such a long time getting right? Next time you might find that you can use someone else's plans. There are quite a few web sites for teachers where such input is welcome. In time you may prefer to make your own web page, maybe with your pupils. There are, as we shall see, a great many schools with their own web pages. These can be used for anything from boasting about the school's league-table placement to publishing student work.

Getting in touch

The potentially most revolutionary aspect of the Internet is its communication facilities. A good deal of the latest technological advances are in this part of the Internet. As more and more people get an e-mail address the way we communicate is changing. E-mail combines the best of written communication channels (such as having time to think about what you want to say, and not disturbing the recipient by demanding

instant attention the way a telephone call does) with speed of transmission and an informality of expression which increasingly resembles
the spoken language. While a letter or a fax would be oddly abrupt if
it did not have the form of a traditional letter with its rather formal
salutation and closing phrases, an e-mail of one or two lines is quite
in order. It is even possible to attach other kinds of documents to an
e-mail. Such communication is clearly much quicker than a phone call,
and may in time replace a good deal of communication between, for
example, members of the public and the council or the tax office. We
may choose to use the phone only when the call has a social function.

A **mailing list** is
a group discus-
sion via e-mail.

A **newsgroup** is
one of thousands
of open discus-
sion forums in an
area of cyber-
space known as
USENET.

**Video confer-
encing** is a
communication
system where two
or more people
can communicate
using sound and
images.

The Internet lets us come into contact with people with whom we
have something in common but would otherwise have been unlikely to
come across. It is possible to join a **mailing list**, which is a kind of
discussion group on a particular topic where anything anyone says is
sent to all the list's members. These discussions are sometimes referred
to as computer conferences. **Newsgroups** are open, ongoing discussions which you can listen in on without being observed whenever you
want. The e-mail addresses of the discussion's participants are given
so you can get in touch directly with any one you want to. You can
telephone your friends or colleagues with the Net's help, hold **video
conferences**, play games with friends or other users, and many other
things. The applications of Internet technology are developing continuously. It has jokingly been said that there are seven Internet years in
each human year, just like for dogs. When you read this, this book will
already be somewhat out of date.

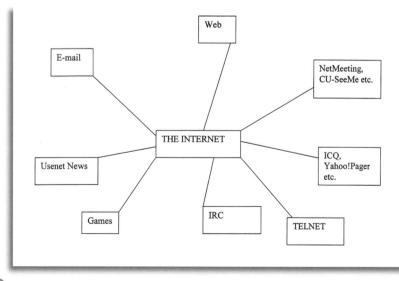

1.2 *Main Internet services*

Intranets

Intranets are computer networks which use Internet technology for communication within a single organisation. An intranet can be used for spreading internal information, for example on web pages or by electronic post. Intranets can be connected to the Internet, although the idea is that unauthorised Internet users cannot gain access to documents on the intranet. To accomplish this the intranet is usually separated from the Internet by a program known as a *firewall*, which regulates what external users are allowed to do inside the intranet while making it possible for intranet users to access Internet material.

 In practice

School intranets

An intranet is a practical way for schools to make best use of their computer network. Internal e-mail is not only a useful way for teachers to communicate with each other, but also a relatively safe way for pupils to learn about e-mail. Web pages with anything from the week's lunch menu to class project presentations or the school telephone list can be placed on the intranet. Different users can be given access to different parts of the intranet. The firewall protects the material from outsiders, but can even be configured to allow certain groups (e.g. parents) access from outside by password.

Getting started

Your first steps out into cyberspace are not difficult, and there is plenty of help and advice available to you. Remember you are not alone! Despite rumours to the contrary, there are still a good many people who have not yet used the Internet. Many schools have gained Internet facilities without giving a thought to the fact that few teachers have been given any training or information. This is, hopefully, a temporary problem. In time, almost all teachers will have had some kind of Internet training, whether as a formal in-service training (INSET) course or as an informal briefing from the school's technician. Newly qualified teachers will often be expected to lead the way in this respect.

It is often left up to IT enthusiasts to introduce the Internet into a school. Schools which are not lucky enough to have such a member of staff may find themselves left behind and be obliged to catch up when pupils and parents start wondering why the school is not online. There is nothing intrinsically difficult or even especially technical about using the Internet once everything is set up. You can leave technical details in the hands of those who enjoy such things (the school technician or an ISP) and move on to the interesting bits.

Prerequisites

There are few schools nowadays which are completely without computer equipment. Even if the number of pupils per computer is higher than you might wish, it may still be possible to use the Internet in a meaningful way. The logistics involved in setting up an Internet server for the school, or for hooking up an existing computer network to the Internet, are beyond the scope of this book. Ask your technician or an ISP. Otherwise, the method of getting Internet access to a school computer is very similar to the position for a private person. Basically, you need a computer and some way of having it communicate with an ISP's computer.

You do not need a very modern computer to gain access to the Internet: if you use a PC (IBM-compatible) computer, you will need at least a 486 processor, 8Mb RAM and SVGA graphics (with at least 256 colours) if you want to see the Web's pictures properly. In general, the better the computer, the faster and easier it will be to use the Internet. A sound card and microphone are becoming increasingly desirable as more and more use is being made of sound files on the Net, for music, sound illustration to web pages, voice communication, for example Internet telephony, or other real-time applications. If you will want to participate in video communication, a faster computer and a simple web camera will be required. These are not expensive. The computer does not need to have a CD-ROM drive.

For users of Macintosh and other computers similar requirements apply – while newer means better, you don't need the most modern computer available. Talk to an ISP about what they recommend. BT Internet, for example, recommend at least the following minimal requirements:

❑ For Windows 95 users, an IBM-compatible PC with at least a 486 processor and at least 4Mb RAM. An alternative is an Apple Macintosh or Power Macintosh with at least a 68030 processor and at least 8Mb RAM.

❑ A hard drive with at least 15Mb of free space.

❑ An internal or external CD-ROM drive (if you're installing from the BT Internet CD-ROM).

❑ A telephone line or ISDN line if you are connecting through ISDN.

❏ A spare serial communication port (PC users) or modem port (Macintosh users).

❏ An internal or external modem capable of 9,600bps or an ISDN terminal adapter.

❏ Microsoft Windows 95 or 98, Windows NT version 4.0 or later, Windows 3.x, Windows for Workgroups 3.x or Macintosh System 7.1 or later – System 7.5 is recommended.

Modems and ISDN

One way for a single computer to communicate with an ISP is by modem. A modem is a kind of telephone for computers. The most modern modems are very fast. A modem uses the normal phone lines to transmit and receive data from the Internet. A major disadvantage of this method of communication is that it may block the phone for incoming and outgoing calls. Unless there is an extra telephone number available for the computer this could be a problem. It is generally a concern for those who connect to the Internet from home. New technologies are becoming available in response to this problem. ISDN lines, for example, allow voice communication as well as faster communication between computers and will even allow you to use the phone at the same time as your computer is online.

ISDN is a good choice for schools who plan to use the Internet a good deal. ISDN is a new kind of telephone connection which enables computers to transmit a great deal of data very quickly. A single computer or an entire network can be connected to the Internet using such a connection via an ISP. Cable companies and British Telecom (BT) have, at the time of writing, offered ISDN connections to schools at rates which compare favourably with the cost of standard telephone connections. Schemes such as BT's popular *Schools Internet Caller* allow schools unlimited ISDN access to the Net during the day for a flat fee. This means that school computers can be continuously online without schools having to worry about the phone bill.

The Office of Telecommunications (OFTEL) Education and Public Access Points Task Force recommend 'a baseline of digital connectivity at ISDN or equivalent (at least 128kbit/sec) to be available to all UK schools'. There are other, more expensive, options, such as dedicated or leased lines if greater capacity is needed. Other possibilities, such as the Internet via cable TV networks, the electricity net or satellite, are being developed.

Internet Service Providers

Your computer needs a program to help it communicate with the ISP's computer via the modem or ISDN connection. If you use a newer Macin-

A **browser** is a program used to view web pages, e.g. Netscape and Microsoft Internet Explorer.

tosh, Windows 95 or a newer Windows version this facility may already exist in your computer. You will also need some kind of web **browser**, and possibly a separate e-mail program. There are other programs which you may want to use, but you will generally download them directly from web sites as they are needed.

Most ISPs provide you with everything you need, usually preconfigured so you need only install the programs in your computer. The quality of their introductory program pack is one of the service providers' most important means of competing with each other.

When choosing an ISP there are several important points to bear in mind.

❑ *The* ISP'*s rates*. Most providers offer unlimited access for a flat rate. There are, however, those who charge by the hour. If you do not expect to spend many hours online each month, this might work out cheaper, but you may find that you soon spend longer online than you had thought possible!

❑ *Your telephone bill*. Many providers offer local call access to the Internet. Others do not, and you may find yourself having a hefty bill for hours of long-distance calling if you are not located near the provider. Several ISPs participate in BT's *Schools Internet Caller*, which provides unlimited access at a flat rate during the school day (till 6 p.m.).

❑ *The amount and quality of technical service available to you*. Most ISPs offer a support number which you can ring. Before you finally choose an ISP it might be worth trying the support number at different times of day to see if you can get through.

❑ *The ease of access to the* ISP. In some cases the ISPs capacity might be underdimensioned for the number of subscribers they have, which means that they cannot accept enough calls at the same time. Before you sign up you can check this by ringing up the **modem pool** number at different times of day. If the number is often engaged you might want to look elsewhere.

A **modem pool** is a group of modems connected to an ISP's server.

Bandwidth is the amount of data sent or received every second.

❑ *The* **bandwidth** *of the* ISP'*s connection to the Internet*. The greater the bandwidth the faster the connection.

Some ISPs specialise in offering connections to schools and other educational institutions. Educational ISPs may also offer attractive educational content to their subscribers. They will often be able to offer complete Internet packages at competitive rates. Any Internet magazine at your local paper shop will give you a list of several hundred ISPs and tell you how to contact them.

Going online

Case study

> ### *Meet Mary Smith*
>
> Let us introduce you to Mary Smith, an English teacher at a fictional comprehensive school in the Midlands. She has been using the Internet at home and at school for the last six months. The school has a network of PC computers: some 25 in a computer room and another 30 spread around the school's classrooms. Arrangements have been made for the teachers to have remote access to the school's computer network, so that teachers can get online from home after school hours if they have their own computers at home. There are many different technical arrangements which can be set up to allow this kind of remote access. When Mary wants to get online from home she starts a program which calls up the school's network server on the modem and asks her for her password. Once she has typed that in she can work as though she were sitting at one of the school's computers.
>
> Mary's teenage daughter Allison also likes to spend time online and has a lively correspondence with a young man in Sydney. She has a private Internet account with a national ISP. Their arrangement is that Allison uses a communication program provided by the ISP to dial up the ISP's modem pool and then she is greeted by a special welcome screen where she can choose which online function she wants to use. Allison does not have to write in her password every time; it is stored by the communication program.

The World Wide Web

As we saw above, the Web has quickly become the most popular Internet service. The combination of the possibility of making an attractive presentation of up-to-date information available to a large number of people around the world and the speed and ease of access to this information has led to the Web becoming a force to be reckoned with. It means not only that everybody, from a schoolgirl in the Hebrides to a multinational company in Singapore, has an equal chance of being seen, but also that there is (as yet) no centralised controlling body which is responsible for the quality of the information on the Web.

Anybody can put anything they want on a web page. While this can be seen a major leap forward for democracy, there is a clear need for web users to view all information gleaned from the World Wide Web as potentially false. This is naturally especially important when young people are to access the Web.

Hypertext and web structure

The World Wide Web is made up of documents which typically contain text and pictures, known as *web pages*. These pages are generally part of a *web site*, which is a group of related pages written by the same person or organisation. Web sites are ideally organised hierarchically. There is usually a main entrance to the site, called the *home page*. From there the reader can choose from a number of options each of which will take them to a different page or group of pages on the site.

Hypertext is a marked word or phrase which users can click on to be shown another document.

Links are web addresses or e-mail addresses associated with text or images in a web page.

One of the most revolutionary and attractive aspects of the Web is **hypertext**. The idea is that you start off by looking at a particular web page; on that page there may be a number of 'hot' words, marked in some way (often written in blue and underlined). These words (or phrases, or even pictures or buttons) are known as hypertext or **links**. When you guide the mouse pointer to a hypertext link the shape of the cursor changes and you can click on the word. What happens then depends on

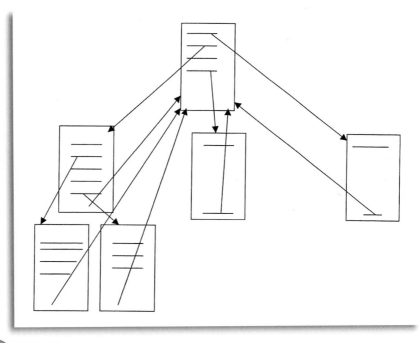

1.3 *Web site organisation*

where the author of the page wants to take you. You might jump to a place further down the page you were reading, or to another page in the same site or to a page on another computer in another country. In this way you can be given further information about a topic by another source.

How big is the Web?

The number of documents on the World Wide Web is impossible to estimate accurately. At the time of writing, the search engine AltaVista (a program which periodically visits all accessible web sites to index them) claims to cover some 31 million pages found on 627,000 servers. Many web sites are, however, protected from automatic visits of this kind for security reasons, so the total number is likely to be considerably larger.

A web address is an example of a **Uniform Resource Locator**.

Each web page has a unique address, which is called an URL (**Uniform Resource Locator**, sometimes pronounced *earl*). For example, the URL *http://www.thornes.co.uk* is the address of the home page of Stanley Thornes Publishers. The address tells you something about the site. Starting from the right:

.uk means that it is a UK site

.co means that it is a commercial site (as opposed to, say, *.ac* which is an academic site or *.sch* which is a school site)

Domain names *are registered names which refer to an individual's or company's space on the Web.*

thornes is the **domain name**, which is usually the name of the host computer

http://www indicates that it is a web page.

Other pages on the web site are usually located in the same directory on the server's hard disk or in subdirectories. Their name is tacked onto the main page's name, so that *http://www.thornes.co.uk/latest/newbooks.html* might be a page (*newbooks.html*) on the Stanley Thornes site in the subdirectory *latest* where a presentation of newly published books is given.

Did you know?

Domain names have to be registered with a central authority so that computers all over the world know where to find them. The number of registered domain names in the world exceeded one million in February 1997 and is still increasing rapidly.

A recent international agreement has expanded the number of top domain names. The *.com* top domain is popular with large companies but dominated by American corporations. Other top domains are *.org* for organisations, *.net* for network providers, *.gov* for governmental domains and *.edu* for education. There

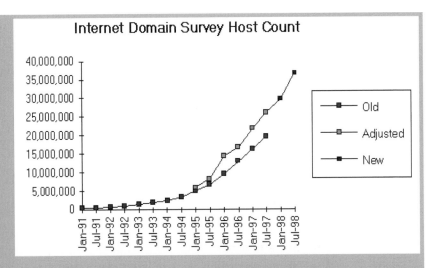

Internet Domain Survey Host Count

1.4 *Registrations of domain names, 1991–8*

Source: Network Wizards (www.nw.com)

have been many disputes about the right to the often fairly short domain names as companies with similar names have wanted to register the same domain name. These are now to be joined by a number of new top domains, such as *.nom* for individuals, *.firm* for general business and *.store* for the growing online shopping sector.

The alternative has been to register with a national organisation giving a local top domain, such as *.uk* for the UK, *.fr* for France and *.aus* for Australia. Some of these national top domains have further divisions, such as *.co.uk* for British commercial sites or *.nhs.uk* for National Health sites. The *.sch.uk* ending is for schools. Because of the large number of schools with similar sounding names, schools are to be registered according to a special convention: in England and Wales, the system is to use the LEA as the sub-domain, giving domain names like *school.derby.sch.uk*.

Web pages are of many different types. Some are very richly illustrated with image maps (large pictures which are made up of several clickable areas) or button bars. Others are mainly text, perhaps with a logotype and a coloured background. Some pages are such a riot of colour and complicated backgrounds that it is hardly possible to read the text on the page.

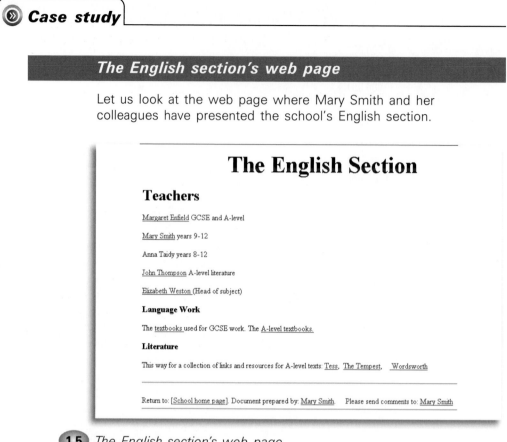

Case study

The English section's web page

Let us look at the web page where Mary Smith and her colleagues have presented the school's English section.

The English Section

Teachers

Margaret Enfield GCSE and A-level

Mary Smith years 9-12

Anna Taidy years 8-12

John Thompson A-level literature

Elizabeth Weston (Head of subject)

Language Work

The textbooks used for GCSE work. The A-level textbooks.

Literature

This way for a collection of links and resources for A-level texts: Tess, The Tempest, Wordsworth

Return to: [School home page]. Document prepared by: Mary Smith. Please send comments to: Mary Smith

1.5 *The English section's web page*

Each of the teachers, except Mary's colleague Anna Taidy who has not made her personal web page yet, has their name as a hypertext link. If the reader clicks on one of the underlined names he will be immediately transported to another web page where that teacher has put together some details about herself. Further down the page the reader can click on a link to a web page where there is some information about the textbooks used in language teaching. From that page there might be links out to the authors of the books or to the publishers. Under 'Literature' there are links concerning particular texts which are currently being taught. These may lead to student essays, external sites concerning Hardy, Shakespeare and Wordsworth, web pages and teaching resources put up by other teachers in other schools, or universities, or material written by the staff at Mary's school. This kind of page can be of interest to several groups of readers: other teachers at Mary's school who can keep up with what is going on in the English section, English teachers at other schools, parents and, not least, the pupils themselves.

Since it was Mary who put together the information on the page, she 'signs' it with her name at the bottom. This is a special type of hypertext link. If a reader clicks on it they are presented with a form which they can use to send an e-mail directly to Mary's e-mail address.

HTML

Web pages are written using HTML, a special kind of code which tells the web browser how to present the information. The HTML code contains, among other things, the addresses behind the hypertext links.

You can view the code used in any web page by selecting the option *Page Source* from the *View* menu. Fortunately, you do not have to write all these HTML codes yourself. There are a number of excellent editor and word-processor programs which transform ordinary text into HTML. The Netscape browser, for example, has an easily used editor, Netscape Composer, while Microsoft Explorer has Front Page Express (a budget version of Front Page, Microsoft's full-scale web editor). The newest versions of popular word-processor programs such as Word have a function whereby documents can be saved as HTML.

Browsers

Web browsers are programs which interpret the HTML code in which web pages are written. The browser turns HTML documents into easily read web pages with pictures, hypertext links to other pages on the site or to other sites and perhaps even the possibility of viewing a video clip or listening to a sound file, and attractive layout and backgrounds. A browser is generally part of the program package an ISP will provide for subscribers. New versions of browsers can be downloaded from Microsoft's and Netscape's web sites. Browsers are also usually included on the CD that comes with computer magazines.

There are several different web browsers available, but by far the most popular are Netscape Navigator and Microsoft Internet Explorer. These two browsers are really very similar, and which you choose to use has no real bearing on the way you will experience the Web. Both Netscape and Microsoft update their products frequently in their bid to outdo each other. They tend to add new features which they hope will make users switch to their browser. This means that they also strive to keep up with each other and thus remain reasonably compatible.

⊗ **Did you know?**

The first web browser, Mosaic, has now almost disappeared from the scene. Netscape took over the market almost completely by allowing their browsers to be downloaded free from the Net. Microsoft's browser, Internet Explorer, seized a large part of the market when it began to be sold as an integrated part of Windows 95. Subsequent updates of Internet Explorer can currently be downloaded at no charge from Microsoft's web site.

Netscape have attempted to hold on to the market by introducing new features to their products, so that web authors often had to warn readers that they needed Netscape's browser to view their pages. Microsoft developed their product to handle Netscape's enhancements, and added a few of their own, such as a parental control option (the possibility for parents (or indeed teachers) to block out pages containing certain words). And so it goes on. In their effort to outdo each other, these Internet giants continuously improve their products at little or no cost to millions of delighted users.

Netscape was for some time the standard browser preferred by most users. Microsoft's Internet Explorer is, however, currently more popular. Other browsers have similar functions. Let us look more closely at the functions browsers offer.

Microsoft's browser, Internet Explorer (Version 5.0, which is almost ready for release as we write) opens with a screen which has a menu

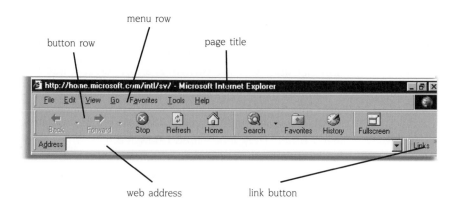

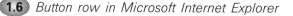

1.6 *Button row in Microsoft Internet Explorer*

row at the top and under that a row of buttons. The buttons are labelled *Back, Forward, Stop, Refresh, Home, Search, Favorites, History* and *Fullscreen.*

❑ The *Back* button is very useful, since it allows you to retrace your steps to the previous page from wherever you are, so there is no risk of getting 'lost'.

❑ *Forward* lets you go back to where you were before you pressed the *Back* button.

❑ *Stop* lets you stop the browser while it is loading in a page.

❑ *Refresh* tells the browser to load in the page again: this is useful with pages that are continuously updated or if the browser stops loading the site midway.

❑ The *Home* button will take you to whatever web page you have chosen to have as your starting-out page. That page will be loaded into the browser every time you start it up. You might have chosen your ISP's home page, or your school's web noticeboard, or perhaps a search engine's entrance page. (You can set a new page to start up on by entering the page address in the *Internet settings* under the *Edit* menu.)

❑ If you press the *Search* button, the browser will take you to a page where you can choose which of a selection of search engines you want to use. It is often quicker to go directly to whichever search engine you find suits you, but when you are starting out this selection can be useful.

❑ The *Favorites* button will save the URL of the page you are on in a special list so you can easily find it when you want to return to the page. It is possible to keep your favourites organised in separate files according to subject.

❑ *History* shows you (and anyone who wants to keep tabs on you) which pages you have visited. You can set *History* to save information about a certain number of days and you can also remove compromising pages from the History (by clicking on them with the right mouse button and choosing *Remove*) or erase the entire History (by choosing *Internet alternatives* in the *View* menu).

❑ *Fullscreen* hides all the buttons and menus so you can see more of a web page on the screen. Click the icon again to return to normal viewing.

Below this row of buttons there are some other functions, for example the *Address* panel where you can enter URLs. It also tells you the URL or file name of the page you are currently viewing. You can write in any address you please in this panel and as long as you are online, the browser

uick tip

If you are a PC user you can use your right mouse button to click on text, buttons or pictures. You then get a pop-up menu of the options available to you right where you are. This works for both Netscape and Explorer.

page title

menu row

button row

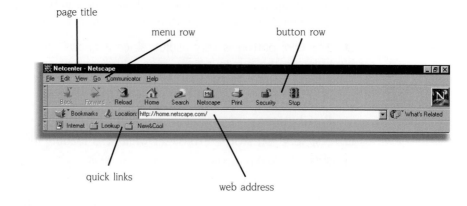

quick links

web address

 Button row in Netscape Navigator

will take you there if it can. To its right there is a button for collecting links so that you can easily find them again.

The differences between Netscape's and Microsoft's browsers are primarily cosmetic. The row of buttons at the top of the Netscape screen corresponds more or less to the Explorer buttons. Both browsers allow you to reduce the space taken up by these toolbars. Explorer has *Favorites* instead of *Bookmarks* and has an additional *Links* button where you can store a few currently important links. Otherwise, your choice of browser will not handicap you in any way.

Searching for information

Once you have got your browser up and running the next thing you will want to do is to start investigating the potential of the Web. You may have a few good addresses that you have seen in a newspaper or been given by a friend. You can just go ahead and type them in the location/address panel at the top of the screen. Make sure you copy the URL accurately, otherwise you will just get an error message. You must be careful about full stops and slashes and getting capital letters in the right places. Sometimes you can get an error message even if you have copied the address correctly. Perhaps the newspaper got it wrong, or maybe the page no longer exists. The Web is, after all, a dynamic environment and pages get changed all the time. There is a list of links for the sites mentioned in this book in Appendix 4, but by the time you read this a good few of them will be out of date. (Visit our web site for an updated list.)

If the address you have does not get you to where you thought it would, you might like to try to go back a step, to the page above the one you were looking for in the hierarchy of the web site. For example, if you typed in *http://www.school.lea.sch.uk/teachers/msmith*, which was the personal home page of our friend Mary Smith, and found yourself getting an error message, you could try deleting the final */msmith* or even */teachers/msmith* and see if that works. If it does you may find that the web site has simply been reorganised so that you can follow new links to the information you were looking for.

If that fails, the best way to find a page with information on a particular topic is to search for it. Sometimes when we talk to teachers who are learning about the Internet they say 'Just show me where the index is and I'll be able to find my way around'. Unfortunately, the Internet is not neatly catalogued and indexed like a library. Finding useful information on the Internet requires patience, imagination and a fair amount of luck. That said, there are some excellent tools at your disposal in the shape of search engines and web catalogues.

Search engines

A **newbie** is a person who is new to the Net.

Search engines scan the text of web pages keeping track of which words occur on which pages.

The easiest way for the beginner (**newbie** in Internet usage) to find **search engines**, i.e. programs which will find web pages containing the word or words you specify, is simply to click on the browser's *Search* button. This leads to a web page full of links to search engines.

1.8 *Netscape search page*

On this page there are a number of search engines, though the list is far from complete. Most of the engines listed here are American. There are several British and European search engines which may be more useful. Some of the American engines have British mirror sites (sites located on servers in the UK) and may be faster to access. They also give you the choice of whether you want to restrict your search to information held on British sites or whether you want to search through the entire World Wide Web. Which you choose will, of course, depend on the nature of the information you are looking for. These search engines work in slightly different ways, and we will look at three of them, *AltaVista*, *Infoseek* and *Excite*, to see how they compare.

AltaVista is a very popular search engine. Its searches will generally span the entire Web unless you specify otherwise using the advanced search facilities. Infoseek is one of the biggest engines around. Excite is currently our preferred search engine, because of the excellent facility for sorting results according to the site the pages found appear on. Both Infoseek and Excite have UK-based sites where you can easily choose to restrict your search to the UK only.

Refine your search

Making a well-defined search is a skill you will need to learn. Often when you search for a word or words you will be given thousands of suggestions in the form of information about pages on which the word occurs. The information you are given (the page's title and the first few lines of text unless the page's author has specified otherwise) is often not enough for you to decide whether or not the page is what you are looking for. Fortunately, there are ways to reduce the number of irrelevant pages turned up as a result of your search.

The following applies to all three engines:

❏ A search word written in small letters, e.g. *birmingham*, will also turn up pages where the word occurs with capital letters – *birmingham*, Birmingham, BIRMINGHAM, BiRmInGhAm, but the reverse is not true: BIRMINGHAM will find only BIRMINGHAM and none of the other variants.

❏ If it is important that words occur in a particular order you can enclose them in double quotation marks: "*the battle of britain*".

❏ Words that must occur in the documents the engine turns up can be immediately preceded by a plus: +*perfume* +*french*.

❏ Words that may not appear in the documents can be indicated using a minus: + "*Cliff Richard*" –*Shadows*.

In AltaVista only:

❏ If you write two or more search words, AltaVista will find pages where any one of the words occurs, although pages with more of the search words will be listed first. The other engines look for all the search words.

❏ You can use an asterisk as a wild card to match 0–5 lower-case letters as long as you have at least three letters preceding the asterisk. This is useful for finding variant spellings: for example, *hono*r* will return both *honour* and *honor*, or various forms of a word; *sing** will return *sing*, *sings*, *singer*, *singing* (as well as *singe*, *Singh*, *single*, etc.).

In Infoseek only:

❏ If you capitalise two or more adjacent words, Infoseek treats them as a single name or title, e.g. *Cliff Richard*, even without quotation marks. If you do not capitalise, *cliff richard* will turn up sites on seashore cliffs as well as the singing kind. If you want pages where both Cliff Richard and Paul McCartney are mentioned, you will have to separate their capitalised names with a comma, otherwise Infoseek will treat *Cliff Richard Paul McCartney* as a single long name.

There are other, more advanced search options, using the Boolean logic operators, AND and OR, etc. If you find you need to refine your searches further, you can consult the individual search engines' help facility.

❯ *Case study*

When was Tony Blair born?

uick tip

Remember to always ask yourself who stands behind the pages you get from this kind of search. A search engine will return a satirical attack on Tony Blair's character just as easily as official information.

Mary Smith was looking for some biographical background on Tony Blair. She decided to consult Excite's UK search to see if she could get any leads. She typed *"Tony Blair" +born* in the hope of getting some personal information. This proved to be a good tactic, and gave her several interesting leads to follow.

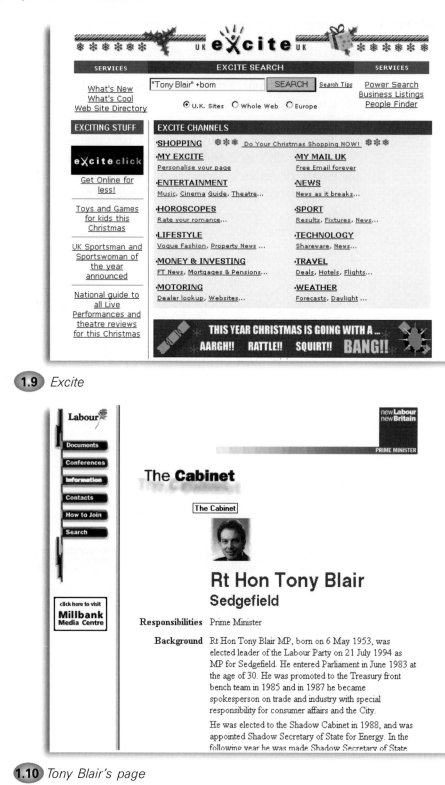

1.9 *Excite*

The Cabinet

The Cabinet

Rt Hon Tony Blair
Sedgefield

Responsibilities   Prime Minister

Background   Rt Hon Tony Blair MP, born on 6 May 1953, was
elected leader of the Labour Party on 21 July 1994 as
MP for Sedgefield. He entered Parliament in June 1983 at
the age of 30. He was promoted to the Treasury front
bench team in 1985 and in 1987 he became
spokesperson on trade and industry with special
responsibility for consumer affairs and the City.

He was elected to the Shadow Cabinet in 1988, and was
appointed Shadow Secretary of State for Energy. In the
following year he was made Shadow Secretary of State

1.10 *Tony Blair's page*

Catalogues

The search engines are only one of the possible ways you can look for information on the Web. There are also a few catalogues of pages – indexed and often summarised and even graded for the quality of their material. You will find them with the search engines when you click the browser's Search button. *Yahoo!* is the name of the first and biggest of the Web catalogues, but there are others. Yahoo! has a special catalogue for the UK and Ireland. Both Infoseek and Excite have catalogue components, and if you visit Infoseek's UK site you can use the UK catalogue UK*Plus*. These catalogues are organised hierarchically in directories.

Which way you choose to help you find the information you want depends on the kind of page you want to find. Had Mary instead been looking for information about the political parties of the UK she would have done better to consult one of these catalogues rather than a search engine. Under the path from *Regional* to *Countries* to *United Kingdom* to *Government* to *Politics* to *Parties* in Yahoo! we found a long list of links to parties' own information about themselves. UKPlus did even better with a brief description of each link in its list of parties which could be reached directly from the main UKPlus page.

There are other catalogues too: some aim to help you find the e-mail address and /or telephone number of private persons, or businesses. These catalogues are called White Pages and Yellow Pages respectively by analogy with the telephone directory. These services are not very well developed on this side of the Atlantic as yet, but they are on their way.

⨠ Communication

The potentially most revolutionary part of the Internet is not the deluge of information which is instantly available to anyone who wants it, although that is a major breakthrough. The Internet's communication capacity is beyond anything we ever imagined. Not only can you send a message to a person on the other side of the world in a matter of seconds at almost no cost, you can also come into contact with people you would otherwise never have met.

E-mail

E-mail is at the heart of the Internet's communication. It was one of the first services to be developed. It is as useful for communication between continents as for communication between teachers in a school. E-mail addresses are appearing everywhere now, from your bank statement to the credits of TV programmes. If you have Internet access at home or at school you probably have already been given an e-mail address. This is made up of two parts separated by a 'commercial *at*' symbol, @. The part after the @ is the same as we saw in web addresses: the domain name followed by the top domain.

⊗ *Case study*

E-mail addresses

Mary Smith's e-mail address is *msmith@school.lea.sch.uk*. Many school web sites and e-mail addresses follow this hierarchical convention with the name of the school followed by the name of the LEA and finally *.sch.uk* which tells us that the address belongs to someone associated with a UK school. The part before the @ is Mary's user name. Her school wants all the teachers to have their first initial and their surname as their user name. Unfortunately this means that Mary would have the same e-mail address as Michael Smith, the French teacher, so his user name was changed to *mike.smith*.

Using e-mail

Not all of your mail will require an answer from you. You can use mail to participate in mailing list discussions (or just to passively read the discussion) or to exchange personal messages with your friends and family. It can also be useful to communicate with your colleagues and

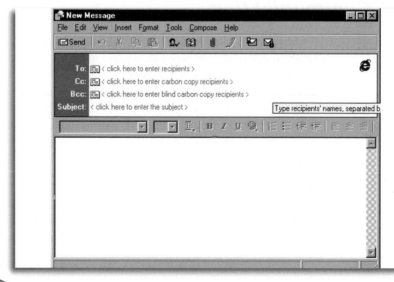

1.11 *The Cc: feature in Microsoft Outlook Express*

the parents of your pupils. When you want to reply to a mail, you need only click on the reply button at the top of the screen. Then you will be presented with an e-mail form with the address of the recipient already filled in. The program will also include the text of the message being replied to unless you set it not to (under *File*), and the subject line will be the same as the subject of the message you are replying to with the word *Re:* in front. You can change the subject line if you want. You can send a copy of messages you send to others, either openly (using Cc:) or without letting the primary recipient know that you are sending a copy to another recipient (using Bcc:).

⊗ Case study

E-mailing colleagues

One of Mary's mails has been sent to all the English teachers by a colleague in the geography section. He wants to know if anyone is interested in collaborating with him and his GCSE classes in an Internet project with a school in South Africa. The idea is that the pupils will exchange climate-related essays, discussing anything from 'The farming year in my country' to 'The worst thing about the weather here'. Mary sends an affirmative reply to him and copies her reply to the rest of the English teachers so they know the request has been dealt with.

Several different mail groups have been set up by the school technician so that some of Mary's mail comes to her as a member of *engteach@school.lea.sch.uk* (English teachers), some as *allteach@school.lea.sch.uk* (all teachers) and some as *GCSEteach@school.lea.sch.uk*, which is used for information for all teachers at the school who are preparing classes for GCSEs.

E-mail programs

Both Microsoft's and Netscape's web program suites have included acceptable e-mail facilities since version 4. Previously, the e-mail facilities built into web browsers have not been nearly as good as dedicated e-mail programs. *Eudora* is a widely used e-mail program. As it has both a **freeware** version and a professional commercial version with further refinements, it became popular with many users, ourselves included.

Freeware programs can be copied and shared at no cost.

The e-mail programs included in Microsoft's and Netscape's web suites have become progressively more advanced, but at the same time easier to use in successive versions. The help screens in the programs contain all the guidance you are likely to need. For the normal user, therefore, there is no longer any real reason to use a separate e-mail program.

Once you have your e-mail program up and running and you have got yourself online, the first thing you can do is to test the system by sending an e-mail to yourself. You may have to click on *Send and Receive* or *Get Msg* once or twice, but after a very short time you should be able to read your mail. The major advantages of e-mail over what is jokingly known as *snail mail* (ordinary posted letters) are the speed of delivery and the low cost of sending messages. While you can never be sure that an e-mail has arrived, it will often be returned if it has not been delivered.

Mailing lists

Writing letters to yourself is a pretty sad way to spend time, so you will probably want to make some new Internet acquaintances. One of the most productive ways to use e-mail is to join a few mailing lists, also known as mail groups, computer-mediated conferences (CMC) or e-mail discussions. Mailing list discussions are dedicated to a particular subject or group of people, organised so that all the list

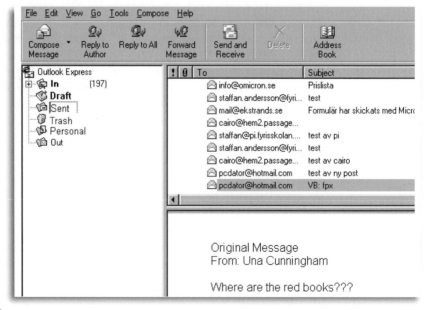

1.12 *Outlook Express*

members receive all the messages that are posted to the group as e-mails. Joining mailing lists does not generally cost anything, although some online service providers such as *CompuServe* and *America Online* do have their own discussion groups which are open only to paying members.

Finding a list

There are mailing lists on every imaginable topic, from pop groups' fan lists to lists where research scientists discuss the latest developments in their fields. There are several web sites devoted exclusively to helping you find a list suited to your professional or personal interests. *Liszt Search*, for example, allows you either to search among over 70 000 lists or to browse in their subject categories. Other similar sites are *Tile Net* and *List of Lists*, or for UK-based lists, *Mailbase*.

On a mailing list you can ask questions and hope to get an answer, either privately to your e-mail address or through the list if the answer is thought to be of interest to more people. When you are new to a list it is considered courteous to get a feel for the kind of discussion that is going on before jumping in to introduce yourself or ask a question. Many lists have a list of Frequently Asked Questions and answers (FAQ) which will be sent to you on request. If you can get hold of such a list you will not inadvertently bore list members by bringing up matters which have already been discussed at length.

Joining a list

There are several different kinds of mailing list. The difference lies in the kind of system which is used to administer the list. The two most frequent kinds of lists are LISTSERV and *Majordomo*. There is also the UK-based system, *Mailbase*, mentioned above. The commands associated with these are slightly different. You know which is which by looking at the list's administrative address, which is generally part of the information you will find in the list resources sites above. Which system the list uses has little practical importance for you. One minor difference is in the instruction you need to send to the list's administrative address if you want to join the list: to addresses with the word *majordomo* you send an e-mail with nothing in the subject line and the word *subscribe* followed by the name of the list. In LISTSERV lists you also need to include your name after the name of the list, otherwise the procedure is the same. Mailbase uses the command *join* instead. Some lists will require you to confirm your interest in joining them by replying to their initial message within a short period. Others will have a person to screen all applications for memberships. Some lists are moderated, which means that editors will read through all submissions before passing them on to the list – a safeguard against commercial messages (known as *spams* and totally inappropriate) or against unsuitable or irrelevant material. One of the lists we have been on is the UK-SCHOOLS list. You can join it if you send the words *join uk-schools* in the body (not subject line) of an e-mail to *mailbase@mailbase.ac.uk*. You will find other mailing list suggestions in chapter 3.

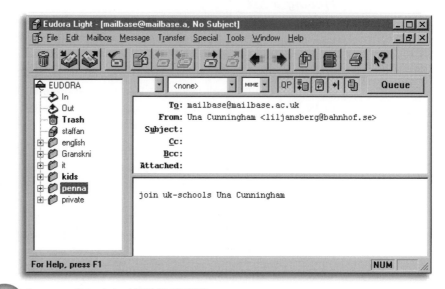

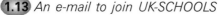 *An e-mail to join UK-SCHOOLS*

Case study

Mary joins a list

Mary has found a list for teachers of English as a second language, *TESL-L*. This is an area of some interest to her and she decides to join the list. According to the instructions she has found on the Lizst resource she needs to send an e-mail to the administrative address, *listserv@cunyvm.cuny.edu* with the text: *subscribe TESL-L Mary Smith*. This she does and within seconds she receives two messages from LISTSERV.

One of these is just a confirmation that she has subscribed while the other is a long message with all sorts of information about the list, for example that it currently has some 16800 members in 110 countries and a message average of 17 per day. The message gives the address to use to send mail which is intended for all the list members to read, and stresses the importance of not mixing up this and the administrative address. The information message has also a list of commands (such as the *subscribe* command) which must be sent to the administrative address where they will be automatically dealt with. The most important of these is the *unsubscribe TESL-L* command, which Mary will need if she ever wants to leave the list. Other useful LISTSERV commands are *set nomail TESL-L*, which can be used to stop mail filling the mailbox if it cannot be checked for a while, and *set digest TESL-L*, which means that Mary gets the mail from the list in one bundle each day with all the subject lines first, rather than getting each message by itself.

You will probably find existing lists to suit you, but you may at some point want to start your own mailing list. There are several possibilities here, but they are beyond the scope of this book. You can visit LISTSERV's or Mailbase's web sites for ideas. Your ISP or network administrator might be able to set up a mailing list for you. There are sites where you can arrange to have a free (financed by advertising) list hosted on a server somewhere in the world.

⊗ *In practice*

Too much mail!

A computer which **crashes** stops working and will need to be restarted. Valuable data can be lost in a crash.

A teacher at an FE college in Scotland had mixed experiences of using mailing lists with his students. While the students found it easy to join the list many forgot to unsubscribe, building up huge quantities of unwanted mail in accounts they were no longer checking. This actually caused the college server to **crash.** His advice is to insist that the students print out and retain the instructions for unsubscribing and do actually unsubscribe from the lists.

Mailing lists are sometimes used for special purposes, such as an intensive online conference where, during a period of a few days or a week, participants discuss certain subjects in depth. There are, however, other, more immediate, ways to conduct this kind of intense discussion which will be considered later. Another possibility is to have all the members of a class sign up on a mailing list which can then be used for communication between the students and the teacher. The teacher need not be the only one to answer questions, and any homework assignments and the like can be discussed in the entire group without taking up valuable class time. This is especially useful for courses where there are relatively few contact hours.

Newsgroups

It is not always necessary to belong to a mailing list to join in discussions with the thousands of other Net users out there. Newsgroups offer another possibility which is simpler for occasional browsing. Newsgroups, also called USENET discussion groups or USENET news, were originally designed to carry news about the Net to its users. These groups soon began to discuss other matters too, such as science fiction, which was a major interest for many of these early netters. Things developed until the present state of affairs with 15–20 000 newsgroups discussing as many different topics.

Newsgroups are often very similar to mailing lists. There are even a few mailing lists which are redistributed via USENET as newsgroups, although you have to have subscribed to the mailing list before you can make a contribution. The advantage of mailing lists over newsgroups is that you can be sure not to miss any of the group's discussion – all the messages come straight into your mailbox. In a newsgroup the messages are on the server for only a few days. If you do not read them and save the messages in a file they will be gone.

Quick tip

One side effect of this is that anything you write in a USENET newsgroup or a mailing list which is redistributed as news can be traced back to you for years to come. Some American employers are said to search for job applicants' names in Deja News' archives to see what kinds of interests and personal inclinations they have. Make sure you never write anything you might regret!

There is, however, a way to catch up on a discussion that has taken place in a newsgroup, or even to find complete discussions about subjects that interest you even if you do not generally follow any newsgroups. Several special search systems allow you to search among the newsgroups. *Deja News* is one such service, with its own dedicated web site. Others are Infoseek, Excite and AltaVista. These web search engines also allow you to choose to search among newsgroups.

A **news server** relays the latest contributions to news groups to computers elsewhere on the Net when requested to do so by a news-reader program.

Both Microsoft's Outlook Express, which is included with Internet Explorer, and the Netscape Communicator Suite have newsreading components which let you read and contribute to the discussion on the newsgroups. Click *GoTo/Discussions* in Outlook or the *Discussions* icon to enter Netscape's Message Center. There you can subscribe to any of the thousands of discussion groups (in the File menu). Subscribing to a group means that messages from that group will be read in from your ISP's **news server** every time you start up the newsreader.

There are a number of conventions concerning the naming of newsgroups. Most groups are primarily American unless they have the element *uk* or some other national prefix (e.g. *.za* for South African groups) in their name, although in some groups there are contributors from many countries.

Category	Example
comp (about computers and computing)	comp.multimedia comp.society.development
sci (all about science)	sci.edu
soc (discussion about society and culture)	soc.culture.british soc.culture.german soc.culture.nordic soc.culture.french soc.college
rec (recreation)	rec.music.classical rec.arts.books
talk (all kinds of discussion)	talk.politics.china
news	news.newusers.questions
misc (other subjects)	misc.kids misc.handicap misc.education misc.education.science misc.education.home-school.misc
alt (no official approval required)	alt.education.distance alt.education.disabled alt.culture.usenet alt.irc alt.kids-talk
uk (specifically British groups)	uk.education.16plus uk.education.misc uk.education.schools-it uk.education.staffroom uk.education.teachers uk.rec.walking uk.media.radio.misc
k12 (school groups)	k12.chat.senior k12.chat.teacher k12.ed.health.pe k12.ed.music k12.ed.tech k12.ed.business

Newsgroup categories

Just as for mailing lists, some newsgroups are moderated. This is particularly important if pupils are to access newsgroups, since newsgroups are open and easily accessible to malicious individuals. There are, however, a large number of newsgroups which are dedicated to the exchange of pornographic pictures and other material or to discussions which are otherwise unsuitable for use in schools. There are ways to ensure that only handpicked newsgroups are made available to the pupils. Netscape has, for example, a facility whereby a password is required to subscribe to new groups. Your ISP may also limit the newsgroups available. Some ISPs have their own discussion groups as well as or instead of access to USENET news.

IRC

Internet Relay Chat (IRC) can be thought of as an area of the Internet, separate from those occupied by the Web, USENET newsgroups and e-mail. With IRC you can communicate in real time (*chat*) with Internet users all over the world. This kind of chatting usually means exchanging written messages. It is a superb way to train keyboard skills as the tempo can be very high in some channels. For some pupils chatting can be extremely motivating and may be the only way to get them to write willingly.

If you want to use IRC you will need a special program, known as an IRC client. You can download for example the popular client *m*IRC as shareware from the Web (address in Appendix 4 and on this book's web pages). There is a comprehensive help file with the program which will tell you exactly what to do. If you know which IRC net you want to use, you can choose a server near you to connect to. Otherwise you can just choose a server at random to have a look around. You will need to choose a screen name (*nick*) to be known by when you are online and you will be asked for your real name and your e-mail address.

Beware of anyone who seems too helpful, especially if they invite you to chat privately. There is every reason to be suspicious of strangers in IRC, but that is no reason not to investigate it. Pupils on IRC may need close supervision and/or guidance. Some schools have a system whereby the pupils are chaperoned by an adult when they chat.

The perceived anonymity of chatting may allow shy pupils to express themselves freely, but it is important to remember that the other chatters are real people, and there is no more excuse for rudeness than there would be talking to strangers while waiting for a bus.

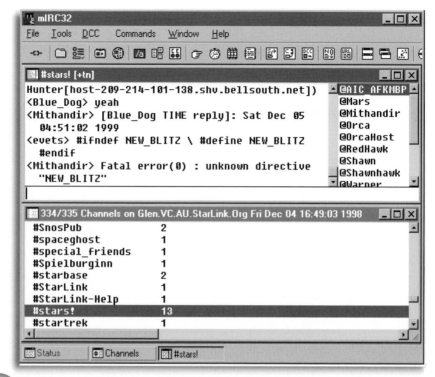

1.14 IRC chat in mIRC

Webchat

The World Wide Web's popularity is not to be underestimated. New applications for web technology are constantly being found. One such new development is the possibility to access online discussions actually on a web page. Some sites have this facility, which is called **webchat**. This is usually arranged so that participants can enter one of a number of *chat rooms*. You can search for webchat facilities using a search engine or catalogue. Some of these webchat rooms arrange events at special times. One that we visited, WBS, offers weekly teacher chat sessions. There is a British room in this facility too, but most chats will welcome all comers.

Webchats are live two-way communication via a web page.

There are several kinds of webchats. Some webchats work in almost real time. What you write will be sent off for immediate incorporation in the web page at the same time as the next set of other people's input is retrieved, using either the browser's *Reload* button or a special receive button on the web page. Others use the programming language Java to achieve real-time chatting via the webchat. Java chats feel more like IRC than do other webchats. The advantage of Java chats over IRC is that Java chats do not require special programs. A disadvantage is

33

that there are not as many chat rooms to choose from as there are on IRC. Webchats are simple to participate in, and can be very useful and enjoyable if you find the right group. The scheduled webchat events are likely to be more rewarding than just dropping into a chat room and hoping to find a kindred spirit at a loose end.

Sound and video conferencing

IRC and webchats are not the only kind of real-time communication available. There are other systems which are not limited to text like IRC. CU-*SeeMe* is a video-conferencing system which has been used in some schools for quite a while. The *Global SchoolHouse* site has a register of schools who are looking for other schools to video conference with. CU-SeeMe requires participants to have a multimedia computer with a microphone and a simple video camera (these are known as webcams and are relatively cheap). You can watch a conference even if you do not have a camera. The CU-SeeMe program is available in a scaled-down freeware version as well as in a full commercial version. The program is not all that simple to install as it requires users to load in a *phonebook* with the addresses of CU-SeeMe reflectors (computers which relay communication to users).

A more recent development is the systems developed by the browser giants Microsoft and Netscape. Both of their browser systems (from version 4) include advanced conferencing systems. Microsoft's NetMeeting and Netscape Conference are free programs (at present) and with their help you can share a document (e.g. Word or Excel) with other participants; write on a joint whiteboard; chat in writing or speak to other participants via a microphone. In NetMeeting you can also see and be seen by the other participants. Nescape Conference allows joint surfing where one participant leads the others on the Web.

ICQ and other direct chats

Joint surfing is also possible for some of the direct chat systems which are appearing. ICQ (from I *seek you*), *Yahoo! Pager* and the Netscape/AOL system *Instant Messenger* are some of the better-known systems. These systems are usually free and will notify you when your friends who use the system come online. Then you can contact them directly via the system and chat in privacy. You will be assigned your own personal number which you can give to your friends or project partners if you install one of these programs.

ICQ is the most advanced of these programs. It allows you to transfer files to other users, or even to set up a personal file server so that your friends can browse and download files from you. ICQ also has a conference function for IRC-like chats with an unlimited number of participants. It is possible to hide in this system so that only those you choose to authorise will know your whereabouts. Alternatively you might allow your contact information to be listed in ICQ's own directory. You can use ICQ at the same time as you are surfing. It will work quietly in the background and allow you to be paged if somebody wants to reach you, or let you page those you want to talk to. You can get the program from the *Mirabilis* web site or from time to time from a computer magazine CD. The program is currently free for personal use. It is simple to use and growing in popularity.

Netiquette

In all successful communication we observe the unwritten rules of give and take, mutual respect and courtesy. When we are using the Internet's communicative facilities to communicate with people we do not know, who may not have English as their language of preference, we must pay extra attention to these matters. Because of the disparate cultural background of the Internet community very little can be taken for granted. Jokes and ambiguity are liable to be misinterpreted. The concept of *netiquette* (from Net etiquette) has developed to refer to a set of guidelines, primarily for communication in newsgroups and mailing lists.

There is no official definition of netiquette, just as we do not agree on what constitutes good manners in other situations, but there are many written lists of netiquette rules 'out there'. Some of the more common features are the following:

❑ Use normal capitalisation. Using all capital letters in a message is interpreted as SHOUTING.

❑ Avoid antagonising or provoking people. This is called 'flaming'. If you want to criticise a person do it by private e-mail, not to a group. 'Flame-wars' between two or more members of a discussion group or mailing list can break out periodically.

❑ E-mail is not necessarily private or transient. Your message can be forwarded to many people without your knowledge. In addition, mail servers may have programs that archive the e-mail messages that they handle.

❑ Before sending a message, read it over, make sure it's what you want to say, and double check the recipient(s). Be especially careful not to send what you intended as a personal reply to the whole group. Many people mix up the administrative and list addresses and send unsubscribe messages and the like to the entire list. This is very irritating and quite ineffective.

❏ When replying to a newsgroup or mail list posting you can include a portion (a few lines) of the original message that you are responding to. Including the entire contents of the original message is not usually necessary.

❏ Always identify yourself and keep messages as brief and to the point as possible.

❏ Avoid *spamming*, the practice of sending unsolicited commercial e-mail messages in bulk, or making similar postings to newsgroups. Most mailing lists and newsgroups do not welcome any kind of commercial activity. Spammers are liable to get mail-bombed – the act of purposely overloading someone's mailbox or server with messages.

❏ It is considered courteous to attempt to repair misunderstandings and apologise for not making yourself clear.

❯ *Did you know?*

Spam is the name given to unsolicited messages, generally containing advertisements for get-rich-quick schemes and scams, especially when the amount of spam threatens to make any real discussion impossible. The name comes from a Monty Python sketch where Vikings demanding spam to eat drowned out other speakers.

Smileys and abbreviations

Communication in newsgroups, mailing lists and other e-mail is a strange kind of intermediate form, somewhere between spoken and written language. E-mails are typically written in a very informal way. Unfortunately they do not carry the writer's facial expression and body language with them. To partially compensate for this a set of symbols known as emoticons or smileys are used. They are supposed to represent a face when viewed sideways. The most common smileys are *smile*, *frown* and *wink*, although if you search for them you can find hundreds of variants, most of which are explained when they are used.

:-) *smile* (humour, happy, encouragement)

:-(*frown* (sad, disapproval)

;-) *wink* (kidding, joking)

1.15 *A smiley*

These are used in combination with a long list of abbreviations. In some groups these are used so often that it is almost impossible for a beginner to read the message. Examples are:

<g> or <grin>	*grin*
<s> or <smile>	*smile*
lol	*laughed a lot* or *laughing out loud*
imho	*in my humble opinion*
fwiw	*for what it's worth*
ttfn	*ta ta for now*
bfn	*bye for now*
rtfm	*read the f*ing manual* (an unkind remark aimed at newbies who ask too many questions they could easily find the answers to themselves).

Summary

In this chapter you have been introduced to the Internet and learned how to start using some of its services.

❑ We have discussed various ways in which you may be hooked up to the Internet at school and/or at home.

❑ You have learned about the way the World Wide Web is structured into collections of pages known as sites and how the pages of a site are organised and connected by hypertext to each other and to other parts of the Web.

❑ We have shown you the main browsers available to decipher the HTML in which pages are written to present it as colourful, attractive web pages.

❑ You have learned how to find information on the Web in a structured search or by using a catalogue.

❑ You have learned about sending and receiving e-mail and about the ways you can meet people to exchange messages within mailing lists and newsgroups.

❑ You have learned to take part in the real-time written conversations known as chatting.

❏ Finally we have discussed the rules which you should observe in your encounters with strangers in cyberspace. The kind of knowledge you have gained from this chapter is useless if it is not applied. The more you use the Internet the more confident you will become.

Does the **Internet** belong in schools?

Newspaper and television journalists find the combination of the Internet and schools to be a never-ending source of story material. Banner headlines raise the alarm: *Schoolboys buy drugs from the Internet!* or *Paedophile masquerades as a 10-year-old on the Net!* Nonetheless, schools are continuing to get connected, convinced that the advantages of Internet access outweigh the disadvantages. In this chapter we take a look at the pros and cons of having access to the Internet in schools, and consider ways to lessen the risks.

New ways of working

The Internet is quite unlike any other kind of material or resource that can be used in the classroom. The Web can be compared to an encyclopaedia with half the pages missing where half of the remaining pages were written by experts and the rest written by enthusiastic amateurs. At the same time, the Web is similar to a newspaper or television with up-to-the-minute reports on what is going on in the world. Official information often becomes available on the Web as soon as it is made public. All this is interspersed with advertisements, spoofs and pages that only the writer's closest friends would find interesting.

But the Web is only part of the Internet. E-mail lets pupils communicate quickly and cheaply with the world outside the classroom. This kind of contact could otherwise be established with the use of the telephone, fax or post, but these are not generally available to pupils. The Internet also lets people know about each other. It is a lot easier for a class to get in touch with another class somewhere in the world if they have looked at a web page and want to compare notes. This kind of contact is unlikely to be arranged without Internet access.

Newsgroups and noticeboards for pupils and teachers are another potentially rewarding area where the Internet brings totally new ways of working to the classroom. Real-time communication via chat and computer conferencing systems can make genuine cooperation between groups of pupils at different schools or even in different countries a real possibility. This kind of cooperation does not have to be centrally organised – the Internet offers many places to meet others who are only an e-mail away.

The Internet has many features which can be used to enhance learning. A lot can be accomplished without very much in the way of technical know-how. Nonetheless, it can be a great help for beginners to have someone more experienced to accompany them when they first venture onto the Net. Minor technical setbacks can otherwise be very frustrating. The Internet is relatively new, and its benefits can sometimes be overshadowed by reports of its downside, particularly given the media's propensity for reporting the shocking rather than the productive. There is a real risk that parents and teachers will be put off before they start by the unbalanced picture of the Internet which is generally shown.

Political factors

There are unmistakable signals coming from the powers that be: computers and the Internet are seen as an integral part of classroom equipment as we move into the new millennium. There is a fervent desire to avoid having Britain fall behind countries where the Internet has become more established in the world of education.

The year 1998 was proclaimed NetYear in a public–private joint venture launched in January 1998 by Dr Kim Howells MP, the Minister for Life-Long Learning, together with Cisco Systems, ICL, Sun Microsystems and the *Daily Telegraph*. The Prime Minister, Tony Blair, referred to NetYear as 'the biggest public–private partnership in any education system anywhere in the world' (Labour Party Conference, September 1997).

According to the NetYear documents, at the beginning of 1998 only 6 000 schools out of 32 000 were connected to the Internet, with the majority of these having just one computer connected. An estimated 60 per cent of all computers in schools were then out of date, and 80 per cent of UK teachers needed to be trained in the use of information and communications technology (ICT). The aim, as stated by NetYear Executive Chairman David Wimpress, was to have 'an additional 10,000 schools using the Internet as an educational tool' by the end of 1998.

The NetYear aimed to 'help schools use modern information and communications technology (ICT) for teaching and learning, and by so doing accelerate implementation of the government's vision for a National Grid for Learning'.

BECTa is the British Educational Communications and Technology Agency, formerly NCET (the National Council for Educational Technology).

The Government has given **BECTa** a remit to develop and run the National Grid for Learning (NGfL). The intention is to connect all of Britain's 32 000 state-maintained and independent schools, with over 450 000 teachers and over nine million pupils, by 2002. Virtual teacher centres are to be developed to maintain teachers' standards and every child over the age of nine is to have an e-mail address.

The National Grid for Learning is essentially part of the Internet. The target is to give schools Internet access and provide ways for teachers and pupils to interact. The NGfL's main web page serves to coordinate services to teachers. At the time of writing the most interesting part of the site was the Virtual Teacher Centre (VTC). The structure and content of the VTC is based on the vision set out in the Government's consultation document, *Connecting the Learning Society: National Grid for Learning* (published by the Department for Education and Employment (DfEE), October 1997).

In schools around the world

In the rest of Europe, and indeed the world, similar massive injections of time and money are being administered to the school systems. Germany's *Schulnetz* and Sweden's *Skoldatanät* have been around for quite a while as the result of earlier investment. Ireland's Action Programme for the New Millennium is called *Schools* IT 2000. Estonia's *Tiger Leap* project seems set to project Estonian schools into the thick of things. In Singapore, the Department of Education has launched a *Masterplan for* IT *in Education* to raise standards substantially by the year 2002. The Internet is, of course, known for its international nature, and these national schemes will not need to stand in isolation. There is, for example, a European Schoolnet which manages international projects, and the Global SchoolNet is a very active American organisation sponsored by Microsoft, among others, for this kind of collaboration between schools across borders.

The European Union has many programmes for various kinds of international exchanges and joint ventures which can be greatly enhanced by the use of Internet communication. An important recent development is the notion of European guidelines for the use of ICT in schools under the auspices of the Education and Training Sector of the Telematics Applications Programme. *Technologies for Knowledge and Skills Acquisition* is a part of the INFORMATION SOCIETY Programme in the European Commission's Fifth Framework Programme. (Further details about this can be found on the I*M *Europe* site.)

Economy

These political decisions to earmark funding for information and communication technologies in education mark a political eagerness to jump on the Internet bandwagon. This eagerness is often shared by pupils but less often by parents and teachers. Parents may be worried about security and the risk of their offspring gaining access to adult material. Teachers' worries may be more complex. For a teacher with no background knowledge of computers or interest in the Internet, the major obstacle to incorporating the Internet into the classroom is that of motivation. It may not be immediately obvious what the benefits are. There is also a fairly steep learning curve for anyone who has not dealt with computers at all in the past. Teachers may resent being obliged to learn about the new technologies if they cannot see any practical advantages for themselves or their teaching.

With ventures such as the NetYear and the launch of the National Grid for Learning, vast amounts of public and private funding become available. In January 1998 the Government announced that £250m. was being made available to train teachers in the effective use of ICT as a teaching and learning aid. In November 1998, Tony Blair announced investment which would support over £700m. expenditure on ICT for UK schools. This was in addition to the £300m. already available under the National Lottery for teacher and librarian training, and digitisation of learning content, giving a total investment over the four years up to 2002 in excess of £1 billion.

Also internationally, in the European Union and elsewhere in the world, unusually large investments are being made to maximise the impact of ICT in education. Sights are set high. The ambition of the NetYear was to come some way with the estimated 80 per cent of British teachers who are in need of training in the use of ICT while updating the 60 per cent of school computers which are out of date and increasing the number of schools with Internet connections.

The balance of investment is, however, very fine: it is pointless to invest in the latest computer equipment and fast connections to the Internet if corresponding investments are not made in training the teachers who are to use the equipment with pupils. Before teachers can be trained they need to be motivated – to see what their colleagues are already doing with ICT in the classroom, and to glimpse ways in which they might themselves embrace the new technologies and all they imply.

This training takes time for the teachers. Other kinds of INSET are likely to fall by the wayside in the next few years as resources are funnelled into ICT. Plans exist to provide computers for teachers to have at home, the understanding being that teachers will devote a good deal of their free time to becoming proficient users.

Computers are becoming cheaper. Technological advances mean that even the simplest computers now on sale are quite adequate for Internet connection. The increased telephone bills associated with Internet connection put off many schools, but there are now standard solutions to this problem, such as the BT *Schools Internet Caller* offer regarding ISDN2 lines which give faster connection to the Internet than ordinary telephone lines for up to 30 networked computers. Other similar offers are likely to follow.

The document *Connecting Schools, Networking People*, prepared by BECTa at the request of the DfEE (June 1998), suggests four stages when considering the cost of investing in ICT:

1   *Research and development*. In this stage comes the time staff spend researching alternatives, planning meetings and liasing with ISPs and other companies.

2   *Initial investment*. This refers to the cost of installing the new system: computers and peripheral equipment, software, furniture, network cables, etc.

3   *Operating and support costs*. This refers to the training of staff, telecommunications, technical support and maintenance as well as software upgrading, disks, paper, printer cartridges, etc.

4   *Replacement, disposal and salvage*. When equipment has outlived its usefulness it needs to be disposed of and replaced.

There is a risk that the hidden costs surrounding an investment in ICT will eat up much of a school's resources, leaving little for other activities. This is why the extra funding from central sources is so clearly needed.

Making room in the curriculum for the Internet

If you have worked successfully for many years without access to the Internet at home or in the classroom you may wonder what you are to do with it. Fortunately there are many people who are willing to share their experiences of what has worked for them and to point you in the right direction. The Internet can offer information and contact. It has been said that the advent of ICT will change the face of teaching, giving teachers an advisory role as pupils gather their own information. In fact, the Internet has very little information which is immediately accessible to pupils in terms of being written at an appropriate level and covering the curriculum material.

Teachers cannot just leave pupils to it and expect the Internet to take over where textbooks leave off. The teacher is still very much needed to interpret material from the Internet, especially for use by younger pupils. Teachers will often prefer to find appropriate material and adapt it before making it available to pupils either on computer or on paper.

That said, the Internet's unequalled communication potential can pave the way for pupils to contact individuals, other classes and organisations, which they would not otherwise do. With the right kind of planning and preparation these contacts can be very rewarding.

The Internet can potentially become part of every school subject and activity, as we will show in later chapters. There is material on the Net which is relevant for every subject. The teacher's role is to take the material and use it in such a way as to enhance the learning experience. Take school meals, for example: if the menu is on the school web pages parents can see what the pupils are eating; the pupils can comment on the meals, vote for the week's best lunch, and so on. Or the school football teams: present the team, results, forthcoming home and away matches on the school web pages; use e-mail to inform players and supporters about changes, and so on. There is no shortage of ideas. Once the technology becomes fully unremarkable in the school setting many more uses for it will emerge. ICT will enrich the curriculum rather than fundamentally alter what has traditionally been done. Its function is *as well as* rather than *instead of* other resources. Nonetheless, the Internet has the potential to affect the way we learn if teachers choose to allow it to do so.

The home–school connection

A large and growing number of families with school-age children have Internet access at home. These parents can become involved more intimately in the doings of their children if the week's homework is posted on the class web page along with the notes that otherwise come home scrunched in the bottom of a schoolbag several days too late. E-mail or the Web can be used in all kinds of communication between the school and home, for example for information about the coming parents' meeting or the minutes of the last one; details of sports' day, school outings and other special days, and so on. The pupils can perhaps write a class diary on the class web page telling parents (and anyone else who is interested) what work they have covered in each subject during the week. The e-mail addresses of all the teachers and the school administration could be made available on a web page or sent as a mail to parents. Parents and teachers could then communicate informally by e-mail – so much less serious than calling each other at home, and less time-consuming too! This will obviously work only if there is a common wish to increase the level of communication between the school and the pupils' homes.

➤ *Against the Internet*

As we have mentioned, the Internet has had a very poor press. This has tended to slow down its introduction in schools. Let us consider what the disadvantages of Internet access are considered to be, and why parents and teachers have sometimes been put off before they ever got started.

Pornography, terrorism and crime

The Internet is a medium where text, pictures, sound and film can be sent from one computer to another. All sorts of people use the Internet for all sorts of purposes. A tiny fraction of the material on the Web is what is often called 'adult' material. This can mean anything from the kind of so-called erotic pictures found in the tabloid press to much more advanced pornography. Some of this material is illegal in the UK but legal in the country from which it originates. Other material is illegal almost everywhere. Parents and teachers are generally very anxious to ensure that children do not happen upon any of this material.

In fact, children are unlikely to follow a link while surfing the Web and suddenly be confronted with disturbing or offensive pictures. It is possible that a curious teenager might use a search engine to find this kind of page, but generally this material will not be found without some kind of activity on the part of the user.

There are a number of newsgroups which devote themselves to sexual discussions, some of which use the Net to distribute pictures and links to adult web sites, but again, this material does not appear on the screen without an active choice on the part of the user. On IRC there are a lot of chat channels which are intended for adult participants, and which may be dangerous or unsuitable for young people to frequent. This means that there are opportunities for interested pupils to gain access to unsuitable material with very little effort unless precautions are taken.

Most of the Internet activity involving the distribution of this kind of adult material is carried out with the aim of selling access to pictures. This means that some kind of registration is generally required before gaining access. This alone offers a certain safeguard, even for curious youngsters who are in fact attempting to gain access to inappropriate material.

Adult material is not the only kind of content that may be considered inappropriate for children. The Internet is also a very useful channel for those who make a living selling illegal substances. This is primarily done through post-order from addresses outside the UK, although this is certainly not as visible to the average Internet user as is the Net's pornographic content. Another illegal business that thrives on the Internet is the sale of illicitly copied software and decoder cards for satellite-TV reception.

The Net is, however, also used by all sorts of underground movements, such as Satanists, hackers, extreme political and religious groups, terrorists and common criminals. Generally the purpose is for members of groups to keep in touch with each other, although there are sometimes attempts to recruit new members or to spread propaganda. Young people may, of course, be particularly vulnerable to the influence of these people.

Some schools have been so concerned about the availability of adult and other inappropriate material on the Net that they have decided to abstain from access altogether. Fortunately there are ways to protect pupils from innocently happening upon this material and to thwart older pupils' efforts to still their curiosity. We will return to these later in this chapter.

Variable quality

Let us now leave the relatively small amount of material that many would find offensive for one reason or another and move on. The Web contains millions upon millions of pages. No one knows exactly how many millions. Many of these pages belong to companies and organisations. These pages are often well designed and generally give the same kind of information about the company as a brochure might. Vast numbers of pages represent more or less reputable businesses and people trying to earn some money through the Net.

Other pages belong to universities and schools, governments, municipalities, radio and TV operators and newspapers. They have a steady stream of mainly reliable information about their areas of influence and responsibility.

But what of the rest? Many pages are written by private persons. These pages can be very good indeed – full of information about a specific subject gathered by enthusiasts – but they can also contain very biased or incomplete or even inaccurate information about the topic. A browse through Yahoo! shows that there are pages on everything from skydiving to scuba, written for clubs or just by individual devotees. Some seem to offer just pages of links which send the reader to other similar pages of links without ever finding very much in the way of real information. Other pages have minimal information about some tiny aspect of a subject because that is all the page owner felt like writing. Those who publish material on the Web are under no obligation to make their material useful to others!

People who are new to the Internet often want to make personal home pages. While it is interesting to know something about the people behind information you read, personal information for its own sake has very limited interest for a wider readership. Personal pages can, nonetheless, be fun to make, especially for young people. *Yahoo!* (UK & Ireland) lists over 70 000 personal home pages. Many more can be found hidden in school and college web sites.

A useful rule of thumb is that about one web page or newsgroup posting in ten that you come across when searching for information about a given topic will be useful. The rest will generally be too irrelevant, biased or incomplete to be of much use to anybody.

Doubtful sources

When you are searching the Internet looking for material to use with a class you need to consider your sources. If you do not know where the material comes from you cannot judge its reliability. Schoolbooks and other materials traditionally used in schools can generally be assumed to have undergone some kind of quality control. The publishers who produce textbooks are very careful to check facts and provide a balanced picture of the subject area they cover. Arguments and counter-arguments are weighed against each other and conclusions drawn. Educational broadcasting and information brochures from commercial companies are subject to the same requirements of impartiality. This is not, however, true of the Internet. Anyone can publish anything they please, and there is no easy way for you as a user to separate the wheat from the chaff. Reliable sites from the authorities or established companies are not marked in a special way to distinguish them from other sites when you sift through the results from a search engine. All web pages have more or less equal prominence.

⊘ *Case study*

Check your sources!

Let us take an example. Mary Smith's colleague John Hill is teaching the Holocaust to a GCSE class. He wants to find web pages which illuminate different aspects of the Holocaust, from different points of view. He uses Excite and AltaVista with *holocaust* as the search term. Among many other pages he finds one which details the various execution methods used in the Nazi concentration camps. It is not until he has read the entire page that he becomes suspicious and starts to wonder about who lies behind the information he has read. He follows a link on the page to the site's home page and finds that a revisionist organisation has written what he read. The purpose of the page was to sow doubt about what actually happened in the camps.

John Hill goes back to Excite and limits his search to the UK since he feels more confident about his ability to judge the credibility of British sources. He finds excellent sites on the Holocaust through a link to a BBC News story the year before.

BBC NEWS

Front Page		Relevant Stories
UK	Tuesday, March 31, 1998 Published at 11:33 GMT 12:33 UK	27 Mar 98	World
World	**UK**	Swiss banks dodge sanctions in Holocaust deal
Business	**Holocaust survivors wait on**	04 Dec 97	Special Report
Sci/Tech	**compensation**	The greatest theft in history
Sport		05 Dec 97	World
Despatches		Swiss banks make first payouts from holocaust accounts
World News in Audio ◀))		
On Air		**Internet Links**
粵語廣播		Tripartite Gold Commission
Talking Point	Many Holocaust victims put their money in British bank accounts	London Jewish Museum
Feedback	Holocaust survivors and their families are waiting to hear	Yad Vashem Memorial Museum
Low Graphics	from the UK Government to see if it will pay compensation for money deposited in British bank	Holocaust Memorial Museum
Help	accounts before and during the Second World War and never returned.	The BBC is not responsible for the content of external
Site Map		

2.1 *A BBC news story*

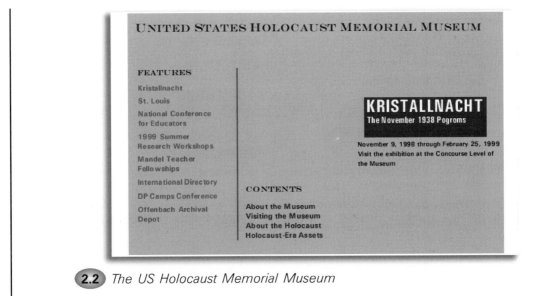

UNITED STATES HOLOCAUST MEMORIAL MUSEUM

FEATURES

Kristallnacht

St. Louis

National Conference
for Educators

1999 Summer
Research Workshops

Mandel Teacher
Fellowships

International Directory

DP Camps Conference

Offenbach Archival
Depot

CONTENTS

About the Museum
Visiting the Museum
About the Holocaust
Holocaust-Era Assets

KRISTALLNACHT
The November 1938 Pogroms

November 9, 1998 through February 25, 1999
Visit the exhibition at the Concourse Level of
the Museum

2.2 *The US Holocaust Memorial Museum*

To a certain extent John Hill in our example can use the fact that the BBC referred to the site, although there is, of course, a disclaimer on the BBC page stating that they are not responsible for the content of external sites. In any case he would do well to attempt to find out who is responsible for the information he is reading. When pupils are learning to find their own material on the Internet they need to be taught techniques for questioning and evaluating the reliability of material they find.

Sometimes the web address of a page can tell you something about the source of your information. As we saw in the last chapter, domain names often are the same as the name of the organisation behind a site. The address *www.whitehouse.gov*, for example, will take you to the White House, home of the US President. But it does not do to rely entirely on this kind of clue to where a web page comes from. In the case of the White House, the address *www.whitehouse.net* also exists. It is the home of more or less satirical attacks on the person of the President.

Games, games, games!

Many young users become completely enthralled by computer games. The most fascinating games are often those which can be played against real opponents over a computer network. There is no shortage of games to choose from. Yahoo! UK & Ireland lists almost 2000 sites associated with Internet games. Microsoft, Yahoo! and others have set up areas where players can join in existing games or start their own. Often these games require the player to already have the CD version of the game

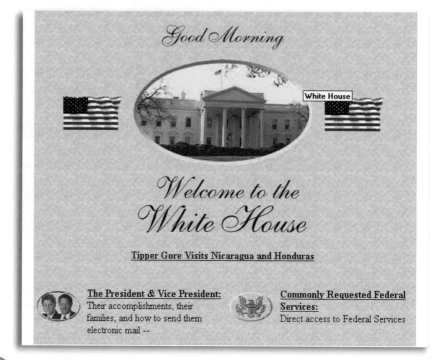

2.3 *The official White House site (www.whitehouse.gov)*

2.4 *The alternative White House site (www.whitehouse.net)*

before it is possible to play via the Net. Many kinds of Internet games are devoted to virtual combat situations involving a fair degree of blood-thirstiness in a graphically advanced environment, often with images in three dimensions. There are, however, also sites devoted to playing board games such as chess and backgammon over the Internet. Some games are text-based virtual environments where players come to play, socialise, compete, fight or build onto the environment. These are variously referred to as MUDs, MOOs, MUCKs, MUSHes and MUSEs depending on their orientation and the degree of fantasy or realism involved in their creation. MOOs in particular are sometimes used for educational purposes, such as for bringing a group of A-level Spanish students into a Spanish-speaking environment.

⊗ *Did you know?*

A **MUCK** is a Multi-User Character Kingdom.

TELNET is a primitive way of communicating directly with another computer.

MUD is an acronym for multi-user dungeon; a MUSH is a multi-user shared hallucination, while MOO is said to come from MU* – a multi-user environment which is not otherwise specified. They are virtual worlds built up by users, so that visitors can be told where they are and what they see at any time. In MUDs there is generally some kind of role-playing activity going on, while the other variants have other functions. In furry **MUCKs**, for example, visitors take on the role of the animal of their choice. MOOs often have the form of a virtual building or city. These games have lost a lot of ground to the more graphically advanced adventure games which can be played on modern computers. You can use either **TELNET** or a special MUD program to participate in the MUD.

Of course, computer games are not necessarily only a negative factor in schools. Used judiciously they can function as motivators for some pupils. Text-based MUDs, MOOs, etc., can even be used to train writing skills.

The Internet is also a rich source of games and educational programs which can be downloaded from central databases for playing on the user's own computer. Many of these games are distributed as **shareware** or *freeware* (these distribution systems will be discussed in chapter 4). Schools with networked computers may find it necessary to regulate the installation and playing of games. Otherwise they might find that pupils are playing games with each other when they should be working. Many pupils have access to computers at home. They may bring diskettes with them to school with the aim of downloading games

Shareware programs can be copied freely, and used for a test period. Longer use means you will have to pay the programmer a small sum for the program.

from the Internet for use at home. Some pupils spend so much time playing games that they have little time for other activities.

Controlling pupils' use of the Internet

We have seen several reasons why it might be necessary to control pupils' access to the school computers and particularly to the Internet.

❑ The Internet itself, particularly the Web, can be so appealing to some young people (and even adults) that they would spend a large portion of their day surfing from page to page and participating in chats if they were given the opportunity. This kind of aimless Internet activity is unlikely to contribute to a pupil's education. The same must be said of unlimited access to computer games.

❑ Some pupils will know about the availability of sexually explicit material on the Net and be keen to satisfy their curiosity. Other pupils might be disturbed and made uncomfortable if they were to happen upon this kind of material. Parents are often extremely anxious about this side of the Internet.

❑ It is generally desirable to shield pupils from illegal transactions and material of all kinds. Traditionally, schools have been protected from this kind of activity.

❑ Young people may not be able to protect themselves from the attentions of strangers trying to make contact. They may need supervision so they do not play into the hands of malevolent individuals.

❑ Information obtained from the Internet may sometimes be false, misleading or unbalanced. Also, most web pages and other information on the Net are written for adults. Young people will often need help in interpreting and using information they obtain from the Net.

Schools have to find their own solutions to these problems, but there are several recognised ways to go. Censorship, supervision and pupil contracts are the usual paths taken. Schools need to decide whether they want to use the introduction of the Internet into the school as an opportunity to teach responsible behaviour or whether they would rather make it almost impossible to behave irresponsibly. There is no easy answer here.

Technical solutions

A few years ago American attempts to control the kind of material which could be put out on the Internet were thwarted by outraged free-speech advocates. There is, if anything, even greater parental concern about the effect of access to the Internet on young minds in the USA. A number of technical solutions enabling parents and teachers to block certain kinds of material before it appears on the screen have been developed.

These technical solutions generally involve some way of categorising the content of web pages (and sometimes other Internet information such as e-mails, chat rooms, etc.) and then in some way acting on the categorisation. Some systems exist to help children to find their way to appropriate material such as child-oriented web sites and search tools such as *Yahooligans*! They suggest suitable places for children to visit, but do not prevent them visiting other places. *Net Shepherd*'s newly developed search service only returns matches that have been judged as appropriate for children. Some ISPs, such as Research Machines' (RM) *Internet for Learning*, filter access to inappropriate material.

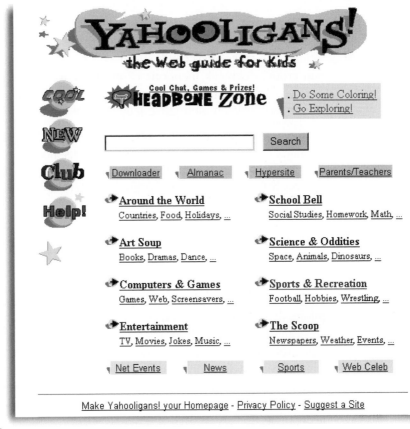

 Yahooligans!

Classification of sites

Other systems make use of tags or labels in a classification system such as PICS (Platform for Internet Content Selection). These systems can either inform the user that the page they want to visit has a certain classification, or block the browser, preventing the page from appearing on the screen, depending on how they are set up. Microsoft's Internet Explorer (version 3 and later) has a function to enable parents or others to set the amount of strong language, nudity, sexual content and violence that is to be accessible. A password is required to view pages which have been 'banned' according to the PICS labels assigned them. Other examples of systems which use PICS labels are *Evaluweb*, which displays a banner indicating the age-appropriateness of web pages, and *Alexa*, which gives information about any PICS labels which have been assigned to a web site in a special toolbar. The problem with this method is that relatively few sites have yet been evaluated and assigned labels and those that have are predominantly in the USA. This kind of system is also dependent on the values held by the body responsible for the ratings. The technology can be used as easily by, say, fundamental Christian groups to block mentions of evolutionary theory in biology texts as to block out pornography and violence. It is possible in some systems to choose between alternative labelling organisations.

There are also censoring systems that deny access to any page containing certain words that have been deemed inappropriate, or to any site which is listed as not being suitable for children. Another approach is to deny access to any site that has not specifically been listed as acceptable. These systems include *Cyber Patrol*, *Evaluweb*, *Net Nanny*, AOL *Parental Controls* and *SurfWatch*. You can find out more about these systems by following the links on this book's web pages and in Appendix 4.

The technical censorship devices discussed above are sometimes difficult to use, because they are so insensitive to the context and style of information filtered out. You may find that not only the 'right' kind of sites are being blocked but even perfectly innocent and useful sites. If you prohibit sites that have not been classified you are only giving access to a tiny fraction of what the Internet has to offer. If you prohibit sites that have 'blacklisted' words you may find that recipes calling for *chicken breasts* are inaccessible while those using *drumsticks* are quite acceptable.

A quite different method of controlling a pupil's Internet activity is to monitor a log of all sites they visit and incoming and outgoing activity. Just letting it be known that a log is kept and that it is possible to later see where an individual has been while online can be enough to deter inappropriate use of school computers. Some blocking systems keep a log of all attempts to access inappropriate material. The browser itself keeps a record of sites visited (known as *History* in Netscape and *Previous* in Explorer). These cache-memory records can, however, be erased fairly easily by any computer-literate user.

Supervision

These technical solutions do have disadvantages, and they are an additional cost to be taken from the school's ICT budget. Some schools (and parents) prefer a simpler approach, simply refusing pupils Internet access unless they are under adult supervision. This method works well in the many schools where only a single computer has an Internet connection, but it is impossible to implement in a situation where classroom computers and entire computer labs are connected in a network which is online more or less continuously.

It is possible to have a system where pupils are freely able to access material on the school's intranet but a teacher is required to enter a password (an indication that the teacher is supervising the activity) to gain Internet access. This kind of requirement is likely to reduce the overall amount of time pupils spend using the Internet. An alternative is to set up online computers in a well-supervised, fairly public setting, such as in the school library in full view of the staff, or just outside the staff room.

⊗ In practice

Lunchtime supervision

In a school for 11–18-year-old girls in Northern Ireland the pupils were allowed to use the only computer with access to the Internet during their lunch hour. The school technician was then responsible for their supervision and instruction. The pupils were able to carry out a class e-mail exchange project with a school in Scotland under these circumstances. This school made extensive use of offline browsing of entire sites which had previously been downloaded and were saved on the computer's hard disk. The teachers at this school were concerned about how to organise the supervision of pupils using the Internet when the school got more online computers.

Offline browsing

A site you **subscribe** to will be updated as often as you specify and be available for offline browsing.

It is possible to let pupils use web material without actually being online. Several programs, such as *WebWhacker*, let the user download entire sites from the Net for later offline browsing. Newer versions of Netscape and Explorer also have this function – you can **subscribe** to a site and specify how often you want your subscription to be updated. This means that you can, in the course of your preparation, find what you deem to be useful material and load the entire site onto a single computer's hard disk or the school intranet (bearing in mind that this may be an infringement of copyright). Alternatively, you can incorporate chunks of the web material into a document in your word processor or even into your own web pages for use on the classroom computer.

Quick tip

You can easily copy material from the Web into other documents (e.g. word-processor documents) using the Windows commands Copy and Paste. Simply mark the material you want to copy by holding the mouse button down as you move the cursor over the screen and select Copy from the Edit menu (or use the shortcut Ctrl+C). Move the cursor to where you want to insert the copied material and select Paste from the Edit menu (or Ctrl+V).

It is possible to carry out quite advanced work involving pupils on the Net even if you do not have many online computers. You can select web material you want the pupils to access offline, and even involve them in e-mail contacts. E-mails can, of course, be read and written offline and sent by the teacher after they have been checked. If it is seen as of primary importance that pupils do not get any opportunity to access unsuitable material, then this might be the path to choose.

Acceptable use policies

The other end of the spectrum of methods to regulate pupils' access to the Internet is the idea of an 'Internet Contract' or 'Acceptable Use Policy' (AUP). This is a document signed by the school, the pupil and parents (if pupils are under 18) which states the terms of the pupil's access to the Internet via the school's computers. The contract will usually explain what kind of access the pupil will have, whether and how this access will be controlled or filtered, adding a disclaimer to the effect that no method of policing is foolproof. The rest of the contract is generally devoted to outlining the standards of Internet behaviour expected from the users (often including specific netiquette rules) and what will happen if the user is found to have broken the rules.

This kind of contract is quite common in other countries, including the USA. Many schools have their policy documents on the Web. You can look at a few via the addresses on this book's web pages.

A potential problem is that parents might be put off by the defensive tone of such a document. The alarmist press coverage the Internet has been given has led to very negative attitudes on the part of some parents. It might be a good idea to ensure that parents understand and support the basic notion of having access to the Internet in the school. Schools have dealt with these issues in various ways. One way is to open the school's ICT facilities to parents in the evenings, either for their own informal exploration of the Internet or for formal courses. This can be a good way to show parents why the school wants to use the Internet with pupils. Making school facilities available for courses for others can also be a useful source of funding.

⊚ *In practice*

Sharing facilities with the community

Some schools have made a point of being at the service of the local community. Oak Farm Community School in Farnborough, for example, offers many courses in cooperation with the Hampshire County Council under the *Colleges and Schools in Partnership* scheme, including one called 'What is a Computer – For Parents and Grandparents'.

An Internet permit

In some schools the signing of the Internet contract is the final point in a preparatory Internet course. In such cases it makes sense to talk about an Internet driving licence. The course itself corresponds to driving lessons, including the rules of the road, courtesy to other users, etc. (Appendix 2 gives suggestions for a series of five lessons leading to certification as independent Internet users.) This can be followed by a 'driving test' to establish whether the pupil is familiar with the rules as well as with the browser and the computer, whether she can search for information and send/receive e-mails, etc. Having passed the test the pupil would then be invited to sign the contract giving freedom of access to the Internet.

Any failure to observe the terms of the contract would usually result in the confiscation of the licence for a period of time somehow related to the seriousness of the offence. This might, however, cause problems if the pupil needed access to the Net for class work.

⟫ *For the Internet*

It is clear that Internet is likely to be around in schools for a long time. The political forces behind its coming seem to agree that the advantages outweigh the disadvantages. What then do those who welcome the Internet in schools see as its positive effects?

An unlimited source of information

Even if the Internet is a somewhat unreliable source of information there is a lot of worthwhile information there that is simply not available elsewhere. There are just so many sources continuously pouring information into the Net, and this information is quickly, easily and cheaply retrievable.

Where else can a class in an English village study the way breaking world news is handled in the newspapers of the English (or Spanish, French or German, etc.) speaking world? How would it otherwise be possible for special education teachers to compare notes and offer each other support in international groups with dozens of messages daily? How would teachers otherwise find the time to collect data about a country from the CIA's databases? In what other way could children in Britain cooperate with Australian children in the writing of book reports? The Internet brings a world of information right into the classroom.

All sorts of authorities and official bodies have both a web site with the information that was previously spread between dozens of brochures, and a way for the public to get in touch by e-mail, often to named individuals. Tax offices and welfare authorities all over Europe are using this new channel for spreading their information. Public libraries are making their catalogues available via the Web.

Democracy

One of the more unexpected developments in the Internet has been that the distance between the authorities and the public seems to have decreased. Writing a letter to your MP is a much more serious business than sending her an e-mail. Have a look at the web pages of any government department – it is easy to find the e-mail address of the people behind the information you read. Drop them a line with your questions! The informality of e-mail means that even what used to be stilted formal letters can be concise and unceremonious. Even local politicians are becoming more accessible (and thus more answerable) to the voters through e-mail.

As more and more official bodies get e-mail addresses which are available to the public, this trend will snowball. E-mails are also more

| Offices & Contact | Forms & Publications | What's New | Technical Information | FAQs | Search & Help |

Inland
Revenue

Quick Reference ▼

go

The Inland Revenue is responsible, under the overall direction of Treasury Ministers, for the efficient administration of income tax, corporation tax, capital gains tax, petroleum revenue tax, inheritance tax and stamp duties. The Department's job is to provide an effective and fair tax service to the country and Government.

Tax for Individuals	Individuals who would normally pay tax through Self Assessment and/or PAYE, or Sub-Contractors in the construction industry.
Tax for Business	Employers, Directors, Company Accountants or Contractors in the construction industry.

If you have visited the site before, you may wish to use the 'Quick Reference menu', located in the top-right corner, to gain quick access to the section which interests you.

If you are a first time user and are unsure which sections of the site apply to you, please indicate above whether you require information on 'Tax for Individuals' or 'Tax for Business'.

2.6 *Tax information from the Inland Revenue*

likely to be directed to the right person, unlike phone calls to large workplaces which tend to go through exchanges. E-mails reach their destination instantly and will wait until the recipient has time to deal with them. Even very busy people will often answer their own e-mails – it is just a matter of a click of the mouse and a line or two in reply and it is done. People will often read their e-mail even when they are not in their offices, thus being more easily reached by those who use this channel.

This means that is relatively easy to give pupils direct contact with decision makers as a part of their civic and political education. Not only is the democratic process more accessible than it has ever been thanks to web sites such as the 10 *Downing Street* site and the *Open.gov* site, it is also possible for pupils to have their say and to put leading politicians on the spot, for example through the open question sessions which are regularly arranged by the 10 Downing Street site.

Web pages compete with each other for surfers' attention on their own merits. A page can generate a lot of attention if it provides what visitors are looking for, regardless of whether it has been produced by a school class in Omagh or a multinational company. Also, on the USENET discussion groups, everyone's voice can be heard. It has been likened to a world-wide page of letters to a non-existent editor. Experts rub shoulders with newbies in the virtual meeting places of the Net.

ICT skills

It is sometimes said that one of the main advantages with ICT in schools is that the pupils learn valuable skills that will be necessary in the workplace when they leave school. In fact, there are those who feel that schools must provide this kind of training for the pupils in an effort to lessen the gap between those pupils who have access to computers and the Internet at home and those who do not. However, while keyboard skills have been widely needed for the past twenty years, and been useful to have for the forty years before that, there is no guarantee that the computers in use in five or ten years will even have keyboards. The ability to perform an intelligent search on the Internet of this year might be of very limited use in a few years' time.

We maintain that ICT's role is important not for ways it might benefit pupils in the future but for what it does for pupils in the present. One of the main benefits of bringing computers and the Internet into schools is that our children become proficient at an early age in those skills which allow them to be informed and active citizens.

Much more important than an understanding of the technical details surrounding computers is that the young adults of tomorrow are equipped to handle the deluge of information which washes over us daily. They need to be able to sift through uninteresting details in search of information they need.

An open window to the world

Classrooms have traditionally been relatively isolated from the rest of the world. A teacher and his class have often seemed to be sufficient unto themselves. The teacher has taught the pupils carefully measured amounts of what he knows about a subject with the help of textbooks. Pupils have learned what they are to learn, hopefully also understanding something of the causes and effects that lie behind. When the pupils have written about what they have learned the teacher has been the only reader.

When the Internet comes into a classroom situation things may change. The teacher and textbooks are no longer the only sources of information. Reference books and the school library have always been available, but the Web is something much wider and deeper. Pupils may be able to find their own information about the subject they are studying. This is not, of course, necessarily a good thing – it is even easier for pupils to put undigested chunks of information into their work if it is on a computer than if they have to copy out what the encyclopaedia says.

> ⊗ *In practice*

Plagiarism

In universities and in schools in countries where the Internet has been widely available for longer than in the UK, deliberate plagiarism is a major problem. There are even sites where pupils can find old coursework essays in a database, e.g. in Sweden where final year high school students are required to produce a coursework project about a topic of their own choice. Different methods have been used to handle this problem. Pupils can be required to hand in the sources they have used along with their work; they can be subjected to spot-check vivas, or they can be required to sign a statement to the effect that the work is their own and not plagiarised.

Pupils can write for a wider public than just their teachers if their work is published on the Web. They gain access to up-to-date material to supplement their textbooks. The classroom can become a part of society rather than being isolated from it.

A new role for teachers

When a teacher begins to use the Internet in her teaching it becomes apparent that the balance of knowledge in the classroom might change. Often some of the pupils are much more proficient than the teachers in the operation of ICT. This does *not* need to be a problem! Let these pupils help you and their classmates to get started. Set them to work searching for information.

Pupils using the Web to widen or deepen their knowledge of the subject at hand may find that they are better informed about just that subject than the teacher. Let them then share their findings with the class. The teacher might find it useful to sometimes be less of a leader and more of a learning companion, responsible for guiding the pupils toward the goals of the curriculum. The pupils need their teacher more than ever in these circumstances: to put the findings into perspective; to explain and interpret the meaning of the new information; and, not least, to judge its credibility.

Summary

❑ There is intense political pressure to incorporate ICT in general and the Internet in particular into our schools. Vast sums of money are being invested nationally and internationally in the purchase of equipment and the training of teachers to make use of computers in the classroom.

❑ The Internet is like society in that you meet a mixture of people there: some are philanthropists, others may be malevolent; some are well informed, others misinformed and others set out to mislead. Those who are out to cheat and bluff their way to financial gain and those who have something to sell rub shoulders with those who are out to help anyone they can.

❑ The Net has the potential to revolutionise the way we learn. It has been described as a car-boot sale of information, opinion and obsession. It offers unlimited information from countless sources and a channel for communication with the individuals who represent official bodies as well as with enthusiasts who are burning with the urge to find someone who shares their interest.

❑ The Internet has come into our schools now, for better or worse. We must learn to use it to our advantage and protect ourselves and our children from its dangers just as we do with cars and electricity and other technological innovations.

The **Internet** for teachers

Teachers are not a homogenous group in any sense, least of all when it comes to their level of familiarity with ICT. Some teachers found their way to computers and the Internet early on and have followed their development for years. These teachers have often taken on the role of the enthusiast who tries with limited success to interest the rest of the staff in using computers (let alone the Internet) with the pupils. Now that the Internet is becoming an ordinary part of school resources these pioneers should be able to step down. Other teachers are catching on to what the Internet can offer them, and are spreading the news. There will always be those who resist the new technologies, and they will be content to carry on working as they have done in the past until someone or something comes along to show them how they and their pupils might stand to gain from ICT.

A day in a teacher's life

Let us look at a day in the life of Mary Smith. She is, as you will recall, fairly new to the Internet. She has had remote access to the Net from home through the school's network for about six months. While she uses the Internet frequently with her pupils at school, she does most of her preparation at home.

Before Mary goes to work she sends herself an e-mail which she will open at school. It contains links to sites she wants to use with a class during the day. She attaches a word-processor file to the e-mail with her notes for the lesson (mostly borrowed from a lesson plan on an American colleague's site). At the same time she checks her e-mail. She has configured her e-mail program to check and send at the same time. This morning she sees that she has received several messages from American mailing lists during the night. There is also a note from her colleague reminding her about next week's tests.

Projects

Mary does not have time in the morning to read the American mail. When she gets to school she starts the day with a class of 13-year-olds who are together writing a web page as a part of the Global SchoolNet project *Community Share Web*. She chose to participate in this project to allow her pupils to write for a large unknown readership (as required by the National Curriculum). They are writing about a waterfall which is a local tourist attraction. The pupils are enthusiastic and have completed their fact-finding. They have discovered that the chemical plant upriver from the waterfall is suspected of having released chemicals into the water, causing the local trout to be less fertile than they should be. The class wrote an e-mail to the managing director of the plant and they have just received a chilly reply denying all knowledge of the problem. They spend most of the class discussing the latest development. They agree to try to involve an ecologist from Birmingham University to comment on what is going on. A group is assigned to track down a suitable person from the university web site and send an e-mail asking for help. Another group is set to plan the web-page layout and a third group to take all the texts written by the class and edit them so they fit together in the web page.

Web information

Mary's next class is a GCSE class. They are in the middle of *Macbeth* and they are finding it tough going. Mary wants to let them see that this text has meant a lot to people all round the globe. She sets pupils on all four of the networked computers in the classroom to search the Internet for Shakespeare sites and *Macbeth* commentaries and discussion. Mary has done some searching at home to see what kind of sites the pupils will be likely to find. Neither she nor they thought they would find quite as much as they do. They decide to make a web page full of annotated bookmarks to add to their class page. Mary cannot give them more class time for this, but a couple of pupils with computers at home are quite happy to do this in their spare time. The other pupils send the addresses of the sites they found and their comments on the sites to these two pupils by e-mail so they can compile a list. Mary promises to see to it that the page is published on the Web when it is ready.

Mary uses the last 15 minutes of class time to have the class read a scene of the play in parts. Several of the pupils have forgotten their books, but the class is able to come up with several sites where the entire text of Macbeth can be found (along with other texts whose copyright has expired), so the pupils can read the text straight off the screen.

Internal information

After lunch Mary sits in on the computer group's meeting. She is one of five teachers who are responsible for the school's Internet presence. They need to discuss how much information to make publicly accessible via the Internet. Should purely internal information like the library opening hours and the timetable be available to all comers? Several teachers want to keep this kind of information internal and let it circulate on the school intranet. Mary does not agree: she has seen a need for parents to be able to access this kind of factual information about the school and argues that this and a good deal more information should be available to anyone who cares to read it. She suggests that each class should have a page which is updated weekly with information about homework, class activities and links to pupils' work. The group agrees to compromise on this point and create an entrance to the school's intranet from the web page. This is to be protected using a password which can be given to parents who have access to the Internet at home or at work and are able to provide an e-mail address which they check daily.

Later Mary has time left over to ask the special needs teacher for help to find some computer games for some pupils who need to practise spelling. She finds a number of educational shareware sites via Yahoo! and downloads a couple of spelling games to evaluate. The rest of the afternoon is spent marking essays. She keeps track of each pupil's work on an Excel spreadsheet which is circulated by e-mail to all the teachers who come into contact with the class. This lets the teachers see if a pupil is slipping behind in several subjects.

When she gets home, Mary checks her e-mail again and finds a note from the headteacher directed to all the teachers. He is looking for volunteers to teach an evening class for parents at the school: 'ICT at our school'. The reason is that some parents have refused to sign the contracts that were sent home at the beginning of the school year acknowledging that their child will be using the Internet at school. The feeling is that the Internet is too dangerous for school use. Mary teaches some of the affected pupils and decides to offer to help. She answers the headteacher's e-mail and also sends a mail to a colleague in a nearby town. She wants to know how the teachers at her school dealt with the problem of resistance from some parents. Then she remembers having read an information sheet for parents on the BECTa site. She clicks on BECTa in her list of bookmarks and goes there to take a look at the parents' activities they suggest.

Private research

While she is on the Web she decides to see what she can find about Janet Greenway, a local author whose second book has just been released. She plans to invite her to come and talk to the older pupils about her writing. She takes a look in the local library's online catalogue to see if Janet's first book is available. It is out on loan, so Mary puts her name down for it (she needs to enter her library card number for this).

Next Mary decides to order Janet's new book. She goes to her favourite online bookshop and finds that the new book is for sale at a special promotional price. Mary orders the book and taps in her credit card number in the secure transactions page. She is informed that the book will be dispatched by post the same day.

Under the terms of the agreement between the staff and the school regarding access to the Internet Mary has a free hand. She may use the Net for private or recreational purposes as well as for work-related matters. This she does. Before she goes offline she checks her bank balance and looks at a detailed statement before transferring a sum to her savings account. Next she looks on a cookery noticeboard for recipe ideas for an oriental dinner party she is planning for a few friends next week.

Suddenly she is interrupted by a notification from ICQ *chat* that her sister in Canada has just come online. Mary hails her using the ICQ system and in seconds they are chatting. When they have said goodbye Mary checks the time of her favourite television serial and goes offline for the day.

Now not all teachers make as much use of the Internet as Mary, but everything she does on the Net is possible right now, given the right technical equipment (a PC 486 or newer or its equivalent and a modem). All Souls School in London's West End is a good example of a (primary) school which makes extensive use of the Web. They boast of being the second school in the UK to have a web page and their site has everything from resources for the literacy hour to an award-winning virtual tour of the Science Museum.

 # *Internet resources for education*

Teachers do not have the time to comb the Internet in search of useful material and contacts. Fortunately they do not have to. There are numerous organisations out there, standing by with massive quantities of tips, specially produced material and links to other material. You will find updated links to the sites we mention on this book's web pages. Some of the following are official or commercial school sites while others

3.1 *ICQ chat*

are written for and by teachers, in some cases with some kind of financial support. The resources we mention here are but a fraction of what there is 'out there' for teachers. If we have not mentioned your favourite educational site please send us an e-mail through the book's web pages so we can add it to the links on our pages.

British official resources

The *National Grid for Learning* (NGfL) web site is just starting up as we write this. It has the potential to be a tremendously influential site for British teachers. The Virtual Teacher Centre (VTC) is based around five 'rooms', Reception, Library, Meeting Room, Classroom Resources and Professional Development. In each of these rooms resources are being created and collected to serve teachers. The meeting room, for example, is a collection of computer conferences (noticeboards where questions, comments and answers are posted). Several different meeting rooms are planned, to discuss subjects like curriculum issues, benchmarking and target setting, sharing schemes of work by curriculum area, peer reviewing of software and reviews of school visits.

The NGfL site also houses the Standards and Effectiveness Database with a collection of documents and case studies pertaining to different areas in which educational standards can be raised, such as homework, study support, summer schools, etc. The site aims to help users to improve effectiveness and raise standards in schools. This section has a lot of very useful information for parents and teachers. There is a section on various kinds of study support, such as homework clubs and summer schools and the full text of consultative documents with national homework guidelines for primary and secondary schools – the direct result of the Government's White Paper *Excellence in Schools*.

In addition the NGfL site has a Governor Centre with advice for school governors and those considering becoming governors, and a further education site. This part of the site was not in service when we visited.

 The NGfL home page

BECT*a* is the organisation entrusted with implementing the DfEE vision of the National Grid for Learning. BECT*a* have their own extensive web site with a most useful series of information sheets about IT in curriculum subjects, about older projects, and with general advice about IT.

International official resources

The *Canadian Schoolnet* is a site intended to help Canadian teachers make use of the Internet in their teaching. This means that it has everything you would expect from such a site – a staffroom with discussion groups and links to teaching resources and lesson plans; links to pages for young people; a library with links to reference material and library resources on the Web; information about online projects that schools can join – and much more. An interesting feature is the Schoolnet MOO where visitors and 'residents' can meet and chat in a virtual environment. Even if a lot of the Schoolnet material is of limited interest outside Canada, there is plenty to engage and inspire British teachers too. Non-Canadian teachers frequently visit the Schoolnet discussion groups.

The *Irish Education Web* describes itself as a site created by and for teachers. It is maintained by the (Irish) National Centre for Technology in Education. It has a listing of Irish schools with a web presence, information about Internet projects, curriculum links, careers information, education links, pages for children and teenagers, a software guide and environmental pages as well as pages for special education and adult education.

The *European Schoolnet* offers many exciting possibilities. There are pages where pupils can find penpals, information about European projects and about the European Union itself. The News and Information page has links to news media from all over Europe. There is a database where you can look for project partners, and links to official education sites in the European Community countries. There is even a European Virtual School with access to teaching and learning resources provided by networks, publishers and schools, and a European Virtual Teacher College (both under development). In the Virtual School each curriculum subject has a 'room' staffed by a group of teachers who will offer resources for teaching and learning and invite you to discuss or share information about different subjects.

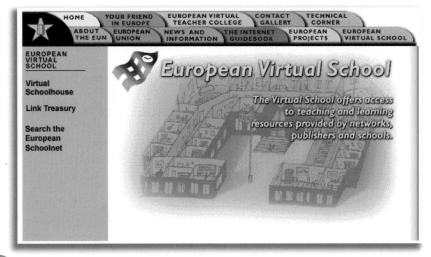

3.3 *European Virtual School*

Other resources

AngliaCampus (CampusWorld and Anglia Interactive)

CampusWorld has been BT's contribution to ICT in British schools. CampusWorld has now joined forces with its competitor *Anglia Interactive*, an Internet service for schools developed by Anglia Multimedia, in a resource known as *AngliaCampus*. The idea is that material from both resources will be available to subscribers. CampusWorld has been an attempt to provide both a valuable resource for teachers and a sheltered environment for schoolchildren to hone their Internet skills.

You can access AngliaCampus via the Web. The AngliaCampus material encompasses over 30 000 pages covering various parts of the curriculum at all levels. The site's major drawback is that it is only accessible to paying members.

The material in AngliaCampus is indexed by subject area, including cross-curricular resources for use by teachers or pupils. There are separate sections for primary and secondary pupils aged 4–18. The secondary area has material to support the National Curriculum in art, design and technology, English, geography, history, languages, maths, music, PE, RE and science. The Learning Exchange links to recommended and approved sites outside the site. While AngliaCampus boasts links to thousands of vetted sites, it offers a 'guided but not constricted approach to web navigation'.

Like CampusWorld before it, AngliaCampus offers subscribers the chance to meet in discussion groups on a large number of topics. This

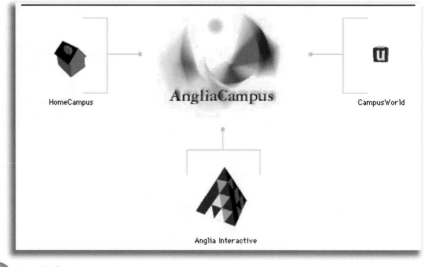

HomeCampus

AngliaCampus

CampusWorld

Anglia Interactive

3.4 *AngliaCampus*

kind of discussion group is one of the most interesting aspects of the site, since it has so many users. AngliaCampus regularly organises special events and projects. A recent example of an event was a virtual visit to Istanbul, where schools from around the world linked up with students at an international school there to find out about similarities and differences in their daily lives. The event is documented and presented in the site as a curriculum resource.

Subscribers also receive the content of the site on a CD-ROM every term. The service offers curriculum-based content for all age ranges, learning activities for home or classroom use, projects involving communication with other learners, and interactive events.

AngliaCampus includes various kinds of projects which offer the opportunity to exchange and combine information with others throughout the world using email, interactive chat and bulletin boards.

The curriculum material makes ample use of video, animation and sound, for example to show the functioning of muscles or historical scenes.

EduWeb

The educational Internet Service Provider RM's *Internet for Learning* is behind *EduWeb*, a site for teachers which has quite a few interesting features. There is a collection of discussion forums (noticeboards) where pupils and teachers can 'link up' with each other, an area where you can get help to search or build school web sites, and a staffroom with teaching resources such as a weekly round-up of the educational news. The site also has links to other educational resources and professional bodies and to topical education information (league tables etc.). In addition, subscribers can get access to what is called the Living Library, where they can browse information about careers, a picture library, quotations and recent news. An interesting feature is a newspaper archive where subscribers can search for articles about any topic in the *Mirror* and the *Sunday Mirror*, the *Independent* and the *Independent on Sunday* since 1992. EduWeb's *Pathways* is a searchable catalogue of over 5000 links to vetted age-graded external sites.

The EduWeb Living Library includes dictionary and thesaurus material from Oxford University Press; encyclopaedia entries from World Book; newspaper articles from the *Independent* and the *Mirror*; images from the Corbis picture library and revision guides from Letts; foreign-language and business/technology news from Reuters; the complete Oxford University Press *Children's Encyclopaedia* (including illustrations);

historical images from the National Monuments Record and maps from Philips. There is so much information here that you and your pupils might never need to look further! Everything is adapted for school use and you can specify the age of your pupils when you search, so the material returned will be on the right level, which cannot always be said of the material you might otherwise find on the Web. EduWeb claims that the Living Library material is extended with a staggering 10 000 new articles each week. The only disadvantage is that you have to pay to access the EduWeb material.

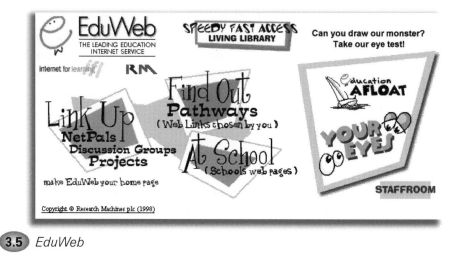

3.5 *EduWeb*

BBC

The BBC education site has a lot more to offer than just information about their educational radio and television programmes. Their Learning Station is a collection of online services aimed at teachers, children and parents, for use in schools and at home. There are educational sites based on BBC school programmes and other children's programmes, and many pages for teachers.

The most interesting parts of the site are the discussion forum *Teacher to Teacher* and the *Resource Centre* with advice on classroom use of all BBC radio, television and online resources. The Web *Index* is a guide to curriculum-related content on the Web categorised according to subject, age range or level according to the National Curriculum for England and Wales (curriculum differences for Scotland and Northern Ireland are said to have been accommodated wherever possible). Teachers are encouraged to contribute their own favourite sites to the Web Index.

The BBC site is developing continuously and looks set to be really useful. There are lists of relevant contacts (educational organisations and institutions) with web and e-mail addresses and a monthly newsletter from the BBC Learning Station. The BBC's Net guide is an explanation of what the Internet is and how you can use it.

Teacher Grid UK

Teacher Grid is a joint effort by RM, BT and Microsoft. It offers curriculum resources, discussion groups, teacher training resources and education news as well as organising live events, such as a visit from the Chief Executive of BECTa to the discussion forum to answer questions about the NGfL. Teacher Grid should become a very important and useful resource, which is not surprising given the calibre of its sponsors.

Microsoft

Microsoft have an extensive education area in both the UK and main US sites. They offer news and resources to parents, teachers and pupils. Their UK Teacher's Page is as near a complete guide to the Internet for British teachers as we have come across. They link to newsgroups (including Microsoft's own teachers' staffroom, EFL resources, online newspapers with education information, distance learning, educational publishers, examination boards, teaching unions, bullying, teaching overseas, as well as having dozens of annotated links to other educational resources.

Global SchoolNet

Global SchoolNet (GSN) is an extensive American resource funded by commercial sponsors (including Microsoft) that is open for schools everywhere. It has a projects database where you can find a classroom project to join or register your own project, as well as about 30 mail lists including the inspiring HILITES list with information about classroom projects which welcome participants. There is also information about video conferencing in schools. GSN has many articles and other resources for teachers as well as a tutorial on using the Web.

Global SchoolHouse was previously a separate site but now it is being merged with the Global SchoolNet site under Microsoft's patronage. There are a number of exciting projects here, such as the Thinkquest project (more about that later) and the Well-Connected Educator pages with collections of articles, discussion about a topic in educational technology (when we visited the topic was 'Student Internet Access: To Filter or Not to Filter?'). The main idea behind this resource is to encourage the development of the Microsoft initiative, the Connected Learning Community.

Web66

Web66 is also American. Its aim is to enable schools to contact each other. It has information about government bodies (the equivalent of the British National Grid for Learning or BECTa sites) supporting the development of ICT in schools in countries in every corner of the world. These bodies in turn usually have a good deal of information about the way ICT is used in the schools of that country. Web66 also has lists of schools with an online presence for every country. The site also contains a fair amount of information for teachers wanting to use the Internet in the classroom, some of it aimed at more technically inclined users who might be interested in setting up their own web servers.

ERIC and AskERIC

ERIC (the Educational Resources Information Center) is an exceptional American resource from the US Department of Education. ERIC has 16 subject-specific clearinghouses for educational information. In each of them you can search for resources although you will only get summaries of articles and journal papers dealing with the subject at hand in some cases.

Quick tip

To request education information, address an e-mail message to:

askeric@askeric.org

The AskERIC service is more useful. You can pose a specific question on the theory or practice of education and the information specialists will respond within 48 hours with ERIC database citations, Internet resources, and, when appropriate, full-text ERIC Digests.

Another useful service of the AskERIC system is the virtual library which offers 125 topical guides to the Internet, over 1200 lesson plans and the archives of over 20 education mailing lists. There are also several development projects, including one to develop a graphical MOO environment for disseminating information.

Classroom Connect

Classroom Connect is another large American site. Its Resource Station has many articles of interest to teachers who use the Internet with their classes: one about citing Internet resources, tips on writing acceptable-use policies, information about global projects and CU-SeeMe video conferencing and advice on how to make the best use of a single modem connection to the Internet. There is also a searchable database of more than 1000 annotated educational links (GRADES), links to lesson plans and tips on where to find more and how to make your own work useful to others, a meeting place (noticeboard-based discussion), and the inevitable monthly guide to Internet educational resources. The site also

An **FTP-site** (File Transfer Protocol) is a directory on an FTP-server connected to the Internet. Files can be downloaded using a web browser.

includes stories of how other teachers have successfully used the Internet in their teaching, help to understand copyright on the Internet, a teacher contact database for finding project partners, a mailing list, an **FTP site** with lesson plans, educational software, etc., and links to USENET newsgroups.

In touch with colleagues

Most of the education resources mentioned above have some kind of noticeboard or discussion group where teachers can get together for a chat. Some of these are better frequented than others. The BBC education site has a number of noticeboard-based chats. These provide a simple way to get in touch. All you need to do is fill in what you want to say on the web page and send it off. If you are lucky you might be able to read a response after a few days.

These discussions are usually closely associated with the web site on which they appear. But there are other ways to get in touch with like-minded colleagues. In the first chapter we discussed mailing lists. Mailing lists provide a relatively sheltered environment for a discussion. The

Contributions to a discussion are either **on-topic** (relevant to the forum's general topic) or **off-topic** (a side-track).

A discussion **thread** is all the contributions on a single topic.

discussion is usually fairly **on-topic** and commercial messages are rare. The discussion on a topic can continue for quite a while until the **thread** tapers off and is replaced by a new subject.

The table below shows a few mailing lists which might be of interest to you as a teacher, with instructions for joining them. We have been members of many of them.

Another way to extend your circle of colleagues is to participate in newsgroup discussions. A number of USENET newsgroups deal with the subject of education. We have already mentioned *uk.education.16plus*, *uk.education.misc, uk.education.schools-it, uk.education.staffroom* and *uk.education.teachers*. There are a few other uk.education groups for maths, home education and expeditions.

You can find other interesting groups if you set your newsreader to search for newsgroups with the word *education* in the group name. Microsoft have their own news server with their own newsgroups on it, including their *Teachers' Staffroom (msn.uk.education.teaching)*. Their other education newsgroups are *msn.uk.education.debates, msn.uk.education.homeworkhelp, msn.uk.education.parents* and *msn.uk.education.students*. You can get to them from Microsoft UK's web pages or from the links in Appendix 4.

The discussion forums we have mentioned do not require participants to be online at the same time as each other. The messages will wait to be read at the visitor's convenience. There are, however, live webchats for teachers. On these you can chat in real time with one or more other

BULLY- L	Message text: sub bully-l <your name> Administration address: listserv@nic.surfnet.nl *For teachers to discuss preventative* *measures*
C-EDRES	Message text: sub c-edres <your name> Administration address: listserv@unbvm1.csd.unb.ca *An excellent source of high-quality* *educational web resources*
DYSLEXIA	Message text: join dyslexia <your name> Administration address: mailbase@mailbase.ac.uk *Forum for issues of particular concern to* *dyslexics, especially computer tools useful to* *dyslexics*
ENGLIT-VICTORIAN	Message text: join englit-victorian <your name> Administration address: mailbase@mailbase.ac.uk *Forum for discussion of research topics in* *Victorian literature*
GENTALK	Message text: subscribe gentalk <your name> Administration address: listserv@usa.net *Discussion of genetics in education at all* *levels*
HILITES	Message text: subscribe hilites Administration address: majordomo@gsn.org *Information about collaborative projects* *seeking partners around the world*
ITS	Message text: sub ITS <your name> Administration address: listserv@unmvma.unm.edu *Implementing IT in schools*
K12-EURO-TEACHERS	Message text: subscribe k12-euro- teachers Administration address: majordomo@lists.eunet.fi *A good source of contact with teachers all* *over Europe*

Some mailing lists of interest to teachers

KIDLINK	Message text: subscribe kidlink <your name> Administration address: listserv@vm1.nodak.edu *A world-wide large-scale project for 10–15-year-olds and their adults*
NEWSLETTER	Message text: subscribe newsletter Administration address: majordomo@teachnet.com *Not a discussion list – a newsletter for primary school teachers*
NUKOP-EDUCATION	Message text: join nukop-education <your name> Administration address: mailbase@mailbase.ac.uk *Offers regular updates of the latest education-related UK government publications and a forum to discuss matters arising from them*
PHYSHARE	Message text: sub physhare <your name> Administration address: listserv@psuvm.psu.edu *For physics teachers*
RELIGIOUS-STUDIES-UK	Message text: join religious-studies-uk <your name> Administration address: mailbase@mailbase.ac.uk *Discussion of problems and opportunities regarding teaching, research, resources, etc.*
SCHOOL-MANAGEMENT	Message text: join school-management <your name> Administration address: mailbase@mailbase.ac.uk *For discussion of education in schools, in particular their management and government and the curriculum*
SENCO-FORUM	Message text: join senco-forum <your name> Administration address: mailbase@mailbase.ac.uk *For researchers, students, teachers and others interested in supporting pupils with special educational needs*

Continued overleaf

SUPERK12	Message text: sub superk12 <your name> Administration address: listserv@listserv.syr.edu *Implementing IT in schools*
TEACHER-2-TEACHER	Message text: subscribe postings Administration address: majordomo@teachnet.com *Discussion list for exchanging teaching tips and information about web resources*
TEACHING-STATISTICS	Message text: teaching-statistics <your name> Administration address: mailbase@mailbase.ac.uk *For those concerned with the initial teaching of statistics in all phases of education*
TESL-L	Message text: subscribe tesl-l <your name> Administration address: listserv@cunyvm.cuny.edu *Teaching English as a second language* *If you join TESL-L you can also join its branches, TESLCA-L and TESLK-12.*
TESLCA-L	Message text: subscribe teslca-l <your name> Administration address: listserv@cunyvm.cuny.edu *About the use of IT in the teaching of English as a second language*
TESLK-12	Message text: sub teslk-12 <your name> Administration address: listserv@cunyvm.cuny.edu *About the teaching of English as a second language in schools*
UK-SCHOOLS	Message text: join uk-schools <your name> Administration address: mailbase@mailbase.ac.uk *For teachers and others interested in the use of the Internet in UK schools*

Mailing lists of interest to teachers, continued

persons. You can locate them by searching for, for example, *teacher chat live* with a search engine. Some of these have scheduled times one hour a week when teachers can get online at the same time for informal discussion. Some of these chats are intended to include parents.

 ## Teaching material on the Web

The education sites and resources we have discussed in this chapter have offered a lot of material about teaching with the Internet. Some teachers are willing to go a step further and share their own teaching preparation (lesson plans) and material with others. The idea is that you can contribute work you have done and maybe use somebody else's work in your own teaching.

Lesson plans

There are any number of sites where teachers can pick up lesson plans and ready-to-use web-based lessons for their classes. You can search for them using Yahoo! or you can use some of the lists of dozens of lesson-plan sites you can find in teaching resources such as the Global SchoolHouse. It is difficult to recommend one site over others because teachers are looking for such different things. Most of these lesson-plan sites are American in origin. Nonetheless they might be useful if you are looking for a fresh way to approach a subject.

The *Teachers Helping Teachers* site claims to provide basic teaching tips to inexperienced teachers with ideas that can be immediately implemented in the classroom. In addition they attempt to provide a forum for experienced teachers to share their expertise and tips with colleagues around the world. There are lesson plans for students on different levels in the areas of classroom management, language arts, maths, science, social studies, the arts and special education.

The *Busy Teacher* has a list of lesson plans, reference tools and other interesting material for many school and non-school subjects, for example archaeology, geology and palaeontology. The maths section, for example, gives lesson plans for calculus for high school as well as for basic primary school concepts.

The *AskERIC* site has lesson plans for different subjects and levels (physical education, maths, science, foreign languages, arts, social studies, health, etc.). We chose to look more closely at the maths section and were able to choose from a number of topics: algebra, applied math, arithmetic, functions, geometry, measurement, probability, process skills and statistics. Within the geometry area there were lesson plans for tangrams and exploring the geometry of the sphere among other things.

On the UK side there are things happening too. *Teacher Grid* UK, sponsored jointly by BT, RM and Microsoft, has an online database with teaching resources, the Curriculum Resource Archive. Here you can find ideas and ready-made classroom activities. The Curriculum Resources of the National Grid for Learning's Virtual Teacher Centre also has a lot of leads, although in many cases both these resource collections will take you to sites outside the UK.

Ready-to-use lessons

The material you can find on the Net that is produced by and for teachers is generally on the level of lesson plans, ideas or collections of links to web sites where you can find material about the subject at hand. If you are looking for something to print out and put into your pupils' hands or to load into their hard disk you may often be disappointed. The material you will find on the Web is often not at the right level for pupils. The notable exceptions are the sites such as EduWeb, AngliaCampus and the like where you will find carefully graded material which has relevance to the curriculum. This kind of material is generally available to paying subscribers. There is, however, some suitable material in the education sites mentioned above that is free. The Net has a long way to go before it will be a serious rival to traditional printed educational material.

If you are looking for online material written for a particular age group you might do better to consult an educational CD-ROM instead. However, if you need to follow the news with your pupils you might find up-to date information at the right level on some of the media sites, such as the BBC education pages. Many teachers take material from the Web and adapt it for use with their classes. Older pupils are, of course, more likely to be able to use material written for a general audience.

 *Teach yourself*

Preparation and research

You may find that the biggest difference the Internet makes to your life as a teacher is that it becomes much easier to research a subject. As new topics crop up you can quickly access information. You may find that you go further into a subject than with printed sources, and at the same time that you also find out about related subjects so that your knowledge becomes both wider and deeper. While knowledge is always a good thing you may find yourself spending more time than you wanted to on a subject.

Also, neither the Internet nor life is ordered into neat categories according to the curriculum. It is very difficult to limit research to what you need to know. If you do not, you find that the time you spend finding out what you needed to has been quite excessive, even if you learned a lot of other things along the way.

» *Case study*

Volcanoes

Mary Smith's colleague Jane Jameson teaches geography and is preparing to teach about volcanoes next week. She has heard that there is a lot of good, up-to-date information about active volcanoes and wants to see how she can use it in her teaching.

Jane searches for *volcano* with Yahoo! UK & Ireland. She comes to a long list of volcanology links in the *Science: Earth Sciences: Geology and Geophysics* section. Yahoo! uses the symbol of a pair of sunglasses to indicate recommended sites. These sites are usually more than just a single person's input – more like a gateway to the study of the particular subject on the Web. The recommended *Volcano World* site is such a site. Jane goes to it and finds a massive site with hundreds of pages for schools and others. There are lesson plans on volcanoes, and articles showing how teachers have taught volcanoes.

Jane follows a link in the lesson-plans page to a site called *Volcano Lovers* which seems to have material written at just the level she is looking for. Concerned as always about checking her sources, Jane traces the page via bottom-of-the-page links to a collection of pages about science behind the news for children – the *Why Files*, under the University of Wisconsin web server, funded by the American National Science Foundation. Reassured, Jane looks at other pages from the *Why Files* and finds it to be a resource she just has to share with her colleagues. There is detailed information ready to put in children's hands about every-thing from elephants to cloning, all at an appropriate level. Every week new material appears and old material is archived for easy retrieval.

By the time Jane is finished she feels quite overwhelmed by all that she has found. Not only has she found all she ever wanted to know about volcanoes, far more than she actually needs for her class, she has also stumbled onto a source of scientific background information about current events written for school-children. The trouble is, she has spent three hours online, which is a lot longer that it would have taken her to get the information she actually needed from a children's encyclopaedia (whether printed or on CD-ROM). While it is of course a good thing that a teacher is well prepared for her teaching, the time spent at the computer is not really commensurate with the results.

3.6 *Volcano World*
Copyright VolcanoWorld (volcano.und.edu)

Ask the experts

One of the features of the *Volcano World* site mentioned above is that you can *Ask a Volcanologist* any question about volcanoes. If your question is not among the 101 Frequently Asked Questions you can put it to a panel of three volcanologists in Hawaii, the USA and Australia who will draw on their considerable experience to answer the question. There are dozens of other Ask-an-Expert sites which accept e-mail questions from the public to answer on the Web. Some of these are commercial sites which offer the service to attract visitors; others are sponsored by advertisers; while some are non-commercial sites, often based in a university department.

You can pose questions to an astronomer, a linguist, a geologist, a dentist, a master plumber an engineer or any of several kinds of doctors. You can find addresses on our web pages or by using a search engine. These resources can be useful to you in several ways. First, there is usually an FAQ somewhere on the site so you can see previous questions and their answers. Read it as a source of interesting titbits of information you can use to enliven other material on the subject. You can then put a question of your own to the expert (usually a panel) or have your pupils formulate questions they might be able to ask (checking to see that the questions have not already been answered).

Material from universities

Quick tip

Your e-mail will almost certainly be read by the person you address it to. If you have a particularly interesting observation or question you might even get an answer, but there are no guarantees. You might ask for some tips as to where you can read more about the project that interests you. Be careful not to let a lot of pupils hound a single research scientist with trivial questions that could be better answered elsewhere.

Some university departments make a point of having a lot of information available to all comers via their web page. In most teaching you will manage very well without ever feeling a need to access the latest research in a subject or read university-level sources for your preparation. But occasions can arise when you or a pupil need to find out more about a subject. Many departments have the details of their current research projects presented on the departmental web pages. Usually the name of the researchers working on each project will be given. The e-mail address of each employee will often appear on another page in the same site. Now you can easily get in touch with the people at the sharp edge of research.

Information points

Quick tip

It is a simple matter to choose a start page. In Microsoft Explorer 4, for example, you need to choose Internet alternative from the View menu and there choose General where you can specify the URL of the page you want as your start page. In Netscape Navigator 4 the procedure is similar: choose Settings from the Edit menu and then click on Navigator to come to a box where you can enter the address of the start page you want to have.

There are a number of web sites which serve as gateways to further information. These pages can be suitable to bookmark as links that are always visible at the top of your browser window. Depending on where your interests lie you might prefer a page which leads to a lot of information about society, such as the current front page of the *Times* or the *Electronic Telegraph*, or about educational organisations and resources, such as the National Grid for Learning entry page. You can choose to start up on Microsoft's UK education page or on Yahoo! UK & Ireland or Infoseek's or Excite's UK entry page. If you have access to, for example, EduWeb or AngliaCampus you may want to start up in their entry pages. You might like to set up your browser to open on one of these pages every time you start it up.

December 3 1998   **No. 66 375**

Hague faces Lords mutiny

WILLIAM HAGUE's leadership of the Tory party was in crisis last night after he was <u>forced to sack</u> <u>Viscount Cranborne</u>, Tory leader in the House of Lords, and the remainder of the Tory front bench peers offered to resign.

Lord Cranborne was dismissed after Mr Hague publicly rejected the deal he had unilaterally done with the Government over Lords reform. It would have allowed 91 hereditary peers to survive the Bill stripping them of their voting rights.

Lord Cranborne's exit is <u>just</u> <u>another page</u> in a well-liked Lord's long story

3.7 *A news story from the Times site*

 # Copyright

The whole issue of copyright on the Internet has been riddled with misconceptions, rumours and confusion. The Net's international character has further muddied the waters. Every country has its own copyright legislation, and even if international agreements do exist to regulate the copying of printed material there has never before been this kind of simultaneous electronic publishing in all the countries of the world.

Current confusion

Part of the confusion lies in the definition of copying in connection with computers. Exactly when can you be said to have made a copy of a document?

❏ Is it when you copy a CD-ROM to another CD-ROM?

❏ Is it when you install a program you have bought to your hard disk?

❏ What about if you download a game from the Internet and install it on your computer?

❏ If you save a web page on your hard disk?

❏ If you view a web page on your computer?

❏ If you copy a chunk of text or a picture from a web page and paste it into your own document?

❏ If you use a background pattern from a web page in your own web page?

In fact, all of these activities are copying. Even if you are simply surfing the Web, a copy of the page you have visited is left on your hard disk. Pictures, sounds and text on the Internet are protected by the same laws as other kinds of documents. This is not to say that it is illegal to surf the Web. Exemptions for this kind of activity have been made.

British legislation

In the UK, digital media such as computer programs and documents are protected, be they stored on floppy disk or CD-ROM or transmitted via the Internet. There are exceptions to this protection, namely what is known as *fair dealing* of material, (that copying is permitted if it is for research, private study, for libraries or for educational uses). The problem arises when attempting to decide what constitutes educational uses. A class copying pictures from the Web for their own pages may be infringing copyright. So may a teacher who downloads an interesting site onto the school intranet for her pupils to use.

The Internet causes difficulties for the interpretation of the law because its very use involves the copying of data from one computer to another. Digitally stored text, sound and pictures are very easy to copy, and there is no deterioration in quality when copies are made. The BECTa document *Connecting Schools, Networking People* urges schools to be aware of copyright issues and to monitor their web site, intranet and uses made of web materials with copyright in mind.

Most kinds of texts and pictures are protected by copyright whether or not there is a copyright notice on them. Make sure you and your pupils make proper reference to sources you use (with an URL, author's name and date if known). It is of course plagiarism to attempt to pass off somebody else's work as your own.

The Copyright, Designs and Patents Act of 1988 made it illegal for anyone to deliberately copy someone else's work without their consent. This is complemented by the Copyright (Computer Programs) Regulations of 1992, which give a computer program the same status as a literary work, and the Computer Misuse Act 1990, which states that it is also illegal to secure access to a program or data held in a computer if the use is not authorised. The interpretation of these laws in connection with the Internet is difficult, and it will be some time before praxis is established (when enough test cases have been heard).

European standard solution

In each of the countries of the European Community different kinds of laws are being passed to regulate the protection of intellectual property in the Internet and elsewhere. It is widely felt that there is a need for a common regulatory approach. The most pressing issues are said to be the prevention of illegal copying, the management of copyright clearances (the right to make copies for certain specified purposes) and the negotiation of authors' rights.

The European Commission has presented a proposal for a Directive harmonising aspects of rules on copyright and related rights in the information society. The Directive would among other things harmonise rules on making protected material available on demand over the Internet. In the USA the free distribution of copyrighted material over the Internet has now become a criminal offence.

How to handle Internet copyright

Often when you visit a page you may read a bottom-of-the-page note telling you who owns the copyright (generally the person who created the page). In many cases, particularly in the case of pages with educational content, you might also be told that you may use the material under certain circumstances (often that the material can be used for educational or non-profit purposes) provided you credit it to the author and include the copyright notice on any copies you make. Some such notices specifically point out that you are not allowed to alter the material in any way or use a portion of the material (which would include pasting chunks of a web document into your own documents).

This creates a problem for teachers who want to make selections of web material available to their pupils. It is quite in order to have a copy of a web page in your computer's cache memory and let pupils view it while offline, but not to place the same web page on an intranet. However if the same document was downloaded from the Internet into each of the computers in the intranet there would be no problem. Here the temptation to bend what appear to be inconsistent rules is certainly strong. Hopefully the impending EC legislation will create reasonable praxis so that we can continue to make use of the Internet in schools in whatever way we think most suitable with a clear conscience.

 ## *Summary*

This chapter has given you a quick tour of what there is on the Net specifically for teachers.

❑ Official and commercial agents are outdoing each other in their effort to get as many teachers as possible online and, what is more important, give them a reason to keep coming back.

❑ It is possible to use the Internet extensively to enrich your teaching and to enhance pupils' learning within the National Curriculum. There is plenty of relevant material out there and thousands of people to meet.

❑ Teachers everywhere are using the Net to bring the world into their classrooms and to inform the world (including parents) about the classroom. The time has come for most teachers to be aware of the Net and be able to use it in their teaching.

The **Internet** for pupils

The Internet is often associated with young people. The reason for this is not quite clear but many young people find the Internet very attractive. Access to computers and the Internet can provide both the motivation some pupils need to apply themselves to their studies and boundless stimulation for more able students. But ICT is not, of course, an end in itself. Without careful consideration of the role the Internet can play in the curriculum it can easily devour a larger share of the time and money available to a class than it is worth.

Young people

Perhaps one of the more fascinating aspects of online communication is that we are judged by our ideas and our ability to formulate them rather than by our age, sex, race or appearance. Most of the contact between individuals and groups on the Internet is still text-based. There is no way to know more about people you meet on the Net than they choose to tell you. The positive side of this is that everybody is equal.

The downside of this is that it is difficult to know who you can trust. The 14-year-old girl in Kansas your pupils thought they were chatting with might just as easily turn out to be a 45-year-old man from Ealing. E-mail addresses do not always tell you much about the identity of the person you are talking to, and they can be falsified. The world is full of all sorts of people, and pupils need to learn that they might come across dangerous people on the Net.

Nonetheless, the Internet opens direct channels of communication where none existed before. You and your pupils can easily write directly to decision makers of all kinds, in the knowledge that your e-mail is more likely to reach the person it is intended for than a letter or telephone call would.

What have pupils been doing on the Internet?

We asked some teachers and pupils (via the Internet, of course) to tell us how they actually use the Internet and what they would like to do if they had adequate resources.

A teacher of history and sociology at a school in Sussex has created several Internet resources for his GCSE classes, including a database of information about 'The Emancipation of Women'. An ongoing project is the creation of a 'First World War Encyclopaedia' written by Year 9 pupils, which has developed into a popular resource with over 1000 visits a day. He is currently trying to find schools in other parts of Europe to join the project. One section of the encyclopaedia is a study of the impact of the war on the towns and villages where the children live. This school has only had a single computer with Internet access, although this changed in late 1998.

The International Internet Encyclopedia of the First World War is being created by teachers and students from several different countries. Each entry includes several pages of narrative, illustrations and links to other relevant websites. The strategy is to look at the international, the national and the local dimension of the conflict. By the middle of 1998 we hope to have over two thousand pages of information in the encyclopedia.

The contents page will provide you with details of what the International Internet Encyclopedia of the First World War will eventually contain. However, this is an organic project and only those headings that are gold and underlined have so far been uploaded. Existing entries are constantly being developed.

Please **e-mail** the editors if you have any suggestions on how the Encyclopedia of the First World War can be improved. We would also like you to contact us if you wish to become involved in this project.

 The International Internet Encyclopedia of the First World War

A Scottish teacher in Connecticut comments wryly that his school tries to avoid projects such as extensive penpal e-mail with other schools, with the view that such projects primarily amuse the students and impress parents and visitors. They do have a Spanish penpal project going for younger pupils though (9–13 years old). The school has a project where high school students are individually tutored in the basic use of the Web and shown how to search for material relevant to the curriculum. Then these students are scheduled to individually tutor teachers (starting with the principal) and other pupils. The students in this school correspond socially via an in-school e-mail system. Each student has a personal ID and the system is used enthusiastically and deemed to be an excellent way to learn to use Internet e-mail in a safe environment.

A teacher of 15–18 year old students of literature and something called 'competitive speech' in Oklahoma reports on how her students use the Net to search for information and graphics for school projects, scripts and speeches for competitive speech and pictures of their favourite singers, actors and athletes. Her pupils enjoy trying to get round the security system which prohibits access to some sites. This teacher would like to establish links with teachers and pupils in other parts of the world, with the ultimate aim of having live discussions with them.

Another Connecticut teacher enjoys the educational newsgroups available on the Net. He says, 'The Internet is the reason I have been having the most exciting year in my teaching career. It definitely has carried over into the classroom.' This teacher has had his sixth-grade inner-city class involved in a project where the class filled in an Internet questionnaire about the geography of their immediate area. Their answer was e-mailed in and added to other answers from schools throughout the world. In the next stage of the project the class received puzzles about cities they were to identify. The final stage is to submit answers to the puzzles and possibly win a prize.

ⓥ *Teaching appropriate behaviour*

In those schools where pupils are not given direct access to the Internet, the main reason (apart from insufficient resources) is that the school and parents are uneasy about the relative ease of access to undesirable material on the Internet. Schools where pupils are permitted free access have usually developed some kind of arrangement to regulate or monitor the pupils' Internet activity (various solutions to this problem have been discussed earlier). One of the most effective ways to regulate Internet activity is to teach responsible behaviour. All other solutions leave the pupil unprotected when accessing the Internet at home or somewhere else where the system of control used at school does not apply.

Some schools have the simple rule that pupils should avoid doing things they would not want their parents or teachers to see. If this rule is applied by the pupils it will cover many situations, both in connection with the Internet and otherwise!

Respect for others

It is important to bear in mind that there is a person at the receiving end of all communication. Newsgroups, web noticeboards and mailing lists can be very fruitful forums for pupils' discussions and learning experiences. But these discussions can very often get out of hand: some-body expresses himself less than tactfully; somebody else takes offence and a third person chimes in to agree with one or other of them. In no time at all the exchanges become decidedly unfriendly and you have a full-scale **flame-war** on your hands. A flame is a personal attack on someone with whom you do not agree.

A **flame-war** is a discussion that turns nasty and gets personal.

This kind of dispute is more likely to arise when a group has partici-pants from several different cultures. Most of the discussions on the Internet are carried out in English, but not everybody who is active on the Net has English as their first language. We have seen misunder-standings arise for all sorts of reasons:

❑ Non-native speakers of English may express themselves clumsily, causing offence, perhaps saying something like 'you must always . . .' rather than 'In my experience I have found it better to . . .'.

❑ Non-native speakers of English might also misunderstand the finer nuances of repartee between participants in a discussion. Figures of speech are particularly problematic. Imagine the bafflement caused by an expression like 'I made a pig's ear out of it'!

❑ Humour is wonderful, but very difficult to use successfully in inter-national discussion groups on the Internet. Irony (often seen as a prominent feature of British humour) is particularly hard to get across successfully. We have seen a flame-war started in a mailing list when one participant sent a message beginning 'Dear Susie', obviously intended for a single recipient, to an entire list. Another list member wrote to the list saying 'Dear Katie, I don't like to be called Susie any more' and signing his name John. He later claimed to have done this as a gentle reminder of the netiquette rule which suggests that it is a good thing to avoid sending letters that are intended for an individual to the entire group. The many responses were of three kinds: one group wrote in and criticised John for his transsexual innuendo ('we don't want that kind of smut here!'); another group wrote in and defended Katie, saying that John was being unnecessarily aggressive ('anyone can make a mistake like that, I've done it myself'), and a third group wrote in explaining the joke to the first group and applauding John's humour. The first group then wrote back saying that they did not appreciate *that* kind of humour.

Really all the individuals involved (except the third group) were guilty of not respecting the other members of the list. John could have written a private mail to Katie, allowing her to save face, and avoiding the whole issue. Similarly, those who were offended by John's post could have written privately to him. The third group, the peacemakers, are a valuable part of a mailing list. There is often a need for some kind of referee to explain and soothe hurt feelings.

❑ People can take offence for the strangest reasons, and if you are going to participate in discussions on the Net you will probably sooner or later offend someone. Any kind of religious comment is generally out, especially if Christian in origin. Some members of non-Christian denominations in the USA are very quick to react to any kind of assumption that everyone on the list has a Christian perspective. The same can be true of any comment that refers to a person's colour. The person writing is likely to be reminded that not all on the list are white Anglo-Saxon Protestants!

In fact there is little you can say without upsetting someone. Just bear in mind that mutual tolerance and respect are the keys to successful international communication. If there is a misunderstanding or upset, try to repair the damage. Apologise if necessary, and explain what you meant to say if you think you can without making matters worse.

Many pupils will need to be specifically taught to think before they write in this kind of forum. Internet discussion groups are very unusual in that they involve fairly casual language, much more like the spoken language than the written, but the discussion is in fact generally written. This means that the participants do not have access to each other's body language when they are expressing themselves or reading some-one else's words. They can neither send nor receive a tongue-in-cheek expression or a smile (unless they use smileys). This is something that needs to be discussed before pupils are let loose on the Net. It might be helpful to picture the person at the other end, reading what you have written and interpreting it through the filter of their own experiences.

Safety first!

As we have said before, not everyone you or your pupils meet on the Net will wish you well. In real life we protect our young people from undesirable encounters and equip them with knowledge about how to deal with strangers. They need the same kind of knowledge when they are at large in the online community. In particular, this means that they must be taught not to divulge personal information (full name, telephone number, home address, etc.) to strangers.

In certain circumstances, pupils may find it difficult to avoid divulging information. Some web sites, such as those which supply free e-mail accounts or access to online versions of newspapers, may require visi-tors to become members. This generally involves filling in some kind of form. You may find it useful to discuss this kind of registration with your pupils: What is the information used for (selling to those who wish to send junk mail?)? Why do they ask the questions they ask (income, number of people in the household)? If you decide that you do not want your pupils to divulge such information you can advise them to fill in obviously false information (e.g. name: xxx yyy, address: zzz, zzz, zzz). This can be compared to the practice of systematically entering a false name and telephone number on money-off coupons at the supermarket. If this kind of tactic is not ethically acceptable to you, at least have the pupils enter the school address rather than their home address.

In environments such as IRC and webchat, young people may be invited to a private chat with a helpful stranger. While this may be perfectly innocent, overly helpful strangers should not be trusted at all. Many schools completely ban IRC, and those that allow it sometimes insist that pupils are chaperoned by an adult or chat monitor and expressly forbid private chatting with strangers. A chaperone will help a pupil to get out of a conversation with a too-interested adult (e.g. by setting *ignore* at the adult's name).

⏩ *Outside school*

It is becoming easier to gain access to the Internet. Libraries, Internet cafés and the like are making the Internet available to those who do not have a computer. The Government's policy is to make the Internet and knowledge about how to use it available to everybody who wants it at little or no expense. This is a very important democratic principle. At a time when more and more information of public interest is becoming available via the Net, it is obviously of the utmost importance that no group be excluded from access to it.

This does mean that the stance taken by the school is only relevant to part of the interested pupil's exposure to the Internet. If the school forbids IRC, for example, that does not mean that it is unavailable elsewhere. As in all other matters, the only protection the school can offer the pupils is to have prepared them adequately with enough knowledge and respect for themselves and others to enable them to make responsible decisions about how to behave even when they are not being supervised.

The Internet at home

An increasing number of families with school-age children have a computer and Internet access at home. Many parents feel that this is necessary if their children are not to be left behind by those who use the Internet at home. In fact many teachers do claim to see a considerable difference between those pupils who are used to dealing with

ICT at home and those who are not. One advantage is that the teacher is able to recruit the former as assistants when setting up classroom equipment and as partners to guide less experienced pupils online. That is not to say that the children who spend time online at home will be any better able to use the Internet productively in school after the initial stages. As we have already seen, not all time spent online is beneficial.

Exploring the Internet can be a very rewarding activity for parents and children together. The problem arises when young people have a computer with Internet access in the privacy of a bedroom. If they are permitted to go online without any kind of supervision or guidance they may well find their way to unsuitable sites. Some parents may find it better to have the computer in the family room where the rest of the family pass by and can see what is on the screen. In some families parents may wish to install some kind of filtering software such as was discussed in chapter 2.

If many pupils have access to the Internet at home the teacher might want to set them some kind of homework involving either online collaboration or the use of online resources. They can prepare material to share with the rest of the class.

In some schools (e.g. those Reading schools involved in Microsoft's pioneer project 'The Highdown Hub') the teachers have entered into cooperation with the parents to exchange all sorts of information between home and school. This is particularly suitable in those schools where the pupils have been supplied with laptop computers to take to and from school each day and an Internet connection via the school, thus ensuring that all the pupils have access to the same kind of equipment. This kind of arrangement usually involves informing the parents about ICT and offering instruction to those who need it. All parties seem to be very satisfied in schools where this system operates.

Organised activities

The Internet is a great attraction in youth clubs and other places where young people gather. There are a number of sites on the Web which are intended for these groups. Activities such as scavenger hunts in competition with other youth clubs, online chatting with counterparts elsewhere, web-page workshops, are suitable for this kind of setting. The advantage of having Internet access for these after-school groups is that the activities can be permitted to take time without necessarily fitting in to the curriculum.

⏩ *Special interests*

You will already have noticed that the Internet is a natural home for all kinds of special interests and obsessions. No matter how narrow an interest may be, there will always be at least a few hundred devotees in a world perspective. The Internet is a superb tool for widening your social circles. Whatever interest your pupils have they will probably find it represented on the Net.

Clubs

From football supporter clubs to Michael Jackson's fan club, there are thousands of clubs of all shapes and sizes on the Net. There are official sites and also unofficial ones, which often have a lot more information to offer. A quick search in Yahoo! UK & Ireland for *Nottingham Forest* takes you to the subcategory of *Regional:Countries:United Kingdom:Recreation and Sport:Sport:Football:Leagues:Nationwide Football League:Division 1:Clubs: Nottingham Forest* FC (if they are in the First Division when you make your search!). Here you will find links to over twenty pages about the Nottingham Forest football club, including the official *Nottingham Forest Online* – which offers among other things daily e-mail news to registered fans, daily updates to pages, results, radio interviews and player interviews. You will also find a link to Yahoo!'s special football service *Yahoo! Football* with up-to-date news about Nottingham Forest or any other team.

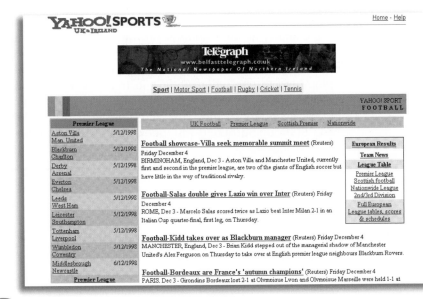

4.2 *Yahoo! Football*

At the other end of the scale, a few minutes' browsing in Yahoo! will take you, for example, to the *Newcastle Kingsmen*, a group of folk dancers in the Northern counties. They pride themselves on performing the Rapper sword dance, together with the Grenoside longsword dance and the Royton Northwest clog Morris dance. The Web has something for everyone!

⊗ *Case study*

Fan club sites

Allison Smith, Mary's teenage daughter, is a great fan of the rock musician Andrew Jenkins. She is member of the Andrew Jenkins fan club, which has an extensive web site for fans all over the world. The web site is used to provide members with an online newsletter. The advantages over a printed newsletter are many – full colour, low cost, no postage charges, and no printing delays. The web newsletter is easy to update, and late-breaking news can be added very simply. Of course there is a whole page devoted to Andrew's tour dates and another with a list of his CDs which can be ordered directly from the site. There is even a short video clip from Andrew's latest hit.

The web site also offers a real-time webchat, and about once a month Andrew himself turns up for the scheduled Wednesday night chat. The fan club uses an IRC channel for unscheduled chats. There is information about which server the chat uses and the channel name #Andrew on the club's web pages. There is also a USENET newsgroup, *alt.fan.andrew-jenkins*, frequented by club members. The club has, of course, an e-mail address for members to use when getting in touch with the club and two mailing lists. One list is used for one-way traffic from Andrew's press secretary to the fans with weekly reports of what Andrew has been doing during the week, the other for club members' own discussions.

Information

Whatever you or your pupils are interested in you are likely to find that somebody has already created a web page with information about the subject. This is especially true of the things that interest young people, given the over-representation of the young in all things to do with computers. Music, sports, outdoor activities such as hang-gliding or bungee jumping, film, comic characters, TV, the environment, animal rights, astronomy, wildflowers or wildlife – there are pages about everything under the sun. Via the Web you can find out about your interest from people who are well informed and experienced. On, for example, a page about cycling you will probably find tips about equipment, good routes to take, what to pack for a longer tour, etc. You might even be able to contribute something yourself. On a page about letterboxing you will be able to learn just what letterboxing is (a kind of individual orienteering where you follow a map to a letterbox with a rubber stamp which you use to stamp a card) and where you can do it.

Contact

The very fact that a person has taken the trouble to make a web page indicates that they are willing to share their knowledge and to discuss the subject with all comers. One of the most important parts of any web page is an e-mail address letting you get in touch with the page's creator. You can write with comments, offer contributions to the subject matter of the page or ask questions. Usually a web page about a particular subject will have a selection of links to other pages about the same subject. There might be information about regular meetings online or in real life (you might come across the abbreviation IRL – In Real Life).

Some pages might have a noticeboard where you can leave messages for other visitors. The purpose of this is to let people who share the same interest get in touch with each other. The narrower the interest, the more valuable this kind of contact is. If you are the only person you know of in your school who is interested in the exploration of Mars it can be very interesting to learn that there are others who share your fascination, even if they are at the other end of the country or on a different continent. If you can get in touch to compare notes and share resources you will have found a way to get a lot more out of your interest. It is a part of the nature of the Internet that people are not excluded from most circles because of their age. A 14-year-old is as welcome in a mailing list discussing space exploration as is a professor of astronomy, and her questions will most likely be taken just as seriously.

Keypals

The Internet has perhaps most to offer those who have clearly defined areas of interest. There are, however, resources for those who simply want contact with others their own age. The traditional concept of the pen friend has an Internet counterpart known as a *keypal*. Writing to a keypal is very much like writing to a pen friend, except that the messages are sent by e-mail instead of snail mail. The young people involved learn a good deal about each other's way of life and they can gain valuable insights. The difference is that everything is speeded up. The messages take seconds rather than days to reach their destination, and this may contribute to the relative difficulty in keeping these exchanges going after the first few turns. Often these exchanges are more useful when organised by a teacher so that entire classes in different countries exchange letters, ideally about a particular topic.

There are several organised sites that pair off young people who are looking for a keypal according to their preferences. One of the largest is *Kidlink*. But keypal exchanges are only a tiny part of what all these sites have to offer pupils working with their teachers or children working individually in their own time.

Sites for children and teenagers

Kidlink

For some reason Kidlink is not as popular in the UK as in a lot of other countries. It is a massive organisation, based in Norway, with thousands of participants up to the age of 15. Kidlink is a non-profit organisation with the stated aim of 'getting as many youth through the age 15 as possible involved in a global dialog'. The network involves 50 public mailing lists for communication between young people, for example in discussions about given topics, or about more ambitious projects, and between adult leaders in various languages. Kidlink also has a private IRC network for real-time chat. Kidlink has hundreds of adult volunteers throughout the world, mostly teachers and parents. Since Kidlink started in 1990 over 110 000 young people in 119 countries have been involved. E-mail is the primary means of communication, but IRC chats, web-based dialogs, ordinary mail, fax, video conferencing and ham radio are also used. The IRC chats are often used as part of a project to enable participants to easily discuss their involvement. All mailing lists and IRC chats are monitored, so they are safe environments for young people.

Kidlink has activities in English, French, German, Hebrew, Icelandic, Japanese, Norwegian, Portuguese, Spanish, Italian, Danish, Macedonian, Turkish and the Nordic languages. Children are welcomed as individual members, or whole classes can join. An interesting feature is that participants are required to give information about themselves and their future plans when they register by answering the four Kidlink questions. Pupils will be required to enter their full names for admittance to Kidlink. The reasons behind this are explained and assurances are given that the information is not made available to third parties. There is no charge for membership.

Yahooligans!

Yahooligans! is owned by the web catalogue Yahoo! Their main site is a web catalogue for children up to the age of about 15. It works in the same way as Yahoo! but all the links are carefully vetted for material that might prove offensive to American parents (who are not known for being more permissive than their British counterparts). The Yahooligans! site also offers *Club Yahooligans*, which children can join on a special web page. There are many features on the site such as *This day in history* where you can look back and see what happened on a given date in years gone by; a sports page with information about (American) teams and results; a news page with the news presented for children but with background provided as links to material written for an adult audience; *Hypersite* which reviews a site for children every week (when we visited the site of the week was devoted entirely to jelly beans). In addition there is a celebrity profile every month, and a selection of web cams to visit (live video cameras on the Internet). When we visited the site we were able to watch kestrels learning to fly via a camera in their nest.

From the Yahooligans! club site there is a link to the *Headbone Zone*. Among many other features, this site offers free e-mail to children (called *hbzmail*). This is a web-based e-mail service with many built-in safety features for the protection of young people. The account registration requires a parent's or a teacher's involvement: an adult's e-mail address

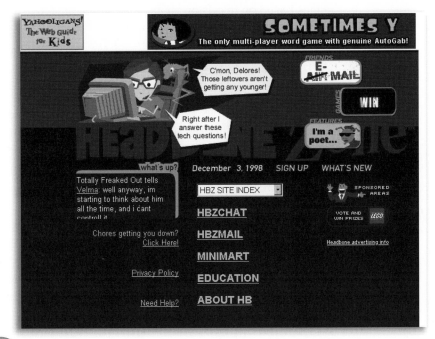

4.3 *The Headbone Zone*

is needed to register and the adult is notified via e-mail when the account is set up. Parents can then select safety features using a password. Being web based, hbzmail can be used from any computer that is connected to the Internet.

The Headbone Zone also offers a live monitored chat for children (in the evenings on this side of the Atlantic). The chat rooms are for up to 12-year-olds, and teens and adult monitors will ensure that the conversation is appropriate.

The Headbone Derby is an Internet learning tool for use in schools (American grades 4 to 8). There is extensive help for teachers planning to use the Derby with their classes. Each Derby is an adventure story with seven episodes. Each episode ends with a puzzle which pupils can solve by accessing other web sites. They can submit their answers online and then move on to the next episode. Teams can compete against each other in the Derby and there are three Derby contests each school year.

TV sites

The *Children's* BBC site leaves little to be desired. It makes heavy use of multimedia technology, which is very attractive but has the disadvantage of taking a long time to load if you are accessing the Internet via a modem. The site offers areas devoted to a number of popular children's programmes, a link to the children's newsroom, a number of games based on television characters, programme information and backstage secrets.

The BBC has another light-hearted site, *Beeb.com*, which will have a lot to interest the young. There is, among other things, information about specific programmes and the actors and presenters involved.

Discovery Channel Online is an exciting site for anybody interested in popular science. There is also a section of the site which is intended for school use, with plenty of lesson plans and other features. The curriculum content might, however, be too American in its orientation to suit British classes.

Newspaper sites

World Magazine Online for children from *National Geographic* includes an *Xpeditions* section with an atlas and discussion forums. The standards section has classroom ideas and family activities for kids and parents. *Xpedition Hall* is an attractive graphical environment packed full of fascinating details and devices to explore, with activities such as painting planetary patterns of biomass and energy, language or hours of sunshine with the world viewer.

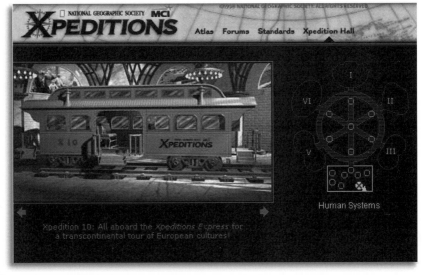

 4.4 *Xpeditions Hall*

The main children's page offers links to keypals, a talkboard for discussion of a particular topic – when we visited the topic was alien invasions, the Crittercam Chronicles accounting for what happened when video cameras were attached to sharks and other sea creatures.

Time magazine has a children's paper *Time for Kids*, which has an interesting site for children. There is a presentation of the news for children; a discussion forum where readers can discuss topics from the news (when we visited the topic was whether the tobacco companies should be required to pay for the treatment of smokers who are afflicted by illness as a result of their smoking); a cartoon area and an amazing facts area.

Other sites

The UK web catalogue UK*plus* has an extensive selection of hand-picked links for children (in their subcategory *Kids*) with information about sites for children of all ages. The links are sorted into sections dealing with, for example, animals, the environment, games, pre-school, junior and teenagers, classroom and teacher resources, science, sport, TV/film, and so on.

Microsoft UK has a *Kids* page with links to other sites. One useful feature is a little-used USENET newsgroup on Microsoft's own news server, *msn.uk.education.homeworkhelp* where school children can get help with their homework. When we visited there was an intensive dialogue going on between a student busy revising for her maths GCSE and a teacher who was able to help her in the weeks leading up to her exams.

Games

Some young people use computers almost entirely for playing games if they are allowed to choose. Games make full use of the advanced graphical capabilities and sound equipment available on modern computers. The Internet is an unequalled source of all kinds of computer games. You can find demonstration versions of games you can buy in the shops, full versions of shareware games, free games, games to download and play on your own computer and games to play across the Net with your friends or with strangers. In schools and homes where young people have unlimited access to computers and the Net there will generally be a lot of game-playing and chatting going on.

Online games

Yahoo! Games is a part of the massive Yahoo! site. You can play chess, checkers (draughts), bridge, spades or backgammon in real time across the Net. All you have to do is to join a table with an empty chair and start to play. In the backgammon section, for example, there are different rooms for different levels. If you join a game in the beginners' room you will be given advice about which moves are possible from the system. If you go online with a friend you can open your own table so you can play against each other. The only disadvantage is that you need to be online for the duration of the game. You can chat while you play, which can be very pleasant, but there is a clear need for caution here as in all chats with strangers.

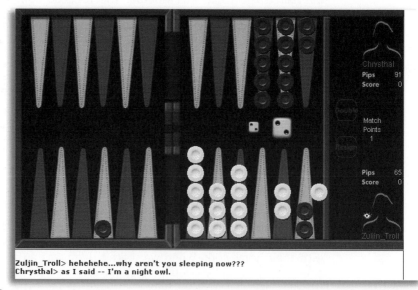

Zuljin_Troll> hehehehe...why aren't you sleeping now???
Chrysthal> as I said -- I'm a night owl.

 Backgammon

The *Microsoft Gaming Zone* is another site with a multitude of online games. Here too you can choose between card games like cribbage, spades and hearts, board games such as backgammon, chess, and scrabble. We enjoyed a few games of backgammon with a couple of Canadians in the virtual bar one evening.

The Microsoft site also has a facility whereby you can play commercial adventure and strategy games such as *Age of Empires* and *Return of the Jedi* with players across the Internet as long as you have your own purchased game CD in your computer. This seems to be very popular with several thousand players simultaneously online.

MUDs, MOOs, MUSHes, MUSEs, MUCKs, etc., are popular with some teenagers. These have traditionally been text-based role-play activities played over TELNET but many are developing graphically with web pages where users can interact. You will find links to dozens of MUDs and the like if you search on Yahoo! These games are losing players to the graphically more attractive strategy and role-play games mentioned above.

IRC is a very popular activity with certain groups of teenagers. They will chat to online friends and perfect strangers but mostly to each other, at every opportunity. Some schools have found that chatting has become a much greater problem than game-playing, and have found it necessary to ban chat software altogether. In situations where the pupils are sitting with an online computer each, the greatest problem need not be that they enter into conversation with potentially dangerous strangers but simply that they will spend hours chatting to pupils at the next desk. It is the electronic equivalent of whispering in class. The pupils can become expert at switching the screen to the program they were supposed to be using instantaneously if the teacher is approaching (the Alt-Esc combination is useful in Windows computers).

Shareware and freeware

Cheat codes can be used in adventure games, for example to make a player invisible or immortal. They are readily available from enthusiasts' web pages.

Young people may sometimes find the Internet's potential as a source of games and **cheat codes** more attractive than its information and contact potential. There are vast databases known as FTP *sites* or *archives* full of games and other programs which can be downloaded at no charge via web pages such as *Shareware.com*, *Jumbo.com* and *Download.com*. These programs are generally demonstration versions of commercial programs (demos), beta versions of programs being developed for commercial release, shareware or freeware.

A *demo* is generally limited in some way. Some demos are fully functional but have a time lock on them so they cease to function after a certain date or a certain number of days after being installed. Other demos are limited in their function: perhaps they permit the use of all functions except the saving of a partially completed game. Some game demos only have a few levels, to give potential buyers an idea of whether the game is what they are looking for.

A *beta version* is a test version – it is released to the public at no charge to let the developers see how the program works on different kinds of computers. Microsoft and Netscape generally release beta versions of their products for download from their web sites some time before the final version appears.

Shareware is a system whereby programs may be freely copied and distributed and used for a trial period (often 30 days). After this trial period the program may become inoperable. In any case, the user is expected to stop using the program after this specified period unless they choose to register the program with its creator and pay a (usually modest) fee. Details about the length of the trial period and instructions for how to register the program are included in the program. There are other variants such as *postcardware* where the creator of a program asks users to send not money but a picture postcard for his collection. Shareware programs are typically, almost by definition, less professionally made than commercial programs, but writing shareware is a great way for young enthusiasts to get started in programming.

Freeware programs are an expression of the slogan 'Information wants to be free!' This ideology was a feature of the early Internet community and still pervades a lot of the thinking behind the Internet. The basic idea is that you should not charge for sharing knowledge and skills. This is not to be confused with the subtle marketing techniques which lead Microsoft and Netscape to offer their browsers free of charge to users (at present).

⊗ *Did you know?*

Downloading programs from the Internet is not difficult but it can take quite a while to download large programs if you have a slow connection. It is a good idea to create a special directory on your computer to download files and programs into. When you install the programs they will often create their own directories.

Screen savers are programs which start up when the computer has not been used for a specified time. They put a moving picture on the screen to avoid damage.

You can browse through different categories of programs, such as **screen savers**, games, e-mail programs or **virus protection programs**, or search for a specific key word. When you find a program you want to download you just need to click on it and you will be asked where you want to have the file (in the directory you have created), and then the download will proceed. When it is complete, you can run the program. Some programs need to be installed while others install themselves.

Virus protection programs will tell you when your computer has been infected by a virus, remove the virus and repair the damage caused by it.

WinZip and **Stuffit** are shareware programs. They are freely available, e.g. on computer magazine CDs and from FTP sites such as *Shareware.com*.

Many files are compressed to make them smaller so they take less time to download. An advantage of using compression is that several files, for example a program and documentation in a *read.me* file, can be downloaded as a single compact packet. If you want to use such a file you will need to uncompress it before you can install it or run it, using a program such as **WinZip** (for Windows computers) or the equivalent for other computers, such as **Stuffit** for Macintosh. The compression programs can also be downloaded from the FTP archives.

When you run a program you have downloaded from the Net there is a risk that your computer may become infected by a computer virus. There are excellent shareware anti-virus programs available from the FTP archives, so let one of them be your first download.

Educational software

There are a great many programs which claim to have some kind of pedagogic value. These claims may, of course, not be well founded. Educational software has often been very grey and boring and quite unattractive. Nonetheless, teachers have often found that children are more motivated to learn their times tables with the help of a program than otherwise. Multimedia technology can be used to make the programs more interesting with the addition of colour, advanced graphics, animation and sound, although a lot of multimedia productions are quite disappointing and do not make good use of the techniques available to them. They are sometimes little more than traditional textbooks transferred to the screen.

Some educational programs are available as shareware, but more advanced productions, such as encyclopaedias, are available commercially as CDs, or over the Net for paying subscribers. Web technology is developing constantly and multimedia can be delivered directly from a web page. The Children's BBC site has several examples of these educational games using these techniques. As Internet connections become faster we will be seeing more of these kinds of pages.

⟫ *Summary*

❑ This chapter has discussed the need to educate pupils so that they know how to behave online. Respect for others is of the utmost importance. This is especially true in communication with people who may not be fully competent in English and who have a different cultural background.

❑ Pupils also need to be informed of the potential hazards involved in dealing with strangers, and be aware that their Internet transactions are not private. Informing pupils of the risks and teaching responsible behaviour is the only way to give pupils protection when they use the Net outside of school.

❑ For many young users, online games are the main attraction. The chance of playing against others via the Net is irresistible. Others will enjoy downloading games and other programs from FTP sites.

❑ The Internet gives enthusiasts a chance to meet each other even if they are in different countries. Many sites exist specifically for young people with the aim of facilitating international contacts and providing educational material or entertainment.

❑ The Internet has plenty to attract young people. Some children's sites are associated with TV or magazine sites. There is material to suit every interest and the opportunity for pupils to add material of their own.

Teaching pupils to use the **Internet**

While many pupils have access to computers and the Internet at home and may be very adept at playing games and even finding their way around the Internet game sites, many other pupils do not have computer skills until they are taught them at school. Those who have experience in using computers will often not have used them for anything more useful than games. Even if these pupils are experts when it comes to using the mouse and knowing how to start up their programs they may lack any deeper understanding of the potential of the equipment they use.

Practical pedagogical matters

There is a case for giving all pupils an introductory course about computers and the Internet as soon as they come to a school where they will have the opportunity to use them. This will often be at 11 years of age, but may be later or earlier. At around 11 years, pupils will usually be able to appreciate the requirement that they use the equipment responsibly. Younger pupils can, of course also benefit from the use of the Internet, but they may need more help to understand the software they need to use.

Different teaching techniques will be needed if the pupils are each able to sit at a computer in a computer room, if they are working in twos or threes at each computer or if there is only one computer for the whole class to share. In the last case there is a choice between having pupils come up to the computer individually or in pairs for individual instruction on the one hand and a whole-class approach on the other hand. If you are going to show a whole class how to use the computer at the same time you will find it useful either to use a screen projector so everybody can see what is happening, or to use still shots of the screen and show them on an overhead projector.

At some point each pupil will need some kind of hands-on experience of using the computer. If there are many pupils using a single machine this may require some kind of booking system so that all pupils can have a go, especially those who are reluctant to try. Those pupils who are used to using computers outside school may feel that they do not need to participate in the course. If you test their knowledge and find that they already know what you plan to teach you might want to let them serve as teaching assistants for their classmates. Let them sit in on the other pupils' hands-on training with strict instructions not to take over but to be on hand to offer advice if the beginning pupil has any difficulty.

First of all the pupils will need an introductory course in which they become familiar with basic computer functions (mouse, keyboard, opening and closing windows, saving documents and copying from one document to paste into another) and the software they will be using (e.g. Excel for spreadsheet work and Word for word processing). After they have had plenty of time to assimilate these new skills and use them in their learning it may be time to introduce them to the basics of using the Internet. A basic course will involve the use of hypertext to move between pages (surfing) and finding information on the Web as well as using e-mail. Depending on the Internet policy adopted by the school, completion of this course (possibly in combination with the signing of a usage agreement by the pupil and his parents) might be deemed sufficient to allow the pupil a level of freedom to navigate the Net independently. The implications of this kind of freedom will naturally be vastly different in a setting where there are several computers permanently online in every room and in a school where there is a single dial-up connection in the school library.

⊚ *In practice*

Knowledge Management course

In Ward Freman school in Hertfordshire all the first-year pupils (Year 9) are given a six-week Knowledge Management programme which includes a regular Internet search by keyword on a given topic, and a CD-ROM investigation. The course aims to demystify the Internet as well as illustrating some of the pitfalls of Net use, but the primary target is to help pupils view the Net as an additional reference tool. Pupils are made aware of the Internet's strengths (wide range) and weaknesses (lack of focus, slowness etc.) as compared to CD-ROMs and the books in the school library.

The Internet as a learning tool

Much has been made of the potential of the Internet as a source of information and the new role of the teacher as guide and mentor to the researching pupil. We have already seen that the content available on the Web is unlimited but unreliable and uneven in quality. The educational content suppliers (e.g. BT, Anglia and RM) have limited but high-quality information available at a price. Whichever way you choose to work, your pupils will be in a position to research a subject relatively independently.

The benefits of using the Internet rather than the school library for this kind of in-depth study of a limited subject are very dependent on the nature of the subject. If the study is about a subject which is topical (a sporting event, or the story behind a news item) the school library may be felt to be quite useless and out of date. If the subject is the first moon landing or the great explorers Columbus and Livingstone, the school library will very likely give a much fuller picture of the subject than can be gleaned from the Internet. The perceived advantages of hypertext, such as the way information can be linked, may equally well be attained by following the cross-references in an encyclopaedia. In a CD-based encyclopaedia you can even have hypertext.

The Internet offers the intriguing possibility of being able to find an expert to ask a specific question about a topic. It does, however, require

---

Message 16 of 26
return to current results

◀◀ | **post reply** | ▶▶   help

previous · post reply · next

Blair's comments on Nationalists.   more options

Author: author profile
Email: view thread
Date: 1998/11/13
Forums: alt.politics.british
more headers

I feel that **Tony Blair** is wrong to criticise the Nationalists plans for an independent Scotlands defence system. They are right to get rid of all the nuclear weapons, as they are expensive to maintain, represent an environmental problem, and are never going to be used anyway!! Secondly, a withdrawal from NATO will leave more funds open to health, **education,** and other more important issues. Indeed, an independent Scotland under Nationalist rule will still remain in certain parts of NATO, just not totally involved like Britain and America are today. Defence in this part of the world(Western Europe) is not as imporatant as it used to be, as any immediate threat of invasion from any neighbour seems very unlikely. Even England wouldn't want to invade, just like they did so that they could annexe Scotland. The Nationalists will get my vote next May, and the votes of many other younger people in Scotland. Their defence policy is one reason why I like the party so much.

5.1 *Newsgroups*

that the teacher is prepared to admit to not knowing the answer to a pupil's question and is able to suggest that the pupil find out the answer on her own, either from information on the Web or by asking an expert. There are many experts and enthusiasts to be found on the Net, as the authors of web sites about the subject at hand, on special ask-an-expert pages, and, not least, on USENET. In many of the thousands of newsgroups that exist there are knowledgeable people who love nothing more than talking about their interests. If suitable precautions are taken to protect the pupils from unsuitable newsgroups and from the spamming (unwanted messages about get-rich-quick scams) which otherwise can result from posting on news-groups, this can be a rich source of information.

Internet technology in the presentation of work

If there are enough computers for every pupil to access one several times a week it will be possible to have pupils regularly, or at least occa-sionally, present their work as a series of HTML (web) documents. This kind of presentation does not require Internet access, and it is espe-cially suitable when several pupils are writing about connected subjects, whether they are working together or separately. Pupils write texts in their word processor or a web page editor and can then insert pictures and even sound, and links to other sections of their own or others' work. The teacher or a pupil-editor can then write an umbrella entrance page that gathers together all the pages in a single structure and shows how they are related. At the end the pupils will have a site about the subject which they can share with each other, other classes, parents, or even the world at large by publishing it on the Web.

Written work from a single pupil can also gain from being written as a web page, even if it is never published on the Web. If the school has an intranet, there is a natural forum for this kind of writing. Producing electronic writing has several advantages:

❑ The pupils practise their keyboard skills. This is important for people in all walks of life now. Who would have imagined 20 years ago that we would all need to know how to type! Fortunately, accuracy is not as crucial as it once was – we can easily erase mistakes without making a mess – although correcting errors takes time. Typing speed and accuracy are a matter of practice and becoming familiar with the keyboard. Even one-finger typists can often type as quickly as they can think. In a few years' time keyboard skills may be quite unnecessary if we move over to another way of communication with computers, for example via speech. There are already excellent systems that allow us to dictate texts to the computer, and these are likely to develop rapidly.

❑ Pupils are able to produce neat, correctly spelled work. The use of spelling checkers should, of course, be encouraged. This can be important for pupils who have difficulty with handwriting or spelling for any reason. The dictation systems mentioned above also are useful to these pupils.

❑ Electronic texts are more easily copied and shared with others via diskettes, an intranet, e-mail or the Web than are texts written on paper, particularly if they are handwritten. This means that electronic texts are more likely to be read by others. This has far-reaching consequences – suddenly pupils are writing for a wider readership rather than for a single teacher as has been the norm. This gives the pupils a reason to make the background to what they write clear and makes for more coherent writing. The more people who are going to read the pupils' texts the more motivated they may be to give the work their best effort.

Pupils on different levels

We have mentioned the situation (which may be perceived as a problem) where some pupils are considerably more at home in front of a computer than their teachers. The solution we have proposed is to allow these pupils to act as tutors to the other pupils, but there are other possibilities if the pupils involved are not likely to be suitable mentors for the less experienced pupils. They may be disruptive and scornful of the other pupils' slow progress.

The most important point here is to make sure that the pupils actually master the basic skills you are teaching the rest of the class. While many pupils know how to use hypertext and seem to understand how it works they may be quite unfamiliar with the finer points of using a search engine. They might, for example, know that they can write in a word (the name of the game they want to read about) but not how to refine their searches. They may be able to work independently with the help of, for example, the online help file to AltaVista. You could have them search for game titles using all the available operators.

A problem with pupils who are used to using the Internet outside school is that they are often very knowledgeable about web sites and other resources within a narrow field, but know very little about what else there is on the Net. One way to give pupils a wider view of the Internet is to set up a resource hunt as a meaningful way to become familiar with the kind of resource the Internet has to offer.

⊛ *Case study*

Putting pupils to work

Mary Smith has a group of four boys in her class who are deeply involved in playing strategy games. They know the gaming zones of the Web intimately, but are very hazy about what else the Internet has to offer. Mary made a list of topics she would be covering with various classes later on in the term, and invited the other teachers to make similar lists. In a day or two she had a list of over a hundred topics, sorted into school subjects. These topics were very diverse, covering things like the poetry of Wilfred Owen, and Dickens' *Oliver Twist* for her own teaching, the Boer War and medieval kings for John Hill the history teacher, the 2000 Olympics and the rules of basketball for Maggie Jones the PE teacher, Islam's view of women and the sons of Abraham for Greg Knight the RE teacher, etc.

Mary had the pupils choose a topic to work on for the remainder of the scheduled course. Their task was to collect all kinds of material about their topic. Mary gave them a list of places to start looking: Yahoo!, AltaVista, Excite, Tile Net for mailing lists and Deja News for newsgroups. Of course, once they found a good resource they could follow the links from it to other resources on the same or related topics. If they knew that someone else was working on a topic they happened upon they were encouraged to mail that person with the URL or other information about the resource.

As the pupils found resources directly related to their own topics they were to explore them and copy the URL or e-mail address into a Word file and write a few sentences about each web page, newsgroup or mailing list. When they had collected as many resources as they could find they were to add the date and their names (hyperlinked to their e-mail addresses) to the bottom of the file and e-mail it to Mary. After she had checked the information she saved the file as an HTML file and published it on the school intranet. The final step was to have the pupils send an e-mail with the location of the finished topic resource lists to the teachers who had requested the information. At the end of the course a more advanced Internet class made the intranet web pages into a structured site for publication on the Web as a resource for teachers in other schools. Within a few weeks some of the pupils were receiving feedback to their e-mail addresses from teachers round the country, thanking them for their work and passing on information about other resources on the same topic.

There are other ways to let the most experienced pupils make use of their skills while broadening their own experience of the Net. They can be 'lent out' as Internet assistants to teachers who are new to the Net but keen to use it in their teaching. This may not be acceptable to all teachers, of course, and it does require that the pupil is able to cooperate with the teacher. Another idea is to have them go round the class's computers to demonstrate particular features of the browser or e-mail software.

Teaching basic Internet skills

Schools deal with the teaching of Internet skills in different ways. In some cases it is the ICT teacher who teaches the pupils what they need to know; in other cases it is a subject teacher who wants to use the Internet in class. In extreme cases the technician might be teaching the teacher and the pupils at the same time. As we have said, it can be convenient to have all pupils take a basic introductory course in how to use the Internet as soon as they are likely to need it, assuming they already have basic computing skills.

When pupils are first introduced to the Internet you may find it useful to establish just how much previous experience each pupil has. At the same time you might investigate their attitudes to the Internet. Have they ever seen a web page? What good things and bad things have they heard about the Net? Do they know any person or company who has their own web page? This will give you an idea of where the pupils stand.

Surfing

The Web is likely to be fairly familiar to pupils. They will probably at least have seen pictures of web pages in newspapers and magazines. When they are first introduced to the browser they are going to be using (Netscape or Explorer) some pupils will probably want to investigate the program fully while others will find the array of buttons and menus confusing. One way to start is by concentrating on the functions of the mouse. (These exercises do not require a live connection to the Internet if you have the relevant pages on your hard disk.)

The **cursor** is usually an arrow on the screen showing you where you are. When the cursor moves over a hyperlink it changes into a hand.

❏ Explain what hypertext is and how it is used to connect documents. Have the pupils move the mouse over a web page that you have loaded into the browser to find any hyperlinks (text or graphics). Point out the **cursor** as its shape changes. Let them choose a link to follow by **left-clicking** (for Windows computers).

Left-clicking involves pushing the left mouse button while the cursor is pointing to the link on the screen.

❏ Explain that every web page has a unique address so the browser knows where to find it. Draw the pupils' attention to the address

113

line at the top of the browser window. Have them press the *Back* button to bring them back to the page they started from. Let them notice that the page address has changed.

❑ Give the pupils a web address to enter in the address window. They will soon see the need for accurate copying!

❑ Have the pupils investigate the right mouse button (for Windows computers). How does the menu change when they push it when the cursor is on a picture, a hyperlink or an empty space on the page background?

❑ Explain how bookmarks work and let the pupils set up a *bookmark* or *favorites* file.

❑ Let the pupils have an online session where they can surf freely to get the feel of the browser. They might have some web addresses that they want to check out. You can start them off with a resource such as Yahooligans! so they will easily find their way to interesting sites.

Finding information

After an initial unrestricted online session you will probably want to structure the pupils' use of the Web. The next logical step is to show them how to use the Internet's search facilities. You might like to have them search for the name of your town, or their favourite football teams or musicians. Let them see the difference between search engines and catalogue-based resources. Show the pupils how to refine their search if they get thousands of links for a single search word. The more search words they use the more likely they are to find just what they are looking for in the first few hits. You might like to have an exercise where the pupils try to come up with as many key words as they can to describe a page on a particular subject.

A good way to become familiar with the various search tools available is to let the pupils search for information on the same topic in a selection of search engines and catalogues. They will then become aware of the differences between the available search tools and should be able to select the most appropriate one.

E-mail

There are many different ways to deal with the question of how best to give the pupils access to e-mail. The school's Internet provider may have some scheme whereby a certain number of e-mail addresses are available to the school users (teachers and pupils). Otherwise systems offering free e-mail abound. Some of these are specifically aimed at school users, others are open to everyone. Generally these systems are financed by advertising, so that every time you access the system you will see adverts for various products.

The school will need to make some kind of policy decision as to whether pupils are to be given individual e-mail addresses at school or not. It might be thought sufficient to have an e-mail address for each class. Of course this kind of decision must be open to review – as the school's involvement in Internet activities increases the need for individual e-mail accounts may arise. E-mails can be compared in this respect to ordinary letters. Most people like to receive their mail unopened. It is no more acceptable to read an e-mail intended for another person than it is to intercept post. If a school feels the need to monitor the content of e-mails being sent and received, the question needs to be asked whether the pupils' letters would be treated in the same way.

There is a choice of e-mail software available. The browsers Internet Explorer and Netscape each have their own perfectly adequate mail programs. There is also a mail program in Windows and there are a number of free stand-alone mail programs too. Which you use is quite unimportant, since most programs will let you perform the same functions. The basic functions you and your pupils will need include:

❑   writing an e-mail

❑   sending an e-mail to the address of your choice

❑   checking to see if you have received mail

❑   reading the incoming mail

❑   replying to a mail you have received

❑   attaching a file to an e-mail

❑   printing out important letters so you can file them on paper (there is always a risk that information stored only on the hard disk will get lost)

❑   transferring mail you want to save to mailboxes (folders) according to your own categories.

The following functions are also useful:

❑   saving the e-mail addresses you use regularly in an address book

❑   filtering post so that post from a particular sender is transferred straight into a given mailbox. This is very useful if you have joined a mailing list with a lot of messages every day – you can have a mailbox for those messages so messages from the list do not swamp your other mail. There may also come a time where you feel a need to discard messages from a particular sender without reading them!

When you are introducing pupils to e-mail you can let them become familiar with the program they are to use, so they know how to access the basic functions above before they start to send mail. The next step is to let them send their first mail, which is best sent to themselves. Then they can check to see if they have mail and read the message they just sent. Then they can send a message to a classmate with a short word-processor file attached. If pupils work in pairs on this they can also retrieve the message and file sent to them. Finally they can answer the message sent by their classmate using the e-mail program's reply function.

Other exercises might involve a study of how to use Internet resources for finding out the e-mail address of a person or organisation, for example the *WhoWhere?* site and the Web search engines. You could ask the pupils to find the Prime Minister's e-mail address or the address of a given person in the news.

 WhoWhere?

Netiquette

While the rules of netiquette are often presented as a list, this might be off-putting to the most hesitant pupils. There may simply seem to be too many rules to take in. For some pupils the possibility of inadvertently offending someone may be seen as such a problem that they do not want to take the risk of using the Internet's communication channels with strangers. It might be useful to simplify the rules of Internet use for younger pupils. The most important rule is to respect the people at the other end of your e-mail or contribution to a discussion, bearing in mind that many Internet users do not have a full command of English.

There is an interesting cautionary tale on the Global SchoolHouse site titled *The Ballad of an E-mail Terrorist*. It is the story of a teenager who sent an obscene e-mail to a younger child who had posted a message to a discussion group asking for information about Disney. The steps taken to trace the teenager and the consequences of his action are related in detail. The moral of the story is that you are not anonymous on the Net (unless you take quite complicated steps to make yourself so) and that there is a real live person at the receiving end of an e-mail address. That person is just as deserving of respect and consideration as she would be in a real-life meeting.

Mailing lists

If the pupils have their own e-mail addresses and the opportunity to check their mail regularly they might like to join a mailing list. There are not many lists specifically for young people, but those who have a special interest such as a sport, music or a specific music group might find others who share their interests in this way. The *Tile.net* resource or Yahoo! (in the subcategory Computers and Internet/Internet/Mailing Lists) may be useful for this. For example, under the sports category of this subcatalogue in Yahoo! we followed a link to UK football clubs and found among other things a page devoted to a selection of mailing lists for Arsenal fans.

There are a number of different list systems and each has its own specific commands for joining and leaving the list. It is very important to keep a copy of all the information sent from the list when you join. One way to keep track of this is to create a mailbox in the e-mail program for every list joined. Welcome messages and instructions from the list can then be stored in this mailbox. When the pupil wants to leave the list the instructions can then be easily retrieved.

Some mailing lists generate a few messages a term while others may have dozens of messages every day. On busy lists it might be a good idea to have pupils get the list in digest form (i.e. with all the day's messages in a single long mail) if this is available. The welcome message will have all this kind of information and instructions about how to change the subscription options.

One of the most important things to teach when dealing with mailing lists is the necessity of keeping the list's administrative address separate from the list address used to send messages to all the list's members.

A useful exercise would be to have pupils join a list which appeals to them and make provision in their mail program for a special mailbox to store list information. It might also be a good idea to set a filter to automatically direct all mail from the list into that mailbox. After the pupils have received about a hundred messages form their lists and read them carefully to judge the tone and style of the list (e.g. whether members introduce themselves when first posting to the list) they might like to send a message themselves. They may have a question or a comment, or even an answer to someone else's question. After monitoring any replies they get (replies may be sent either to the list or directly to the person asking a question) the pupils can leave their lists using the appropriate command. Here they need to be sure that they use the right address to send the command to leave the list.

⊛ *In practice*

Reluctance to use mailing lists

There seem to be few schools who encourage their pupils to participate in mailing lists as yet. One reason might be concern about the kinds of people the pupils might encounter on lists. Another reason is a fear that pupils will receive uncontrollable amounts of post, overloading the mail system. But the most important reason is that few teachers have found a use for the kinds of discussions with outsiders that take place on mailing lists. Closed mailing lists set up for discussing particular projects are more immediately useful. Nonetheless, well-focused mailing lists can be a valuable resource, especially for older pupils investigating a particular topic.

Noticeboards

There are a large number of noticeboards on various kinds of web pages. Many of them are aimed at children and young people. The Kidlink site, for example, has several busy noticeboards for its members. Club Yahooligans is another good site where pupils can exchange views on various matters. A problem with these noticeboards is that they are very public, and are probably not a good place to discuss sensitive subjects. Pupils should also be aware of the necessity to avoid giving away too much information about themselves and their real-world activities which might be misused by strangers.

Newsgroups

A **firewall** protects an intranet from intruders from the Internet while allowing specified traffic to and from the Internet.

There is probably a newsgroup for any special interest a pupil might have. Newsgroups can be a superb source of knowledge for pupils' research into a particular subject. You may, however, not have access to newsgroups at all, depending on the terms of the agreement with your ISP. Schools with their own **firewall** do not always take in newsgroups. They may judge the problems associated with newsgroups to exceed the benefits. The problems are, on the one hand, the large number of newsgroups that deal with 'adult' subjects, and on the other hand the risk of receiving dozens of messages about get-rich-quick scams from Internet spammers who have used a program to automatically harvest your e-mail address from your message.

A good way to access newsgroups efficiently is to go through the *Deja News* web site. Not only will it let you search for recent and previous messages about a particular topic, you can also participate in current discussions without the risk of getting spammed. Deja News provides registered users (registration is free) with a special e-mail address to use for posting to newsgroups. Incoming mail to this address is filtered to remove mail from known spammers, and you avoid compromising your ordinary address.

Often the people who use newsgroups are real enthusiasts and have a lot of knowledge about the subject of the newsgroup. In some newsgroups there is a collection of frequently asked questions (FAQ) that have been answered in the newsgroup. The FAQ is generally available on a web page and the address to the page is then posted to the group at regular intervals along with other information about the group. There are special newsgroups for beginners (e.g. *news.newusers.questions*) which are frequented by helpful experts who will willingly answer beginners' questions. There are also groups which exist for the sole purpose of allowing users to send test messages without polluting a genuine discussion (e.g. *misc.test.moderated*).

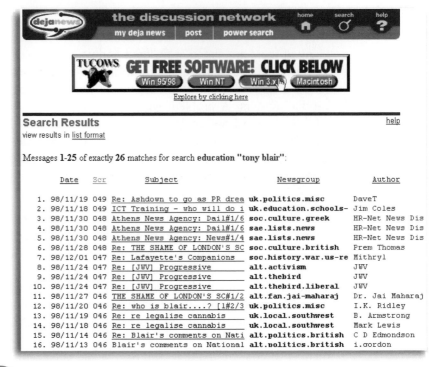

5.3 *Deja News*

uick tip

If you or your pupils do want to use an ordinary newsreader to contribute to the discussion in a newsgroup you would be well advised to protect your e-mail address before doing so to prevent your addresses being harvested by spammers. The way to do this is to find the dialogue box where you enter your e-mail address (look under the Edit or Tools menu for a heading such as Accounts or Settings. Once you find your e-mail address you can insert something obvious into it. If your address is, for example, jbloggs@onenet.net you could change it to jbloggs@no.spam. onenet.net. This means that automatic address collection

There is a newsreader in both Netscape's and Explorer's browser package. These programs are integrated into the e-mail program, and are relatively simple to use. You can either select a newsgroup from a list of those available or write in the name of a group you want to read. It is possible to *subscribe* to newsgroups you want to read regularly so their names will be visible every time you start up the news-reader. If you use Deja News in your newsgroup activity you will not need a separate newsreader, and the whole process will be somewhat simpler.

IRC and other real-time services

Schools may decide that IRC is not a good thing to involve pupils in. On many IRC nets there are just too many inap-propriate discussions going on. In addition, the risk of pupils coming into contact with malevolent strangers is deemed to be not worth taking. There is another reason not to teach pupils how to use IRC – some of them will find it so fascinating that it may occupy more of their time than is healthy. If they are in a situation where they have *programs will be fooled and the spam messages intended for you will disappear into cyberspace. Real people in the newsgroup who want to respond to your query will then simply remove the words no.spam before they send you a mail. This is the conventional way to protect an e-mail address, but if you think there may be confusion you can always write something like 'Remove no.spam from my address to reply'.*

free access to an online computer they may prefer to chat rather than to do what they are supposed to be doing.

Nonetheless, IRC and the other large-scale multi-channel real-time services (i.e. web chat, Microsoft's NetMeeting, Netscape's Conference, ICQ, online games with chat, etc.) can give pupils a real sense of being part of a global community. They can meet pupils from Korea or Mexico as easily as those from the school down the road. For pupils up to 15 the Kidlink organisation might prove to be a suitable forum to try this kind of communication.

Pupils may need quite a bit of practice to become familiar with the programs used for IRC and other chats. Let them contact each other using these systems. Help them to set up private chat channels for this as far as possible. Once they have learned how to use these systems they will be in a position to employ them for meaningful exchanges in many kinds of project work. A tool such as NetMeeting is ideal for collaborative work with classes in other locations.

 ## Practising

Once pupils have become acquainted with the programs they need to make use of the Internet's services they may require a firm hand to steer their activity towards purposeful work rather than idle surfing and superficial contacts. They also need to practise the skills they have learned if they are to become confident in the use of the Internet. The following activities are ways to get your pupils using the Internet.

Treasure hunt

A treasure hunt, or scavenger hunt, can be arranged in a number of different ways. The idea is generally to have pupils discover the scope of information on the Web and become familiar with the search tools at their disposal. There are a few treasure hunts available on the Web, but you can easily arrange your own.

The basic idea is to present the pupils with a list of questions and ask them to find the answers to the questions using the Internet. When they give their answers they must also give the address of the web page or other resource they used to find the answer. It is not enough to know the answer – they have to find the answer on the Web. You can either use general questions or tailor them to suit a specific subject.

Suitable questions are not difficult to come up with. A treasure hunt might include questions about details in various countries' flags, the crops grown in a particular area, the capital cities of certain countries, the latitude of a particular city, the climate of a particular tourist resort, the latest models of a certain make of car, the name and age of the president of a particular country, etc. You will have to test the treasure hunt thoroughly to make sure you do not send the pupils on a wild goose chase. Make sure you can find all the answers before you ask the pupils to do it. If you are reusing questions from an earlier treasure hunt you will probably need to recheck all the answers. The Internet changes rapidly and material that was easily available one week may be gone the week after.

You can vary the basic treasure hunt in various ways. You might like to introduce an element of competition and have the pupils work in teams to see who gets the most right answers in the shortest time. You can even involve other classes or other schools in the chase if it suits your purposes. If you spend time developing treasure-hunt questions you might like to put them on a web page so that others can use them, and maybe even add to them.

Orienteering

Web orienteering involves the pupils following a trail through cyberspace and visiting prepared controls. These can be either numbers or words on web pages that the pupils are sent to visit or messages left on some of the noticeboards on the Web or in test newsgroups.

The participants are issued instructions for how to reach the controls and told that they are to collect the word(s) or numbers at each control. If you want to you can have the words form a sentence and the pupils can e-mail the sentence to you when they have retrieved all the words from the controls.

The instructions might be something like the following (note that these are purely fictitious examples):

❑ Find your way to the Berlin Zoo page and click on the third animal mentioned on the English language *animal* page. The word you want is the second word in the fourth sentence in the page.

❑ Follow the link from the *Berlin* page at the Zoo site to the Berlin Tourist Office's own web pages. You will find a noticeboard there where locals offer bed and breakfast to tourists on a low budget. The word you want is the seventh word in the message with the subject *Room for fellow walkers*.

❑ The room-to-let note was signed by a Wolfgang Schwartz. Search for his name on Deja News and find a message he sent to the newsgroup *rec.walking* with the subject *Great new site*. Go to the site he recommends and the word you want is the second word in the page title.

Contact with authorities

A useful exercise might be to set pupils to find the e-mail address of their local MP or MEP, a member of the municipal council, the local tax office, tourist office, library, etc. The point of this is to show how widespread the Internet has become in our society. Of course, many workplaces (including schools) have assigned e-mail addresses to all employees whether or not they have access to computers and whether or not they possess the necessary skills and level of interest to enable them to check their mail regularly.

You may wish to let your pupils formulate an e-mail to some kind of official address. Bear in mind that there is a better chance of getting an answer and less risk of the recipient getting irritated if they only receive a single well thought out query from a class rather than dozens of trivial questions.

Fact finding

In the last chapter we described how Mary Smith organised her pupils to search for educationally useful material about a range of material on topics which were of interest to Mary and her colleagues. This provides extensive training in the use of the Web and Web and USENET search tools. This can become a regular activity where the teachers make a list of each term's hot topics and are given research help by classes who need to practise their Internet skills.

The most useful way to report on such an activity would be on a web page for each school subject, divided into topics so that new material can be added each term. It would be useful to check that web sites mentioned by other classes are still in existence and still have material relevant to the topic at hand each term when the page is updated. If the idea of making a web page seems too difficult the class might simply e-mail their findings to the teacher concerned. They will still have learned a great deal from the search and will have helped the teacher to benefit from the Internet without spending excessive time finding relevant material.

Class mailing list

The purpose of a class mailing list is to facilitate communication between pupils and with the teacher outside of the classroom. It is an excellent and useful way to practise the use of e-mail for everyday communication purposes. There are several different methods you can use to set up a mailing list. The address-book function in e-mail programs can be used to collect individual e-mail addresses in a group. You can give the group a name and then simply send a single e-mail to the group. The program will then see to it that each address in the group receives a copy of the message. If you show your pupils how to set up a group in the program they are using to access e-mail they can each make a group with the e-mail addresses of all the pupils in the class. These groups can then be used as a simple mailing list.

Another way to make a mailing list is to use one of the free list-hosting services available (e.g. *Coollist*). This kind of list is easily accessible from home or from school and will be more convenient to use than the above e-mail group letters system.

A third way to create the list may be possible if your school has a direct line to the Internet and its own mail server. Then the person who looks after the server should be able to arrange a mailing list for you on the school server.

Once the class mailing list has been set up it can be used for all kinds of purposes, for example group work, discussions about homework, pupils helping pupils, pupils asking the teacher a question in a setting where other pupils are free to chip in with advice or follow-on questions.

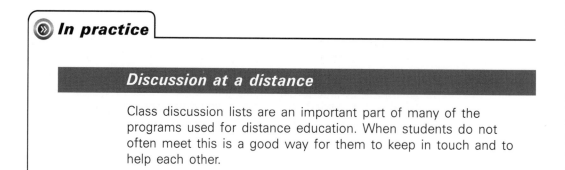

⊗ *In practice*

Discussion at a distance

Class discussion lists are an important part of many of the programs used for distance education. When students do not often meet this is a good way for them to keep in touch and to help each other.

Electronic homework administration

One more way to get in some practice with the Internet is to use it as much as possible in everyday classroom administration. The teacher might choose to place the day's homework on a page in the school's intranet web or even on the Web, or send it as an e-mail to the class mailing list if such a thing exists. Pupils can send their homework to the teacher as a word-processor file attached to an e-mail. This kind of system has been used in the university world for some time.

The teacher can mark work electronically if it is sent from a word processor. Modern word processors such as Microsoft Word allow you to make detailed comments and marks on a text without destroying the pupil's work or having him try to decipher your cramped notes in the margins. The marked work can then be e-mailed as an attachment back to the pupil.

 # *Efficient reading*

Pupils who use the Internet on their own to search for information are in a new situation. Before they find what they are looking for they will have to sift through large amounts of irrelevant material. They will probably also encounter material that is relevant but written at too high a level for them to understand easily. Somehow they have to find their way through all the material which is completely or partially unsuitable in the hope of coming upon what they are looking for.

Working with web texts

Some pupils might find it difficult to read text from the screen. The scrolling motion that changes the position of the text on the screen may disturb them, or they may find it irritating that they can only see a portion of the text on the screen at a time. These pupils might be helped if they could print out texts before reading them, but it is unnecessary (and detrimental to the environment as well as the school's economy) to print out web pages before it is known that they contain valuable information. An alternative is to use a speech-synthesis program which will read the text aloud. Simple text-to-speech programs are sometimes included in the software delivered with computers; otherwise they can be obtained as shareware or demos from shareware archives (e.g. *Download.com*). The SEN teacher will probably be able to advise on this kind of program.

When your pupils have mastered the art of making a good selection of keywords and refining symbols to search for information using a search engine their problems are not over. Hopefully the first 10 or 20 pages listed will contain the most relevant information (pages where most of the key words occur), but how are the pupils to choose which pages to look at first? A search engine is as likely to return a commercial page or a private individual's home page as a page intended for school use.

Consider the following result of an AltaVista search for *"school meals"*:

5. <u>Opintie School in City of Kotka: School Meals</u>

School Meals. Just like in every comprehensive school in Finland the pupils are provided with a free school meal every school day. The weekly changing . . .

http://www.kotka.fi/koulut/opintie/english/ateria.html - size 2K - 15-Oct-1997 - English - Translate

This was one of the first 10 pages returned by the search. The results were very varied. We got everything from the menu from a school in Finland (5) to a nutritional page from eighth-graders in Indiana (2) to several official British pages with regulations about free school meals (3, 6 and 8) and Scottish research on the benefits of milk (10). There was even an illegible (on our system) Japanese page found.

The following clues can be helpful in deciding which page to look at first:

Search engines have **robots** which make automatic visits to all web pages they can access. The robot stores the words of the page in the search engine's massive database for later retrieval by a searcher.

❑ The title of the page should tell you something about what the page covers. Not all pages have titles, however, and those that do are not always useful.

❑ The date is also important. The Web is a repository of out-of-date information. Many old pages are not available (it may be a long time since the last visit from a search engine's **robot**). Those that are still available may no longer be relevant.

❑ The few lines of text describing the page in the search engine's results may be simply the first lines on the page. They can, however, be words that are in the HTML document but not visible when you look at the page. This is done to give the page a greater chance to be found by the search engine. Words can be hidden in the HTML code behind the page or in a special code, known as the META tag, which gives a special description of the page to search engines.

There are several web resources (financed by advertising) where you can arrange for access to web space for your own pages at no charge. Consult Yahoo!'s subcatalogue *Business and Economy: Companies: Internet Services: Web Services: Free Web Pages* for current information.

❑ The address of the page returned by the search engine can often give you a hint as to where the information comes from. If the page is under a university domain (addresses in the top domain *.edu* in the USA and *.ac.uk* in the UK) you will have different expectations than if it is from a commercially registered domain (e.g. *.com* or *.co.uk*) or a page on a **free web space provider** (such as *Geocities*). If you only want to receive search results from British commercial domains, for example, you can specify that in your search. (In AltaVista you would write *+url:.co.uk* as one of the search expressions.)

Skimming, scanning and finding material

Even when they make a reasonable selection of the pages turned up by a web search, pupils are likely to be confronted with a lot more text than they would usually need to read. If they are looking for information about a particular subject they might have to plough through long documents before they find what they need. The sheer amount of text involved can be quite off-putting to those who are not strong readers. Many pupils may require help to read this kind of material.

When a page loads into the browser, the first thing to do is to skim the text to see what it is about. The pupil needs to establish whether the text is actually about the subject being investigated. Sometimes the text in the search results can be misleading or ambiguous. Experienced readers do this without thinking. Less experienced readers often want to start reading the text from the beginning straight away. Pupils may need to be taught to let their eye move over the page to pick out content words and then judge whether the text is relevant. If it does not appear to be relevant they need to move on immediately to the next likely item returned by the search engine.

Once the pupil has found a text to be relevant she needs to find a good place to start reading. It may not be necessary to read the entire document, and with so much potentially interesting material available there is no time to read everything. The technique to use here is to scan the material looking for key words, such as the words used in the original web search.

Sometimes it is not immediately obvious where the subject of the search is on the page. The browser has a search function (in the edit menu) which you can use to search for a particular word in the current page. This can be used to help pupils find where they should start reading if they are only interested in information about a particular matter.

⑧ *Advanced projects*

For many young people the whole point of learning about the Internet is to get the chance to make their own personal page on the Web. Writing and designing a web page becomes easier for each generation of software that is developed. There is no longer any reason why pupils (or their teachers) should hesitate to make and publish their own pages. Just a few years ago writing a web page required an intimate knowledge of the intricacies of HTML. This is no longer true. Web pages can be written in modern word processors as easily as any other kind of document. Alternatively, the web editor delivered in the browser package

Quick tip

(e.g. *FrontPage Express* which comes with Microsoft Internet Explorer 4) lets you put together a page painlessly. In Appendix 3 you will find a step-to-step guide to making a web page.

Putting pages on the Web (or, for that matter, on the school's own intranet web) is also becoming easier all the time. Your ISP or whoever is supplying your web space will be able to provide you with details about the address you should upload your pages to. Netscape have what they call one-button publishing in their browser's editor *Netscape Composer*. Microsoft's fourth-version browser has a web-publishing wizard to help guide users through the steps involved in publishing pages. These publishing aids are quite primitive and later versions of the browsers will probably have much better publishing capabilities.

A web page for the class

Making a class page is a good exercise for a class learning about the Internet. The pupils are required to cooperate and to come to some kind of agreement about the form and content of the page. It might be a good idea to assign various functions to small groups of pupils. You might choose:

General	Startup	Advanced	Firewall

Profile Name: `WS_FTP32`   New

Host Name/Address: `hem1.passagen.se`   Delete

Host Type: `UNIX (standard)`

User ID: `polarb`   ☐ Anonymous

Password: `********`   ☑ Save Pwd

Account: `******`

Comment:

OK	Avbryt	Verkställ	Hjälp

5.4 *WS_FTP*

❑ a group to plan what information the page is to contain

❑ a group to write the text that is to appear on the page

❑ a group to edit the text

❑ a group to make the pictures that will be used

❑ a group to design or choose the graphics (buttons, backgrounds, fancy titles, etc.)

❑ a group to deal with the layout of text and the graphics provided to make a harmonious page.

Individual web pages

If the pupils want to have their own pages they will need to look after all the above functions on their own. The advantage is that they will not need to compromise with others about the contents or appearance of the page. If the pages are to be published in the school's name there may be a need to ensure that the pupils' pages are free from all kinds of potentially offensive material and links. If the class already has a page the pupils' pages can be linked to it.

Before the pupils begin to work on their own pages it is generally a good idea to have them study different kinds of personal pages on the Web. Have them analyse and comment on the pages they see. What makes a page attractive? What works less well? What kind of content is interesting for a wide public?

Too many personal pages are simply a litany of a person's likes and dislikes followed by a list of their 'favourite links'. There is no need for pages to be this uninteresting. Pages are interesting if they contain new information. If a boy says he is a great Spurs fan, don't let him get away with the statement and a collection of Spurs links. Have him write about a match he went to see, giving his impressions of the trip and the match. If a girl is only interested in horses have her write about her riding lessons or about her favourite horse in the field beside the school, or about books she likes to read. That will give visitors to her page a lot more than just a handful of links to other horsy pages.

It is, of course, important that pupils do not give unnecessary personal information on their web pages. In some settings (perhaps with young pupils) there may be a policy whereby pupils do not have their surnames on web pages. Really, the only contact information necessary is an e-mail address. If even this were considered to be too great a risk, it would be sufficient for visitors to the page to be able to send e-mail to a class address that would be opened by the teacher.

Publishing pupils' work

The Web offers pupils a wider potential readership for their work than they have previously had. Once a class page exists it is an easy matter to link from the page to pupils' work. If pupils have their own pages they might want to make a link from their page to their work as well.

It is important that pupils retain the rights to their work, even in a school setting. Pupils should only be invited to publish their work, not obliged to do so. If they are allowed to choose work that they are satisfied with and helped to make any corrections necessary, they can feel proud of their work and pass the web address of the page to their friends and relations. Those pupils who do not want to publish their own work for any reason may be willing to cooperate with another pupil to produce a joint page. There may be many reasons why a pupil does not want to make a page. Sometimes it is a reflection of a lack of familiarity with the programs being used. Alternatively it might be a more general lack of confidence and a feeling that the work is not up to the standards required. In both these cases the pupil will need support to avoid being left out.

 # *Summary*

❏ Pupils are often very keen to learn all they can about the Internet. This means that they will often be motivated and will take every opportunity to practise the skills you are teaching. The problem may be that they will want to surf freely rather than apply their proficiency to their school work. Many pupils will need clear guidelines and meaningful training assignments if they are to be able to resist the temptation to sidetrack.

❏ Pupils need to be able to use at least e-mail and the Web (both passively and actively, making pages of their own). The rest of the time available for training will be needed to teach them about how to make use of the information and contacts they get from the Net.

❏ Once pupils have achieved an acceptable level of proficiency with the Internet they will be able to make use of it in their studies for years to come. Even though web browsers and other programs we use to access the Internet are constantly being improved and becoming more advanced, those who use the Net regularly will easily be able to add new skills as required.

Working with the **Internet**

Even if the Internet has been around for quite a while it is still quite a new tool in the classroom. Some teachers feel uneasy using it for various reasons. The wholesale introduction of ICT into schools is not uncontroversial, and many teachers may feel that the funds involved could have been better spent in other ways. Teachers who have not used computers in the past may find the learning curve quite steep. There is a risk that enthusiastic education authorities and teachers in the schools might overlook the difficulties some of their colleagues have with the new technologies.

⟫ *Pedagogical implications*

Perhaps one of the most off-putting of the notions associated with the full-scale use of the Internet in schools is that revolutionary new teaching methods are called for. This can be a worry for those teachers who are not convinced that the Internet is of any great use to the pupils, but it need not be a problem. There are ways to use the Net in traditional teaching as, for example, one of several sources of infor-mation. ICT in the classroom can be at best a complement to other kinds of resources – it can never replace them. Nonetheless, the Internet opens up the possibility of new kinds of activities for pupils and has the potential to allow the pupils greater autonomy.

In many schools the introduction of ICT has been led on the one hand by teachers who are enthusiastic about computers and have been using them at home for some time, and on the other hand by newly qualified teachers who have used computers and the Internet during their training and are keen to apply their knowledge with their classes. Neither of these groups is especially well placed to fire the rest of the staff with enthusiasm. This problem is likely to be temporary as the government is investing considerable sums in INSET courses for all kinds of teachers.

The fact remains, however, that some teachers will want to make more extensive use of the Internet in their teaching than will others.

Those teachers who are planning to harness the Internet's resources in every way they see to be advantageous will find themselves adopting new methods of working quite automatically. If the class is set to find out what they can about a particular subject, using the Internet as well as other sources, the teacher and pupils will be working together towards a common goal. The teacher's role is to guide the pupils' search for information rather than the traditional model where the teacher imparts knowledge to the pupils. The teacher is also one of several sources of information.

New methods

Unfortunately there is nothing pedagogical about the Internet. It is not a substitute for textbooks, merely a complement. Web pages are not typically graded for difficulty or written to be relevant to the curriculum (with some notable exceptions as mentioned elsewhere). The teacher will often, particularly for younger pupils, need to know that there is an answer to the question pupils are set to answer, otherwise the pupils will become frustrated by being sent on wild goose chases. If the pupils get stuck the teacher can suggest an approach that will give results, although there is no guarantee that the pupils' searching will have the same results even if the teacher has prepared for the class by searching for information about the subject at hand.

For many teachers the first contact with the Internet is to download information from the Web and shape it for use in class as an overhead projector transparency or a worksheet. The step from a situation where the teacher is using the Internet to find supplementary material for the class to a set-up where the class are using the Internet themselves in search of information is often perceived as very large. However, if the teacher is herself to find and form all the web material that is to be made available to the class they will have access to only a fraction of the material which might be useful to them. If the school believes that independent information retrieval is an important skill for the pupils to learn they should eventually learn to find and use their own web material.

⊗ In practice

Narrowing the search

One of the ways in which the teacher can help the pupils in their quest for knowledge is by helping them to clarify and isolate the question being asked. Loosely defined tasks (e.g. go and see what you can find about Islam) may work well when pupils are using encyclopaedias but are not suitable for Internet work. A web search for, say, *Islam* will return millions of web pages. The pupils need to know how to refine their searching, for example by searching for the text string *"Mohammed was born"* if that is what they want to know, or by using the search engine's symbols (e.g. +, – and *) as described in chapter 1.

Younger pupils will often need to be given links to web pages where they can find the necessary information, but for older pupils it is of the utmost importance that they learn to carry out intelligent web searches. A useful way for pupils to approach web searching is to brainstorm for keywords which would probably appear on a page with the information they are looking for. They can then choose a handful of the most likely words to search for. One of the most important skills pupils will need in connection with their use of the Internet, and indeed otherwise, is the ability to process text efficiently. They must be able to disregard irrelevant information and quickly find their way to the information they are looking for.

Classroom management

One of the liveliest debates surrounding the use of ICT in schools concerns the placement of the school's computers. This is particularly relevant for teachers who hope to have their pupils use the Internet regularly. The ideal is of course to have computers available in every classroom as well as enough computers for an entire class in a special computer lab. Of course, financial constraints usually limit the total number of computers in the school.

More and more schools are getting their computers linked into a network (LAN) which can be relatively inexpensively connected to the Internet using ISDN. These computers can be in a single room, or spread throughout the school.

Computers in a computer lab are useful for teaching an entire class how to use features such as e-mail or the web browser. The disadvantage of using the computer lab for incidental work when trying to use the Internet as a tool in other subjects is that it is not altogether easy to send off a group of pupils to use the computers on their own. The computer lab may well be occupied. If there is a booking scheme it will curtail the pupils' ability to spontaneously decide to use the Net for a specific purpose. If the pupils have to go to another room to use the Internet they will be neither supervised nor have anyone to ask if they need help.

One or more classroom computers are a much better option if the target is the active use of the Internet in the curriculum. They are always available to the class. The teacher can more easily control what the computer is being used for and the teacher and peers are available to help when needed. The teacher will generally need to check up on the pupils so that they only do what they are supposed to be doing on the computer. Often there will be others waiting to use the computer, so each pupil may have a limited amount of time to find what they are looking for. The teacher may need to suggest good places to look. If there is no requirement to produce results from the use of the Internet pupils may find themselves being distracted by interesting but irrelevant sidetracks on web pages.

Pupils should be encouraged to save interesting and useful web pages as bookmarks or favourites. They can even bookmark links that they do not have time (or permission) to follow, for later perusal. It is possible for each pupil to have their own subdirectory in Internet Explorer's *Favorites* file.

Generally the teacher will want to retain control of the computers and have pupils ask before using them. On occasion pupils may be assigned to use the Net to find some particular fact or they may be set to find out something using any of the tools available. It is necessary to avoid a situation where everybody has to wait for their turn at the computer with nothing to do while they are waiting.

There is a real risk that a few pupils will try to monopolise classroom computers. In some situations it may be useful to give pupils a sheet with activities that they are to perform independently, such as sending an e-mail, going to a web address, etc. They can then tick off each activity when they have done it. There are several advantages to having the pupils work in pairs at the computer. They can discuss what they find and help each other. If less knowledgeable pupils work with those who have more computer experience they will probably learn more about what the computer can do, but may not get much of a chance to try it themselves. It might be helpful to avoid having the same pairs of pupils together all the time, so that each pupil gets a chance to be active at the keyboard. If more than two pupils work together at the computer one of them will usually be a spectator rather than an active participant.

Information and knowledge

There is, of course, a fundamental distinction to be drawn between information and knowledge. The Internet is filled to overflowing with information in the shape of images, sounds and text. Information can become knowledge held by a pupil only if the pupil processes the information and assimilates it. For this to happen, the information must be at the right linguistic level and not presuppose knowledge not held by the pupil. The teacher has an important part to play in this process.

This means that in Internet work, as in all other kinds of work which involves the pupils' looking for information in reference sources, there needs to be sufficient time allowed for the pupils to work with the information they find. It is no more acceptable for pupils to copy chunks of text electronically than it ever was to copy painstakingly word for word from an encyclopaedia. The teacher will need to guide the pupils' understanding of what they read on the Internet and help them to set it into the context of other material they have covered.

An important element in connection with the Internet is the checking of sources. Pupils need to be able to establish whether the information they have found is trustworthy or not. Even if the pupils learn to trace a web page back to the entrance page of a site and thus find out who is behind the page, they may lack the real-world knowledge to make use of that information. What does it mean if they find that, for example, McDonald's is behind the interesting article about the World Cup in football? How can the pupils take the knowledge into account when judging the content of the web page? There is obviously a need to discuss the role of commercial interests in the provision of information if the pupils are to be able to make sense of the Web on their own.

Project-based learning

The Internet can at best be a slice of life brought into the classroom. It can offer a smorgasbord of information and contacts which do not fall neatly within the subject areas of the National Curriculum or any examination board's syllabus. This means that it is not always possible to limit the kinds of material gathered to suit a single subject. The nature of the Web involves material being connected intuitively to other material by virtue of associations that might never have occurred to educationalists. While this may be a distracting factor in some kinds of work it is a positive advantage in project or theme work. In schools that choose to work this way, studying, for example, the Romans in Britain from a cross-disciplinary perspective, the Internet can be most valuable. There will be maps to study to pick out Roman settlements, roads and fortifications, and further information about each of these can be obtained on the Web from local sources (for example, the City of York's own pages have a good deal of information about local Roman activity). An overview of the entire period can be obtained from sources such as EduWeb or AngliaCampus or any of the hundreds of web sites which deal with this subject (e.g. those listed in Yahoo! in the subcatalogue *Arts:Humanities:History:Ancient History:Roman Empire*).

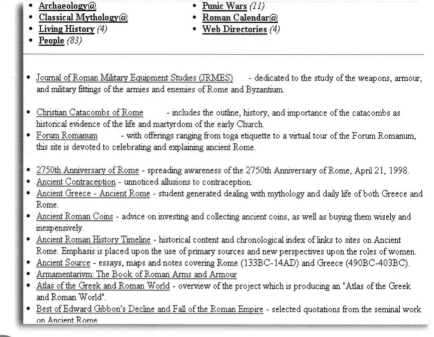

6.1 *Yahoo! Roman Empire*

Individual project work

The Internet really comes into its own in situations where pupils are working individually. When each pupil is looking for information about a specific subject the Web will be a most useful resource. Project work can generally be broken down into a series of distinct steps. First there must be a decision about what the project will cover. This will of course depend on the age and level of the pupils and the requirements of the curriculum. A project about, let us say, Islam will be quite different if it is part of A-level religion or an element in Key Stage 3 history.

Research

Pupils who have learned to use the Internet independently (that is they can navigate the Web, search intelligently and evaluate the sources of the information they find) will be able to find a lot of information on the Web for themselves. Some of the information will not be suitable for one reason or another, but with a little experience the pupils will be able to sort out what they are looking for from the material, just as they learn to do when they go to the school library to research a subject. In the process they are learning valuable study skills which will be useful to them for many years.

When such pupils use the Internet as one of several research tools they will of course find all sorts of almost relevant links. It can be very tempting to click on a link which sounds interesting, even if it is clearly not central to the matter at hand. If there is time, this kind of open-minded surfing can do a lot for the pupils' understanding of a subject area, and is likely to give them an understanding of the way our knowledge of the world is connected. The world does not lend itself easily to a neat compartmentalisation into topics and neither does the Internet.

⊘uick tip

Right-click on a link to save it as a bookmark without first following it.

Nonetheless, there is usually good reason to constrain pupils' online use of the Internet to strictly relevant material. Many pupils need a considerable amount of training and help to stay focused on the subject of their investigation. It might help the pupils to collect interesting links as bookmarks for later perusal.

Presentation

Web techniques can be used to allow pupils to present their work for others. A piece of coursework or a project can be written on the computer as a web (HTML) document, so that pupils can connect parts of their presentation with hyperlinks. This is an excellent way to let pupils produce attractive work incorporating text and pictures (their own photographs or drawings can be scanned into the computer using readily available equipment) and even sound if it contributes to the presentation. Web documents are no more difficult to produce than word-processor documents. An advantage of producing documents in HTML format is that they can easily be e-mailed to others and viewed on other kinds of computers. If the pupil is particularly satisfied with the work she may want to publish it in on the Web, but it can otherwise be viewed on a single computer or on the school intranet.

Some teachers are beginning to produce their own teaching materials in HTML. Test questions, handouts for the pupils, and all of the other documents teachers produce in the course of their preparation and teaching can just as well be saved in HTML as any other format. A few links to other documents or other sections of the same piece can easily be added and the document can be put onto the Web if there is any benefit in making it available to others (teachers at other schools, pupils or parents who can view the document from home, etc.).

Collaborative projects

As we have already seen, the Internet is more than a source of information. The most exciting part of it is the communication channels it opens up. E-mail, IRC, video conferencing, MUDs, web noticeboards and web chats let the world into the classroom. Now, the world is not actually all that welcome – we do want to be able to select those with whom we communicate in classroom situations. One of the most popular forms of Internet communication for schools is teaming up with another class somewhere in the world to work together on a specific project. Fortunately there are plenty of places on the Internet where we can find suitable people to interact with.

Local, national, international

It is fully possible to use the Internet to collaborate with a person sitting at the next desk, but this is not always necessary or desirable. Project partners can be in the same school, in another school in the same town, in another town in the UK or in another country altogether. The choice of project partner will, of course, depend on the nature of the project.

Local projects can be a way of bridging gaps in a town, for example between a private school and a state school, or between a boys' school and a girls' school, or a Catholic school and a Protestant school. Classes can work together to create a tourist guide to their area on the Web, or write a play or a story set in their town. Other possibilities would be a local environmental project (clearing the beach from litter, making an inventory of and documenting the insect life in an area of the local woodland, finding out and documenting how each child's family heats their home, etc.). The results could be displayed on web pages in the site of one of the schools or in some neutral place (e.g. an Internet Service Provider or a free-space provider). These projects can usually be organised by individual teachers who get in touch with each other to suggest and plan a collaboration before the pupils are involved.

National projects can involve many schools or just two or three, or provide the means for schools or classes to join up in twos or threes to work on a common theme. These projects are often organised by some kind of central authority or organisation, such as the Virtual Teachers Centre on the National Grid for Learning site. The Curriculum IT Support (CITS) projects which can be reached from there (on the BECTa site) provide materials and support for activities in a range of curriculum areas. Organisations such as the BBC or Microsoft or the educational ISPs can sometimes organise activities using the Internet where schools are invited to work together on a project.

International projects

Many schools twin themselves with a school in another country, such as France or Germany, and organise their own activities in collaboration with classes in the other school. But there are other kinds of international projects. The *European Union* has several different paths to contact between schools, for example the possibility for schools to find themselves partners in other Community countries and apply for funding for a project of their own design, and the *European Schoolnet* which offers less formal contacts. Many schools have taken part in the Comenius project which supports this kind of exchange. The *British Council* has in the past stood behind international Internet projects, such as one linking British schools with schools in New Zealand. Australian schools are often keen to make contact with schools in Europe for various kinds of projects. They can be reached through the *Aussie SchoolHouse* site, for example. There are also numerous American sites which organise international projects of all kinds and put participants in touch with each other.

Some of these projects are very large and attract thousands of classes. NASA generally has a large-scale schools project on the go

6.2 *Aussie SchoolHouse*

(e.g. exploring Antarctica), while other projects let classes follow the progress of a real adventure in progress (climbing Everest, sailing round the world, etc.). These projects will be discussed further in chapter 7.

Join a project

The first step in joining a project with your class or school is finding a suitable project. The National Grid for Learning, the *European Schoolnet*, the *NickNacks* site, or the *Global SchoolHouse* have many different kinds of national and international projects to choose from. When you are selecting a project, bear in mind that the project must:

❑ Fit into the curriculum as regards the level and the content of the project. Make sure the planned outcome of the project is in line with the aims of the curriculum.

❑ Suit your timetabling (i.e. not have its climax during your half-term or summer holidays).

❑ Not require more advanced technical equipment or knowledge than you can easily manage.

❑ Be attractive to you and to your pupils!

Many different kinds of projects are available. The NickNacks site has, for example, a web-based Jeopardy-style quiz game where students create game questions about a selected global issue or event. It also has annual projects in March and October to chart the progress of spring and autumn in different countries in the northern and southern hemispheres. This project involves students sharing weekly observation and the aim is to help them understand seasonal change on a global level.

Another interesting NickNacks project involves four classes writing four mystery plays in collaboration. Each play has four acts, each act written by a different class. At the end of the writing process the classes have an IRC conference to discuss what they have learned and the dramatic process. They also have four plays they can use for other purposes.

Yet another project involved classes exchanging spreadsheets where they compiled and analysed data on their favourite pets, sports, foods and school subjects. An older, very successful project, organised by a computer instructor at a junior high school in West Virginia, involved letting teenagers at risk ask questions of prison inmates via e-mail. There are links to these and other project descriptions in this book's web pages. Do not hesitate to borrow and adapt others' project ideas for your own purposes!

You can subscribe to mailing lists which will send you details of upcoming projects. There are such lists at the Global SchoolHouse and NickNacks sites. Even if you do not choose to join a project you might get a few good ideas for your own teaching.

Start your own project

If you do not find just what you are looking for in the listings of current projects, or if you wish to use a project idea that you find in a description of an already completed project, you may wish to organise your own project. In this case you will need to have a very clear idea of what you want to accomplish with the project. It will almost certainly take a lot more time than you expect both in the classroom and outside.

The planning stage is probably the most important part of the entire project. Hours put in at this stage are well spent and may save wasted time later on. You may have a subject you want the project to cover or a particular aim you hope to achieve with your pupils. But before you start you must have a clear idea of what the project is going to do and what the outcome or finished product will be (so that you can summarise the project in a few sentences for prospective partners). You also need to know which grades or ages you want to collaborate with (you might want your pupils to interact with younger or older pupils if that is what suits the requirements of the project); how many classes you want to involve in the project; where those classes should be located; and whether they should have any special characteristics (sex, school type, religion, etc.). Then you are ready to start your search for partners.

You can look for partners by posting information about your own planned project in all the places where you can look for other people's projects to join. The NickNacks site is a good place to start – it has also a list of other places where you can post details of your project. You will need to give contact information including the information that this is an individual teacher's initiative rather than a larger-scale centrally organised project. Those looking for a project to join need to know exactly what participation would require in terms of a commitment of time, knowledge and technical resources. Of course they will also want information about the expected outcome of the project and the kinds of pupils you are looking for.

The project's timeframe is very important. You will most likely need to specify start and finishing dates for the entire project well in advance, as well as other dates, for example for the submission of data during the course of the project. It is essential that all parties are very clear about what is expected of them at every stage. You, as project coordinator, must be very punctual, and you might find it helpful to remind the participants of an approaching deadline in good time.

Have a dry run first. Go through all the steps of the project yourself before involving others. If you are going to have participants e-mail files to each other make sure that the files are not too large. If they are you will need to compress or divide them. You might find that your participants are using different kinds of computers and different programs than you are. This does not mean that you cannot communicate, but you will need to know how to ensure compatibility. PC (Windows) computers, Macintoshes, Acorns and others all have their peculiarities. The safest option is really to stick to plain-text e-mails and web documents (which can, of course be attached to e-mails rather than being published on the Web if you are shy). If possible you can try to do what you expect your participants to do from another computer.

When you have found your participants have them do a test run too. In this way you will see whether your explanations have been explicit enough and you can avoid unnecessary delays when the project has started. You can prepare a sample data file that you can send to the participants and have them send back to you.

You may find that some classes will drop out of the project for various reasons before it is over. You can prepare for this eventuality by involving a few more classes than you really need. If you are swamped by classes wanting to participate you can always suggest to one of them that they might like to coordinate a second group. There is a risk that pupils will be disappointed if the project does not live up to their expectations. All classes will not be able to put the same amount of time and effort into the project.

Make sure you deliver what you promised when you posted details of your project. If a web site was to be the result, do not forget to send the web address to all the participants. It is important that the finished product recognises the input of all the participants.

The NickNacks site has some examples of collaborative projects together with the project plans, calls for participants and the outcomes. These projects involve exchanging different kinds of data, such as tables and graphs, multimedia files or text messages.

Communication via the Internet

E-mail

We have mentioned several different ways which can be used for exchanging information via the Internet. E-mail is a very useful tool here, both as a way of sending text messages and as a vehicle for all kinds of files. Some programs (e.g. Hyperstudio, Word and Powerpoint) have a free viewer which you can send along to let others view your files in these programs. If you are going to e-mail large files you will probably want to compress the files. This is a nice way to send a package of several files. They can even be organised into separate hierarchical directories and the directory structure will be preserved when the package is decompressed. You can find compression programs (e.g. Stuffit for Macintosh and WinZip for Windows) in the shareware archives mentioned in the last chapter. If you send too-large files (more than 2 Mb) you risk overloading the recipient's mailbox. A handy rule of thumb is to try to save the file on a 1.4 Mb diskette. If there is room on the diskette for the file you can probably send it without difficulty.

WinZip (Unregistered) - tpi.zip

File   Actions   Options   Help

New   Open   Favorites   Add   Extract   View   CheckOut   Wizard

Name	Date	Time	Size	Ratio	Packed	Path
1 What is the Internet.doc	98-11-24	10:50	123 904	70%	37 749	
glossary.doc	98-12-01	21:46	35 840	76%	8 590	
Appendix 3 Making a web page.doc	98-12-01	22:02	31 744	76%	7 742	
Appendix 2.doc	98-11-23	18:25	22 528	82%	4 143	
Appendix 1.doc	98-11-23	18:26	23 552	81%	4 460	
9 GNVQ subjects.doc	98-12-01	15:19	90 112	72%	24 876	
8 Academic subjects.doc	98-11-26	14:04	133 632	69%	41 014	
7 Cross-curricular Projects.doc	98-11-25	17:08	50 688	73%	13 825	
6 Working with the Internet.doc	98-11-25	16:44	62 464	70%	18 809	
5 Teaching pupils to use the Internet.doc	98-11-25	14:45	97 280	71%	28 008	
4 The Internet for Pupils.doc	98-11-25	13:44	67 072	68%	21 221	
3 The Internet for teachers.doc	98-11-24	21:51	101 376	72%	28 148	
2 Does the Internet belong in schools.doc	98-12-03	13:42	89 600	71%	25 934	
10 Where is the Internet headed.doc	98-12-01	21:34	51 200	73%	13 746	

Selected 0 files, 0 bytes   Total 15 files, 980KB

6.3 WinZip
Copyright 1991–8, Nico Mak Computing, Inc. Printed with permission of Nico Mak Computing, Inc.

Computer conferencing

E-mail mailing lists or dedicated noticeboard-type discussions such as those available on CampusWorld (for subscribers) and the European Virtual School can be a useful complement to class work, particularly for older pupils. These forums offer the opportunity to discuss current affairs or curricular topics with other pupils, and teachers who participate regularly.

The Web

Published web pages are another useful way of letting others see what you want them to see. You can show tables and graphs on the Web, and even those who do not have the same hardware or software as you can view them. Modern spreadsheet programs such as Microsoft Excel lend themselves easily to web presentations. But there are other ways to share files. Some programs accept files created in other programs. There are some basic formats that are accepted by a wide range of programs. You may need to consult your technician about this. Another advantage of the Web is that it is a good way to show pictures and play sound files to people at other locations.

Using chats in class

When live chats are to be used as part of a collaborative learning experience, often as the climax of a long period of e-mail discussion, it is important that the pupils are given support to make the chat as useful as it can be. The chat needs to be focused in advance, so that there are specific themes to be discussed. It is probably not a good idea to have the pupils prepare in detail what they are going to say. That might destroy the spontaneity of the chat and be off-putting to other, less well-prepared participants.

If the participants are tongue tied the teachers may need to get the ball rolling by asking open-ended questions such as 'What do you think we should do with what we have learned in this project?' Depending on the age and level of the pupils the teachers may have to oil the machinery of conversation by elaborating on cryptic comments and the like. The chat may be more successful if the pupils actually have information they want to exchange with each other.

This kind of chat can generally be conducted in a private or secret channel so as not to be open to all comers. It is possible to work with a single classroom computer if there is some way to let all pupils see the screen. If some of the pupils are not actually involved in typing they will need to be included in the discussion in some way, perhaps by regularly asking for a show of hands to report the class opinion.

ICQ or Web chats may be easier to manage than IRC, particularly when several pupils are involved simultaneously. If complicated data need to be discussed a conference program such as Microsoft's NetMeeting or Netscape's Conference will be useful. NetMeeting allows both voice and video contact and can be used even by those whose typing speeds are not up to scratch. In fact, it is difficult to imagine anything you might want to do in a collaborative project that you could not use NetMeeting for. One thing that Netscape's system can do is allow conference participants to surf together. This could be useful to show the results of an Internet search for information about a topic.

6.4 *Netscape Conference*

There are other systems which can be used for video conferencing, such as CU-SeeMe. Many of the schools who have been pioneers in video conferencing have had direct contact with their co-participants rather than connecting up via the Internet.

Information wants to be free!

The Internet is neither more nor less than what its users make it. We must all do what we can to make the Internet a friendly and useful place to spend time. Government efforts to ensure that we find at least some of what we are looking for when we connect our computers to the Net are, of course, very valuable and welcome, but they are but a drop in the ocean.

Sharing your work

All the teacher resources we have looked at are at least partly the work of ordinary teachers who have decided to contribute in one way or another. The lesson-plan collections and discussion forums for teachers would not exist if there were not individual teachers who are willing to share their work with others. If you have spent a lot of time preparing a handout or a test to give to your class you might feel hesitant about giving your work away, but really you have nothing to lose. You have done the work, but your achievement is not lessened in the sharing. Next time perhaps you can use somebody else's material. Maybe someone who uses your material can give you a idea about how to improve your handout for next time you want to use it with a class, or even send an improved and extended version of your handout back to the group.

In fact the entire Internet, or at least the useful part of it, is built up on this kind of give and take. It is an intrinsic part of what the Internet is about. If we pool our resources we can do more than if we struggle on alone.

Sharing your knowledge

As you begin to navigate the discussion forums of the Net with the Web, newsgroups, e-mail and chat you will find that most people you encounter are not out to cheat you or make money from you, but are rather looking for a genuine exchange of ideas and support. People ask questions or describe their problems and others contribute with answers or advice. Most people find it rewarding to be able to answer other people's questions. Those who do not wish to answer need not.

In any forum there will be a number of people who are active contributors to the discussion and a much larger number of *lurkers* (i.e. silent participants who never contribute to the discussion). Lurking is not necessarily frowned on in Internet circles, and it is generally advisable to lurk for a while in a new forum so you can judge the tone of the discussion before you jump in. However if you never contribute you are withholding your opinions and unique set of experiences from the community. The people you might have answered will be the worse off for not having heard your advice. Similarly, if you never ask a question or set the discussion off on a new topic you will probably never learn what the group has to say about that topic.

A global network?

The Internet is often described as global. This is not strictly accurate. The Internet is predominantly accessible in industrialised countries. There are great white areas in Africa, Asia and Latin America where Internet connections are few and far between. The few connections which do exist are reserved for university and governmental use. In some cases the political regime is doing its best to ensure that the Internet does not gain a foothold. But this is changing, albeit slowly, and there are pioneer projects which make the Internet available in other countries too.

The Internet's lingua franca

If you have spent any amount of time surfing the Web you will have come across some material in languages other than English. The search engine AltaVista has even gone as far as to offer an instant translation of web pages from a number of languages to English (and vice versa). But it can generally be said that you need not feel you have missed anything by not being able to understand the site, because no web-page maker in a country where English is not a native language would dream of writing anything but local interest material in the local language. The Internet is international and there is only one language that is widely enough used to be a candidate for use in international gatherings of this kind – English. English has been referred to as the world's second language – not that it is the world's second largest native language but rather that is the most widely spoken language by people who may or may not have another first language.

Now this situation is alarming for speakers of many other languages who are finding that as soon as they set foot outside their country (even virtually) they are being required to use English. It is also a bit of a blow for speakers of other world languages, such as Spanish, French and German. There is considerable Internet activity in these languages, but it primarily involves native speakers. If material is aimed at a wider audience it will generally be in English, often as well as another language (e.g. Swedish, Dutch, etc.). Sometimes this leads to parallel sites being built up in English and one or more other languages. The advantages of having a single, common language throughout the Internet are obvious, but this causes severe problems for those who are not proficient in English. They may have access to only a fraction of the material the Internet can offer, and their participation in international communication is likely to be riddled with misunderstandings.

The privilege of English

Those of us who have English as a native language need to be aware of the privileged position we occupy. Our circumstances have given us an advantage which we must take care not to abuse. This means that we need to be very aware of the problems faced by non-native speakers when we move in international circles on the Net, although there can be as much linguistic and cultural confusion between Americans and the British as ever was caused by non-native speakers. It is, nonetheless, worth considering that a fellow netizen's clumsy comments or failure to get what we are talking about might be attributable to a less-than-perfect command of the language before we get upset.

One advantage our children have over their European companions is that they have access to the greatest part of the Internet's resources at a very early age. Young Spaniards, Greeks and Norwegians, for example, need to wait until they have mastered the English language sufficiently well to venture outside the relative security of web pages and other Internet resources written in the local language.

ⓧ *Summary*

- ❏ The Internet need not alter your teaching style unless you let it. But if you decide to use the Internet's resources to enhance your teaching you will probably find yourself working differently than you have before.

- ❏ The Net is ideal for project work and for pupils' own investigations of well-defined areas.

- ❏ Internet communication channels may lead you to contacts that you would not otherwise have made. The challenge lies in applying the technology where it has a positive effect.

- ❏ The Internet is very democratic, and everybody is welcome to contribute with information, teaching notes, handouts, tests and samples of pupils' work, and by answering the questions of others when possible. The Internet is the sum of all its contributors' efforts.

Cross-curricular projects

In this chapter we will look at some large-scale cross-curricular projects involving the use of the Internet. These kinds of projects come and go. The projects we describe here may no longer be in existence when you read this, but there will be others which have taken their place. Many of these projects are international; others are primarily organised for schools in a certain country but may welcome the participation of schools in several countries.

You can find out about projects like this in a number of ways. One of the best ways is to keep an eye on major educational sites such as the NGfL site, the European Schoolnet and the Global SchoolNet. There are also mailing lists which will send you information about upcoming projects, such as the HILITES list and the K12-EURO-TEACHERS list mentioned in chapter 3.

Organising projects

These projects take a lot of organising and for this reason they are unlikely to come out of individual schools. Projects that are successful tend to become large as more and more schools join in. Organisations like the British Council and the European Union are better able to assign resources to educational activities, although some of the projects described here are organised by commercially sponsored education sites. However, some projects are reliant on the work of volunteers. Teachers, parents and other adults contribute vast amounts of time and energy to online commitments. These projects can be immensely rewarding.

Participation in most projects is free for schools, but it will probably make more work for the teacher or teachers involved. If the project is a governmental or European Union initiative there may be funds available to cover this. In some cases there may be requirements which mean that participating classes need to have more access to computer resources than they would otherwise have had. This too may be fundable in some kinds of projects. But most of the projects we describe here assume that the teachers involved will give freely of their time and effort out of their own interest and for the good of the pupils.

Making space for projects

Even if teachers are sometimes assumed to have unlimited time on their hands which they can put into participation in a project, pupils do not. Their time in school is strictly regulated by their timetable. Unless the teacher can motivate the pupils to devote some of their free time to the project it will have to be strictly relevant to the curriculum. There simply is not time for extensive sidetracks, no matter how interesting they may be.

If the topic of a project that interests you or your pupils is not covered by the curriculum it might be possible to get involved anyway. You might consider starting interested pupils off and having them carry out the project at home or in a school computer club if such a thing exists. If the school allows pupils access to the school computers after school they might be able to participate then.

That said, there are often ways to use a project for your own purposes. If you are planning to teach about a country you can relatively easily enhance the pupils' learning experience with a virtual visit to that country. If you are going to teach about life during the 1939–45 war, who better to ask than someone who remembers how it was. It may be possible to adapt a project activity or focus on some part of it to suit your class.

International projects

The beauty of the Internet is that it lets schools and individuals communicate with each other quickly and easily regardless of the distance between them at very little or no cost (assuming they already have access to the Internet). But since schools are not used to this kind of contact they may need help to get started. Before the Internet made its way into the world of education there were no directories of schools in different countries. There was no straightforward way to find the addresses of schools outside the UK or the names of teachers who might be interested in making contact with a school in the UK.

With the help of the Web it takes no more than a few minutes to find a school in, say, Munich, and track down an English teacher to approach with the idea of an English/German keypal exchange. But even this approach is not really the best way to go about finding project partners. There are hundreds of centrally organised projects that you can join. In addition you can register yourself in a partner database so others looking for partners can find you. The projects described below are good starting points.

European Schools Project

The *European Schools Project* (ESP) is not to be confused with the European Union's *European Schoolnet*. The ESP is an initiative of the Faculty of Pedagogical and Educational Sciences of the University of Amsterdam. Its purpose is to help teachers and pupils to participate in Internet-based communication and to use the Internet's information resources to improve learning and teaching.

The ESP has grown and now involves a number of national coordinators in participating countries. They help teachers and schools to participate in collaborative projects. They work with the basic concept of the *teletrip* or *teleproject*. These teletrips can be on any topic and use any language.

The ESP defines teletrips as 'collaborative distance learning projects designed by teachers from various countries around a part of curriculum that is thought to be mutually relevant'. The principal idea is that a teletrip will involve the pupils carrying out some piece of local research about a particular topic. The next step is that the local results are exchanged and discussed with the partner school. Generally this will involve a foreign language and e-mail. Teletrips can involve subject teachers, language teachers and ICT teachers to make the activities as educationally relevant as possible.

ESP teletrips are by their very nature easy to tailor exactly to a particular aspect of the curriculum. They are very flexible because they involve only two classes at a time. The teachers can easily find a suitable topic to build the teletrip around.

The ESP has coordinated hundreds of these projects in past years. Previous teletrips have covered topics as diverse as 'The Image of the Other' and 'Water Quality' (both have web pages describing the teletrip) as well as 'Everyday Statistics', 'Pollution', 'Tourism', 'Stories about World War II' and 'Power Plants'.

Chatback

Chatback describes itself as 'the world-wide electronic school'. It was started as early as 1986 to provide e-mail communication for some 100 schools in the UK and abroad. Most of these were special schools and all of them catered for children who had some mental or physical difficulty with communicating. Chatback has electronic links with children in Argentina, Australia, Canada, Estonia, Germany, Italy, Japan, Lithuania, Poland, the USA, and even a special school in Novosibirsk in Siberia.

The idea behind Chatback is to encourage young people to correspond with each other for social interaction and for work on classroom subjects. Chatback has a couple of very interesting projects involving a 'Panel of Elders' – a group of elderly Internet users in many different countries, who interact with the young participants of the project.

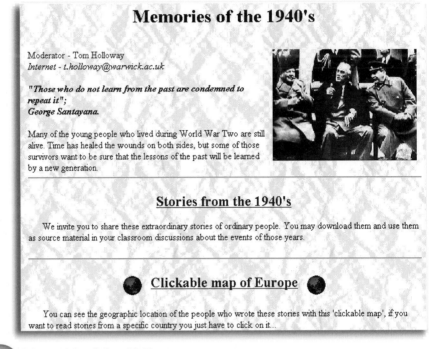

Memories of the 1940's

Moderator - Tom Holloway
Internet - t.holloway@warwick.ac.uk

"Those who do not learn from the past are condemned to repeat it";
George Santayana.

Many of the young people who lived during World War Two are still alive. Time has healed the wounds on both sides, but some of those survivors want to be sure that the lessons of the past will be learned by a new generation.

Stories from the 1940's

We invite you to share these extraordinary stories of ordinary people. You may download them and use them as source material in your classroom discussions about the events of those years.

Clickable map of Europe

You can see the geographic location of the people who wrote these stories with this 'clickable map', if you want to read stories from a specific country you just have to click on it...

7.1 *Memories of the 1940s*

The project *Memories of the 1940s* is based round a collection of descriptions of life in the 1940s. Some of these descriptions were written by individuals from many countries who remember life at that time. Others are written by young people who have interviewed their parents or grandparents. The 'Panel of Elders', who have all written this kind of short description of their lives in the 1940s, invite participants to send in questions which are then added to the web page along with an answer from one of the Elders. This project could be useful for the study of modern history, languages, geography, English and civics as well as ICT.

Granny's Kitchen is another attractive project involving elderly Internet users from various countries. The idea is to investigate the food preferences of today's children and compare them to the childhood preferences of the elders.

European Schoolnet

The *European Schoolnet* has been described in chapter 3. It includes a project archive of active and older projects which can either be joined or used as inspiration for new projects. Projects include a Belgian virtual comic book made by children from all over the world; a Dutch project *Face to Face* in which multicultural secondary schools exchange video letters, e-mail, ordinary letters and fax with a partner class with students of comparable age and level; and a Greek light pollution project.

The European Schoolnet also has an interesting French project which involves Danish, English, French, Greek, Italian, Portuguese and Turkish secondary schools in a European network, *Young Reporters for the Environment*. The students lead investigations on environmental issues faced by their regions through direct contact with local actors such as firms, town councils, laboratories, the public, etc. This kind of project can be relevant to the teaching of languages, geography, civics and environmental science.

Some of these projects are run by individual schools, others by a national educational technology agency (the local equivalent of BECTa). They use the European Schoolnet to publicise the project and help prospective participants to find partners.

The European Studies Programme

The European Studies Programme has been operating for several years and aims to link Irish and Northern Irish schools to schools elsewhere in Europe. It is financed jointly by the Departments of Education in Northern Ireland and the Republic of Ireland. It involves over 400 schools and colleges in Austria, Belgium, Denmark, England, Finland, Germany, Italy, The Netherlands, Norway, Poland, Spain and Sweden. The students work in groups with at least one school from Northern Ireland and one from the Republic of Ireland. The project offers a curriculum-based Junior Programme for 11–16 year-olds with specially produced materials in English, geography and history, as well as a one-year cross-curricular Senior Programme involving topics with economic, political, cultural, technological, social and environmental perspectives.

⟫ *Interactive expeditions*

Another kind of project allows pupils to tag along on a real-life adventure. The idea is that there is an actual expedition or adventure happening and the real adventurers keep the participating classes involved in the expedition by means of web pages, IRC, e-mail bulletins to a mailing list, etc. There have been numerous such projects in the past and new adventures are being planned all the time. If you keep an eye on the web sites for the following projects (addresses in this book's web pages) you will be able to see what is available.

MayaQuest, AfricaQuest and GalapagosQuest

MayaQuest ran from 1995 to 1998. It involved following the exploits of a team of explorers who cycled to ruins in Mexico and Central America, met with on-site archaeologists and attempted to unlock the mystery of the collapse of the ancient Maya civilisation. Their adventures were followed by over one million pupils, teachers and others from around the world. They could follow the activities day by day via the Internet. Every day, different members of the expedition team shared their experiences from the rainforest either in a report or in some kind of online activity. The team reported on the adventures they were having; on their findings and insights into Maya history and archaeology; on the technical set-up involved in transmitting their experiences live from the rainforest via satellite; and on the ecological perspective to various experiments that the team carried out. Efforts were made to give participating schools insight into the environment and culture of the Maya region with regular features covering regional foods, personal encounters with exotic species, and local myths and legends. The adventurers also met local children and put them in touch with the schools following the expedition.

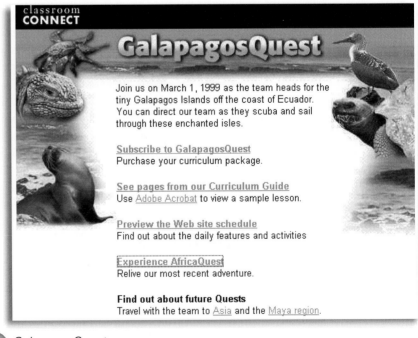

classroom
CONNECT

GalapagosQuest

Join us on March 1, 1999 as the team heads for the tiny Galapagos Islands off the coast of Ecuador. You can direct our team as they scuba and sail through these enchanted isles.

Subscribe to GalapagosQuest
Purchase your curriculum package.

See pages from our Curriculum Guide
Use Adobe Acrobat to view a sample lesson.

Preview the Web site schedule
Find out about the daily features and activities

Experience AfricaQuest
Relive our most recent adventure.

Find out about future Quests
Travel with the team to Asia and the Maya region.

7.2 *GalapagosQuest*
Copyright Classroom Connect. All rights reserved. (www.classroom.com)

A major part of this kind of interactive expedition is that the pupils who follow the adventure are able to communicate directly with the adventurers. In MayaQuest pupils could actually vote on where the expedition would go next.

MayaQuest and *AfricaQuest* are over now, but *GalapagosQuest* is planned to start in the spring of 1999. There is already information available about subsequent planned Quests. They will most likely be set up in a similar way. These adventures are organised by *Classroom Connect*, an American publisher of educational materials for classrooms using the Internet. Schools may observe for free, but a subscription gives them a detailed teacher's guide, a classroom poster with a map of the expedition, and access to all the interactive elements of the adventure.

JASON

The JASON project, which is sponsored by NASA, involves an annual scientific expedition which is the focus of an original curriculum developed for grades 5 to 12 in the American school system (ages 10–18 years). The project currently works with a network of educational, research and cultural institutions in the USA, Mexico, Bermuda and the UK. Pupils take part in the expeditions through live interactive communication.

The JASON project works with the approach that teachers are 'facilitators' or 'managers' of the learning process. They provide their own curriculum for the project. The program involves a two-week intensive programme with an extended programme up to one year. There are programme sessions in the USA, Mexico, Bermuda and the UK. About 14 000 pupils participate every year. The project describes itself as relevant to scientific subjects, ICT, mathematics and social sciences.

When we investigated the JASON programme they were planning their tenth annual expedition, JASON X: *Rainforests – a Wet & Wild Adventure*, to the Amazon Center for Environmental Education and Research (ACEER), located in the Peruvian Amazon rainforest. The plan is to make a comparative study of temperate, tropical and fossil rainforests.

During the two-week long live telepresence, participating pupils will be able to virtually climb to a height of over a hundred feet and explore the layers of the forest and its inhabitants along a quarter-mile long canopy walkway, study an ant colony, investigate the Amazon River and its watershed, and learn about how local people have used the resources of the rainforest for food, shelter and medicine.

The idea is that pupils and teachers will prepare for the telepresence by studying research web sites and carrying out comparative local field investigations and hands-on experiments. Pupils are to be helped to study the plants, animals, climate and hydrology of their own local environment by 'designing and building canopy walkways and insect traps, collecting and analysing leaf litter, ground-truthing satellite data, constructing and monitoring an artificial bromeliad, and more'. The pupils' local research findings will be supported by interaction with an interdisciplinary team of researchers. Pupils will be able to share their local findings with the JASON team.

JASON X will probably be over when you read this, but there will most likely be a new JASON expedition underway that you can join if you wish.

» *Creating web material*

Global SchoolNet

Global SchoolNet (GSN) has had an ongoing adventure project for quite a few years, *Where on the Globe is Roger?*, following the exploits of an American man travelling around the world in a lorry. This project is winding down now, but Global SchoolNet is still going strong.

GSN currently has a major project which is elegant in its simplicity, the *Community Share web*. Classes around the world are invited to create one or more web pages describing an aspect of their local community that they are proud of. The class pages are then collected and made available online and searchable by school, city, project category and language. Each month GSN comes up with a new activity designed to strengthen the bond between schools and their local communities.

The web pages are to focus on one of eight categories: local leaders; community groups and special populations; businesses and organisations; local specialities; local attractions (natural and man-made); historical landmarks; environmental awareness and issues; and local music and art forms.

The GSN site provides discussion questions and starter activities to help classes to get started. It encourages schools to coordinate with other schools in their district, so that different schools choose different categories, rather than duplicate the same information.

In this kind of project the result is not really all that important. The web pages produced by classes may never actually be much use to anybody outside the immediate locality of the school. Nonetheless the pupils will have learned a tremendous amount while working on their page and gathering the information they need to make it.

Kidlink

Kidlink has been described in detail earlier (chapter 4). Here we shall look at a large-scale project planned by Kidlink, *Who-am-I?* This project is not unlike GSN's *Community Share web*, in that it encourages young people to take a good look at themselves and their immediate surroundings. This project has been designed for European teachers of young people up to the age of 15 to use with their classes.

The Who-am-I? project runs for the first time in the 1998–9 school year. The project has several stages which follow each other: Who am I? Where do I live? What are my rights? (starting on United Nations day, 24 October); My friends and family; What are my roots? and finally, Virtual vacation.

Kidlink points out that the main educational objective is not the contents of the web pages generated by the project. The process of gathering the material on each topic is expected to enhance the pupils' education with respect to

> **language arts, writing** (the writing process with step by step support), **research** (finding information, evaluate, use, books, electronic media, searching skills/strategies, evaluating result, documenting results), **social studies** (latitude and longitude/time zones, world cultures, current events), history, geography, economics (currencies around the world – description and history), **mathematics** (problem solving, applying topics to real world situations), **science** (scientific methods, exploring and experimenting, environment), **The Arts** (music, drawing, painting), and **current awareness**, in addition to **personal development, Internet networking skills, Information & Communications Technology skills**, and other skills needed in modern society.

The aim of the Who-am-I? project is to assist teachers in enhancing their existing curriculum. The idea is to give pupils an audience and to give meaning and context to tasks that can otherwise be boring. The project is actually a combination of previously successful Kidlink activities, developed into an integrated, multilingual program tailored for European teachers.

The project will be carried out with the use of Kidlink's mailing lists supplemented by Kidlink's private chat network. Web space will be made available on the Kidlink site for pupils' multimedia web pages. Kidlink will help set up mailing lists for teachers and students in any European language that does not already have them. The programme includes module descriptions, teacher tips, lessons, links to resources, module guidelines and answers to Frequently Asked Questions (FAQ) in English (and translations into all participating languages).

As in other Kidlink activities, the programme has been developed and will be coordinated by experienced teachers. Each official language area will have a language coordinator to work directly with teachers for the duration of the programme, provide help, and act as a mentor. The Kidlink teacher rooms will help teachers to make contact with others who are involved in the project. It is fully possible to participate in a language other than your own.

ThinkQuest

ThinkQuest describes itself as 'an annual contest that challenges young people, ages 12 to 19, to use the Internet as a collaborative, interactive teaching and learning tool'. This project too is run under the auspices of the Global SchoolNet.

The idea is for pupils to work in teams of two or three to produce sets of web pages that can be used as teaching and learning tools by teachers and pupils around the world. There are large cash prizes available for the best entries.

This is a project to appeal to those pupils who are most at home with computers and who are able to harness the power of the Web. Ideally they can work together with pupils who have a lot of knowledge and a burning interest in a suitable topic. ThinkQuest lets pupils combine their interest in technology and web design with curriculum topics. The entries must also be useful for others and somehow help them to learn the material. The end result is what ThinkQuest calls 'a valuable library of Internet based educational materials produced by students, for students'.

Vikings

The *Viking Project* involves individuals and schools in almost all countries where the Vikings made their presence felt: Canada, Denmark, England, Estonia, Finland, the Faeroes, Iceland, Ireland, Norway, Scotland, Sweden and the USA. The idea is that participants become members of the Viking Network and produce an information sheet about Viking activity in their locality. This gives them the right to request sheets from other members. Many of these sheets are now on the Web, since making web pages has become much simpler than it was when the Viking Network was developed in 1994. One of the most interesting pages tells of a simulated raid by Danish Vikings (Balleskolen, Silkebork, Denmark) on an Irish monastery (St Michael's Boys Primary School, Trim, Ireland) in which the two schools took it in turns to describe the raid from their perspective.

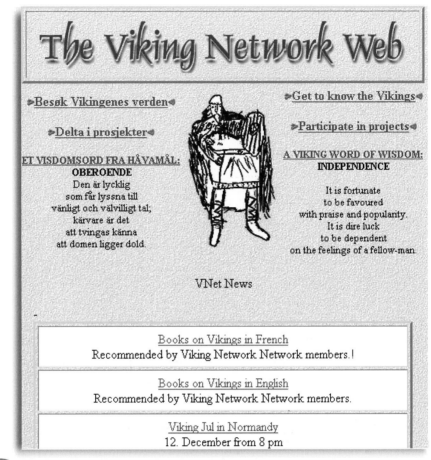

The Viking Network Web

▶Besøk Vikingenes verden◀

▶Delta i prosjekter◀

ET VISDOMSORD FRA HÅVAMÅL:
OBEROENDE
Den är lycklig
som får lyssna till
vänligt och välvilligt tal;
kärvare är det
att tvingas känna
att domen ligger dold.

▶Get to know the Vikings◀

▶Participate in projects◀

A VIKING WORD OF WISDOM:
INDEPENDENCE
It is fortunate
to be favoured
with praise and popularity.
It is dire luck
to be dependent
on the feelings of a fellow-man.

VNet News

> Books on Vikings in French
> Recommended by Viking Network Network members.!

> Books on Vikings in English
> Recommended by Viking Network Network members.

> Viking Jul in Normandy
> 12. December from 8 pm

7.3 *The Viking Network*

The Viking Network's web pages have very detailed information about every aspect of the Vikings' life and history. This project is a really good example of the kind of work that can be done with the help of the Internet and which would simply not be possible otherwise.

Summary

❑ The Internet lends itself easily to large-scale international projects. They are attractive for pupils and teachers alike, and are likely to teach pupils a good deal about the everyday life of pupils in other countries as well as about the actual focus of the project. The Internet allows teachers and pupils to meet their counterparts in other parts of the world and to work together towards a common goal.

❏ Official bodies such as the British Council, the European Union, NASA and the National Grid for Learning find that Internet projects are an excellent way to do what they have been set up to do.

❏ Commercial organisations behind international cross-disciplinary projects also have a lot to gain from sponsoring this kind of activity. Apart from the positive public relations, corporations such as Microsoft stand to gain when more young people start actively using computers. The projects also attract them to web pages where they will be exposed to advertising.

❏ Other organisations, such as Chatback and Kidlink, are run by volunteers who gain nothing but personal satisfaction from their involvement in Internet projects.

Academic subjects

Learning about the Internet is often viewed as an educational goal in itself. However, if the Internet is to be used as efficiently as possible in schools it must become a tool among others, used by teachers of every subject. The aim of this chapter is to give subject teachers a glimpse of the many Internet resources and activities that are relevant to each school subject.

The Internet is overflowing with countless resources, informative sites and enthusiasts in every subject under the sun. Every site or discussion forum you find has information about others. If you start to look for information about a particular subject you will likely find more than you ever imagined possible.

 ## *Fitting the Internet into the curriculum*

The logistics of gaining access to the school's computers may require some creativity on the part of subject teachers. Some schools have their computers (or at least those computers which have an Internet connection) mostly in computer labs or the school library rather than in individual classrooms. The widespread use of the Internet by teachers of all subjects will be made a lot easier if at least one or two online computers are available in the ordinary classroom. Otherwise the effort required to get the pupils to the equipment and to give them suitable supervision in the task they are to do may exceed the benefits of using the Internet.

There are many reasons why teachers might be reluctant to make extensive use of the Internet in their teaching, for example the time required to become familiar with the equipment and to discover resources which are relevant to the subject in question. Even then it is time-consuming to incorporate new methods into your teaching. But teachers everywhere have to learn to use the new technology. There is, on the other hand, a risk of becoming so excited by the possibilities of the new technologies that you get involved in activities that are not strictly relevant to the curriculum. However rewarding these may be, there is rarely classroom time available to devote to extra topics. Nonetheless, if you can find a resource or activity which matches an area of your curriculum and which you feel would add to your pupils' understanding of the topic, there is no reason to hesitate.

uick tip

If you find a link that does not work you might be able to find another way to the page you are looking for. You can try to remove the end of the web address, so that if you are trying to get to, say, www.a.com/x/y/z.htlm you can try www.a.com/x/y or www.a.com. In this way you might get lucky and find a link to the same information from a page higher up in the site hierarchy if the page you want has been moved within the site. If the site has moved to another server it will have a new address altogether. In this case you can try to search in, for example, AltaVista for the page title (enclosed in quotation marks).

In many school subjects the curriculum allows for project work and coursework. This can sometimes be a very suitable spot to fill with an Internet-based project.

Information and contact

The Internet's strengths are, as we have already said, information and contact. This is clearly evident in the ideas and activities described in the following sections. They are intended to be used by subject teachers who are relatively new to the Internet. You can see these ideas as suggestions. As you become more familiar with what is available and more aware of what is possible you will most likely develop ideas of your own. Most of the activities involve gathering and/or sharing information and making contact with other classes.

In the sections that follow we will refer to a great many web sites and other Internet resources. Because of the rate at which the Internet changes we are not giving the addresses to these resources in these pages. You will find web addresses in Appendix 4 and the same list regularly updated in this book's web pages.

Archaeology

The Web has quite a number of resources that are relevant to the study of archaeology at school. These include accounts of archaeological surveys, museums (including interactive virtual exhibitions), archives of reports, maps and pictures.

The Royal Commission on the Historical Monuments of England

The *Royal Commission on the Historical Monuments of England* (RCHME) has an extensive site with many kinds of information. The *National Monuments Record*, a public archive which holds over 12 million items, including old and new photographs, maps, reports and surveys as well as complete coverage of the country in aerial photographs, can be accessed through the site. At present it is possible to order copies of material and to view selected material, but the Commission is committed to making as much material as possible available online. Copies of many documents can be obtained free of charge or for a small fee. The Royal Commission plans to launch a range of services for schools on its site.

The National Monuments Record is a fantastic resource for anyone wanting archaeological information. It holds the archive deriving from RCHME's archaeological field survey projects from 1908 to the present day (around 5000 individual sites or projects). Its MONARCH database has over 250 000 records of archaeological sites and monuments and an Activities Index of over 42 000 archaeological interventions, including excavations, geophysical surveys and watching briefs.

The school services promised on the RCHME site will probably be well worth a visit. In the meantime, the National Monuments Record would be a good source of material about archaeologically interesting aspects of the local area. You can search the online MONARCH database to see what material is available. You might even be able to view the material online.

The RCHME Air Survey is a range of surveys of archaeological sites done through the skilled interpretation of features revealed on air photographs. This is done both to aid understanding of archaeological landscapes and to complement ground survey work. You might like to select a site near you and work through the material, comparing it with other sources available to you. The RCHME material includes detailed surveys and reports of the Roman town of Silchester in Hampshire and the Roman fort, *vicus* and prehistoric henge complex at Newton Kyme in North Yorkshire.

World Heritage Sites

Quick tip

Those who wish to keep abreast of World Heritage issues can join the mailing list WH NEWS by sending an e-mail to majordomo@unesco.org. In the body of the text, type the words 'subscribe whnews'.

The UNESCO *World Heritage Sites* have their own home on the Web. You can find a complete list of all the 552 World Heritage Sites, from the Galapagos Islands to Blenheim Palace, along with a description of each site and links to further web material. Many of the World Heritage sites in the United Kingdom are of archaeological interest, for example Durham Castle and Cathedral, Studley Royal Park, including the ruins of Fountains Abbey, Stonehenge, Avebury and associated sites, the castles and town walls of King Edward in Gwynedd, the City of Bath and Hadrian's Wall.

Activities

The World Heritage Site has an ambitious educational programme which is run through the UNESCO system of Associated Schools in some 90 countries in Europe, English-speaking Africa and the Asia–Pacific region. The project, *Young People's Participation in World Heritage Preservation and Promotion*, is now run as a UNESCO Medium-Term (1996–2001) 'Special Project'. Many activities are suggested on the site, such as building a scale model of a protected site, or working out a strategy permitting people to visit a site without ruining it, or creating a 'heritage trail' in your own home town. There is also a World Heritage Club for children where they can exchange experiences of local World Heritage sites, and a live online chat for children is planned. Teachers can send for an education kit with further suggestions for activities.

Archaeology on the Net

Archaeology on the Net is a guide to almost anything that is even faintly connected to archaeology. It is set up as a web catalogue with categories covering, for example, Internet discussion groups, maps and atlases, museums, fieldwork opportunities, field projects and reports, rock art and underwater archaeology, as well as the option to view links for individual regions.

This resource will be a gold mine for pupils who are looking for project material and ideas. The fieldwork opportunities section, for example, has information about current digs from Belize to the Isle of Man and from Turkey to Kenya. Each of these has its own link to further information on the Web about the nature of the investigation, the conditions and the finds.

Museums

Of course there is no way a web site can be a substitute for a real visit to a museum, but if you are a long way from London it is certainly better than nothing. A virtual visit to a museum can be an excellent preparation to a real visit.

The British Museum

At the *British Museum* site, for example, there is extensive information about some of the more important exhibits, such as the Rosetta Stone and the Portland Vase. The site is richly illustrated with pictures of the Museum's exhibits. The British Museum is enormous and this is reflected in its web site. There are pages for each department: Coins and Medals; Egyptian Antiquities; Ethnography; Greek and Roman Antiquities; Japanese Antiquities; Medieval and Later Antiquities; Oriental Antiquities; Prehistoric and Romano-British Antiquities; and Western Asiatic Antiquities.

York City Walls

The *City of York*'s web site invites you to take a virtual tour of the City Walls. You will be guided round the various parts of the Walls and shown how different sections were added in different periods.

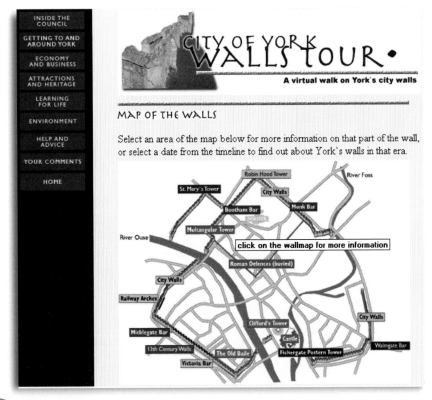

INSIDE THE
COUNCIL

GETTING TO AND
AROUND YORK

ECONOMY
AND BUSINESS

ATTRACTIONS
AND HERITAGE

LEARNING
FOR LIFE

ENVIRONMENT

HELP AND
ADVICE

YOUR COMMENTS

HOME

CITY OF YORK WALLS TOUR •

A virtual walk on York's city walls

MAP OF THE WALLS

Select an area of the map below for more information on that part of the wall, or select a date from the timeline to find out about York's walls in that era.

click on the wallmap for more information

 City of York Walls
Copyright City of York Council (http://www.york.gov.uk)

The Jorvik Viking Centre

The Jorvik Viking Centre is a very exciting place to visit, and the description given of it on the web site leaves little to the imagination. There are pictures and even a sound file with a sample of what authentic Viking speech must have sounded like. This site has a collection of links to all sorts of Viking material on the Internet.

Birka

This Swedish/English site describes the excavations of the Viking town of Birka, and the museum erected on the island near Stockholm where the town was situated. There is a full description of the history of Birka in its heyday in the eighth, ninth and tenth centuries and of the artefacts found in the graves there.

» *Classical civilisation*

The subject classical civilisation is not far removed from archaeology. In this subject pupils are concerned with the history, literature, art and architecture of Ancient Greece and Rome. There is plenty of information about these matters on the Web, including the following sites.

The Hellenic Ministry of Culture

The Hellenic (Greek) Ministry of Culture has set up a massive web site with information about 1000 museums, archaeological sites or monuments. You can either access the material from a clickable map of Greece to choose a geographical area you want to know more about, or you can select an entry from the Archaeological Sites, Monuments or Museums alphabetical lists. If you know what you are looking for you can go straight there with the site's search engine.

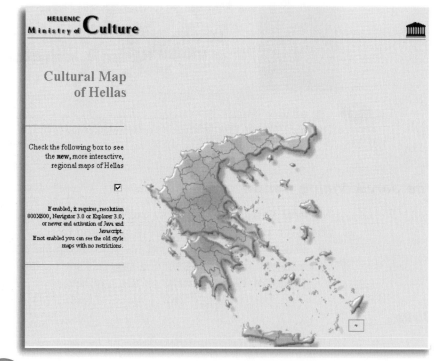

8.2 *Interactive map of Greece, from the Hellenic Ministry of Culture site*

This magnificent resource makes full use of the interactive nature of the Web. You need only click on a particular district or island to be transported to a larger-scale map with links to local archaeological sites, museums or monuments. As you go you are given a full account of the persons and events associated with the locality in ancient and recent times.

The *Acropolis of Athens* and the *National Archaeological Museum of Athens* are, of course, well represented in this site. Teachers and pupils would be hard pushed to find a better source of information about Ancient Greece. Among other things there is plenty of information about the Greek efforts to have the Parthenon Marbles restored to Athens. At the beginning of the nineteenth century, shortly before the War of Independence and the emancipation of Greece from the Turks, Lord Elgin stripped the Parthenon, taking advantage of the post he held as British ambassador in Constantinople. The marble decorations from the Parthenon have been in the British Museum ever since, much to the dismay of the Greeks.

The Internet Classics Archive

The *Internet Classics Archive* is sponsored in part by the MIT (Massachusetts Institute of Technology) Program in Writing and Humanistic studies. It offers a list of 441 works of classical literature by 59 different authors, including comments on the works from readers and 'reader's choice' web links. The works represented are mainly Greek or Roman (some Chinese and Persian), all in English translation.

Since classical works, even in quite old translation, are generally not protected by copyright; you can access the full text of the works online or download it for reading offline.

Dead Romans

The *Dead Romans* site is relatively small. It features information about Roman coins, architecture, and artwork from the Early Roman Empire. There is a 3-D photographic walkthrough of archaeological sites including the Colosseum, Via Sacra and Forum Romanum with a map and historical notes about the buildings. The Coins page has an introduction to Imperial Roman coins, their denominations, metals and minting, with the most common Roman names, titles and abbreviations. There is also a page with a timeline with brief descriptions of the emperors from Augustus to Marcus Aurelius. This kind of site is useful as a source of background information for project work of all kinds.

Pompeii Forum Project

The *Pompeii Forum* site from the University of Virginia provides an in-depth look at the Forum in Pompeii, complete with maps, images and history. The site contains all kinds of information about Pompeii and a collection of pages for teachers and pupils who want to use the site. There are a number of activities for pupils using the site:

❑ A study of the letters of Pliny the Younger to the historian Tacitus recounting the events surrounding the eruption of Vesuvius and the death of his uncle, Pliny the Elder.

❑ Examples of Latin inscriptions from Pompeii including translations for non-Latin readers and help in analysing and understanding the inscriptions in the context of their positions in Pompeii and the people mentioned on them.

❑ Help in understanding a Roman painting depicting a scene from a myth. The visiting pupil is invited either to get more information about the myth depicted on the picture, or to get more information about the painting's background, or to analyse the painting.

❑ A virtual tour of the city of Pompeii, including a discussion of the lessons we can learn from Pompeii.

ROMARCH: Roman art and archaeology

The ROMARCH site is an excellent source of art and architecture from all over the Roman empire. There is a mailing list for discussions and a geographic list and clickable map of Internet resources associated with all parts of the Roman Empire, including Italia, Hispania, Gallia, Britannia, Germania, Raetia, Noricum and Thule, Pannonia, Dalmatia, Moesia and Dacia, Graecia and Thracia, Asia (Minor), Armenia, Mesopotamia, Syria, Judaea and Arabia, Aegyptus and Africa. This map leads to a rich collection of links to local Roman Internet resources from every area of the Roman world. The ROMARCH site is yet another illustration of how the international nature of the Web comes into its own. Web pages from dozens of countries are collected here into a really useful source of information.

AncientSites and SPQR

AncientSites is a bizarre combination of the ancient world and up-to-the-minute web technology. It describes itself as a 'unique Internet community that offers 3D games, quizzes and virtual walking tours to students, teachers and history buffs around the world'. The site includes digital reconstructions of Rome, Athens and Egypt which visitors can explore, but also a communication channel. Visitors can exchange views with a world-wide online community of like-minded ancient history fans through chat rooms, bulletin boards, free personal home pages, Who's Online panel and instant messages. When you connect to the site you get to see the AncientSites Communications Panel with a list of people online whom you can chat to if you are a member of the community.

One of the games associated with the site is SPQR, named after, and inspired by, the Senate and the People of Rome (*Senatus Populusque Romanus* in Latin). This fascinating online web game contains a reconstruction of the Roman Forum that you can walk around in. The year is 205 AD and Rome is threatened by a mysterious saboteur named the Calamitus. The city, and indeed the entire Empire, may be in danger! Your mission is to save Rome. If you are a member of the AncientSites Virtual Community you can exchange instant messages with other players of SPQR as you try to solve the mystery. This is as far from dry and dusty as the study of Classical civilisation gets!

Greek Mythology Link

Greek Mythology Link is another large site, created by Carlos Parada, author of *Genealogical Guide to Greek Mythology* (Paul Åströms Förlag 1992).

It is mainly concerned with the creative, artistic, literary and inspiring aspects of Greek mythology deriving from its tales. The web site has an index of 6460 mythological characters and another index of Places and Peoples including 1191 entries. The material includes text, images, maps and tables. This is a great place to find out about individual characters in Greek mythology and to see their relationship to other characters.

⏩ Art and design

While this subject is characterised by its practical nature, art and design usually includes a programme of study of ways of looking at the work of artists and designers. Pupils often spend a lot of time visiting galleries and museums to view paintings and sculptures as they really are. While the Web cannot hope to be a substitute for experiencing these works at first hand, it can be an excellent complement, and a way to become familiar with works held in museums and galleries in other countries.

There are many collections of art on the Web, as you will see if you look in a catalogue such as Yahoo! With this resource pupils can study paintings and sculptures from the whole world.

Sculpture

The THAIS site is Italian and links you to hundreds of places in Italy and beyond where you can see Italian sculpture produced in the last 1200 years. In Texas, the *Umlauf Sculpture Garden and Museum* web site will take you on a virtual tour of the Gardens. In Oslo the *Gustaf Vigeland Sculpture Park* is waiting to welcome you, offering explanations of the many sculptures to be seen there.

Paintings

Major museums and galleries often have web sites. You can visit the *Louvre*, for example, and stroll from room to room, lingering at the Mona Lisa and the Venus de Milo. You can visit an interactive exhibition of Picasso's early work from the *Boston Museum of Fine Arts* or let Picasso's son Claude show you his private collection. If you would like to study the work of the Swedish painter Carl Larsson you can study his paintings on the Swedish *Runeberg* site which has copyright-free texts and pictures. There are numerous Dali sites, too, with the painter's most famous works depicted.

 The Mona Lisa, from the Louvre site

Activities

The American *ArtsEdNet*'s web gateway is a great place to start your exploration of what there is on the Net. It has links to the biggest online galleries and museums. This site also has a discussion list, mostly for art teachers, which can be joined as a mailing list or used as a web-based noticeboard. ArtsEdNet offers lesson plans and curriculum ideas too.

The National Grid for Learning's *Virtual Teacher Centre* has an area for art education. There is to be a gallery there for classroom exhibitions. The gallery will contain exhibitions of work, both digital and traditional. The site will eventually include curriculum-planning tools for art and advice on purchasing and using computer systems for art.

There are other sites too where pupils' own work can be displayed, for example in CampusWorld's Art and Design area, but there is no reason why your pupils should not create their own gallery pages. They can scan in their work or a photograph or copy of it (alternatively they can use a digital camera to create pictures directly for the Web). The Virtual Teacher Centre Art page has links to several school sites with their own galleries on the Web.

The CampusWorld (AngliaCampus) site has classroom-ready material available for its subscribers in art and design, such as a Year 9 project *From the Real to the Surreal* in nine one-hour sessions. There is also material for younger pupils.

If the class has access to a digital camera there is a lot of interesting work that can be done. Unlike traditional photography, the digital camera gives instant results. A pupil can almost immediately see the results of various kinds of experimentation. In addition, the kind of photo-editing program which accompanies most digital cameras will enable pupils to study the effects of different kinds of picture composition.

Many art teachers are helping pupils to use computer-based image manipulation to create interesting effects in their work. Pupils can either use drawings on paper which are scanned in as a basis for their image manipulation, or they can choose to create their pictures from scratch using a drawing program. While the Web is an excellent forum for pupils to display their art, many may become interested in the design aspect of creating aesthetically and functionally appealing web pages.

The step from web design to the creation of multimedia applications is relatively small, and there is a vast amount of information and products available on the Web for this area. Three-D graphics and the creation of virtual-reality environments are fascinating subjects for those who are both artistically and technically inclined.

 *Astronomy*

Astronomy is not generally considered to be a school subject in its own right, but we will include it here because there is such a lot of material available which is well suited to use in schools.

NASA

NASA is a major consumer of funding from the American taxpayers and is obliged, in return, to make much of its material available to the American public in general and to schools in particular. The result of this is that NASA has hundreds of web pages about, for example, its missions to the moon and Mars (complete with countless pictures from the surfaces), the topography of all the planets and their satellites, contact information for all its institutions, the advanced plans that exist for human missions to the planets (Mars in particular), and so on. Most activities are also open to schools in other countries.

8.4 *Mars*
Source: JPL/NASA/Caltech

NASA activities for schools include live web chats with senior female engineers and other events involving the Women of NASA. These are intended to interest more girls in the sciences.

The Hubble Space Telescope has its own site where teachers and pupils can access images from the telescope. There are also periodically activities for schools where classes submit suggestions for experiments using the telescope and are allotted a slot of time to control it. Visitors can view the latest pictures from Hubble and even movies and animations.

The NASA site leads to a number of pages about human space flight involving the space shuttle and space station. Visitors can consult the shuttle mission schedule or the shuttle reference manual which claims to inform you about 'Everything you always wanted to know about the Shuttle but were afraid to ask'.

Other pages about planetary exploration with space probes and Mars exploration have enough material for any amount of project work. You can even take a virtual tour of the solar system, with pictures and information about all the planets and their satellites as well as various other heavenly bodies.

Nine Planets

The Nine Planets site has been around since 1994, but it is continuously being improved and extended. It is a magnificent resource for schools and anyone else interested in the planets. The site describes itself as follows: 'Nine Planets is an overview of the history, mythology, and current scientific knowledge of each of the planets and moons in our solar system. Each page has text and images, some have sounds and movies, most provide references to additional related information.'

Visitors can choose to take the express tour of the solar system or to go round and browse the site by themselves. The Sun, all the planets and their individual satellites and other small bodies such as comets, asteroids and meteors have pages devoted to them. There are also pages about other solar systems and spacecraft involved in planetary science.

On this site you can find out, for example, about which planets are the biggest, or the brightest, as well as gain an understanding of the origin of the solar system. There is extensive coverage of when and by whom the planets were discovered and the system by which they and newly discovered bodies are named.

8.5 *The Nine Planets*
Source: Bill Arnett (http://seds.lpl.arizona.edu/billa/tnp)

Contact with classes in the southern hemisphere

The Nine Planets site also provides you with guidance for your own observations of the planets. This can form the basis of many activities which pupils can get involved in. It might be fun to get in touch with a school in Australia, New Zealand or South Africa (or any other country in the southern hemisphere) to compare the stars you can see at night. You might be able to exchange star charts, or otherwise discuss the stars.

If you already have contact with pupils in another country you can compare how easily you can see the stars. Light pollution is a major problem in this matter. Densely populated parts of Europe, such as the British Midlands or The Netherlands, are, of course, more severely affected than sparsely populated areas such as the Highlands of Scotland or rural areas of Scandinavia.

Business studies and economics

The Internet's immediacy makes it an excellent tool for following the rapidly changing world of business and finance. There are countless web sites, web chats and mailing lists which deal with these subjects. The following are just a few to get you started. When you start to browse the Web on your own you will find many more.

Online services

Microsoft's MSN UK start page and *Yahoo!* UK & Ireland both have sections where you can get up-to-the-minute news from the UK and world business and financial scene. Both of these have business and financial news headlines that you can click to be taken to the full story. The Yahoo! *Business* section is mainly devoted to news, while *Finance* is more extensive, with stock prices from the London, Paris and Frankfurt markets updated continuously throughout the working day. Yahoo! has plans to introduce a portfolio function for stocks listed for European markets. This already exists for the US market. It is also possible to download spreadsheet files from Yahoo! In the US version of *Yahoo! Finance*, it's possible to get charts showing a company's performance over various periods (one day to five years). This service is planned for the European markets too. Yahoo! has a chat room for those who wish to discuss stocks with each other.

These sites offer all the UK business and financial news you are likely to need, but if you want other sources you can turn to the daily newspapers' business pages. All the major newspapers have online editions which you can find easily in Yahoo! UK & Ireland's *News and Media* sub-catalogue *Papers*.

Biz/ed

Biz/ed is an Internet service from the University of Bristol and its partners. This free service is aimed at teachers of economics and business. It provides classroom materials written specifically for Biz/ed and makes extensive use of the Internet's potential.

Biz/ed has a collection of links to other quality educational sites but is primarily interesting because of the wide variety of primary materials available. It has case studies, work sheets and substantial data sets not found elsewhere on the Internet. It is not to be missed!

Biz/ed offers:

❑ Information on companies, with collections of Company Facts where top companies including BP, Unilever and the Body Shop answer frequently asked questions and offer case studies to help pupils in their coursework. Biz/ed includes Extel Data (part of FT Information) where you can see key features of 500 major plc company accounts. You can compare companies with a Company Report Profiler and you can follow links to the FTSE 100 Companies and other companies' own web sites.

❑ The Biz/ed Data Service, which hosts both original and mirrored data sets for economics, business and finance for the UK and over-seas. Biz/ed gives you access to both Penn World Data Tables and the Office for National Statistics (ONS). This section of the site has advice on student projects and tips for teachers among other things. There are even downloadable spreadsheets from the ONS on average earnings.

❑ Extensive support for teachers including resources to help teachers to use Internet material, information on Nuffield Curriculum Development Projects, teacher notes and worksheets.

❑ Activities such as a *Be Your Own Chancellor* site, and a virtual factory.

❑ Access to *Classroom Expernomics*, a US newsletter dedicated to the use of economic experiments as a teaching tool for the classroom.

❑ A mailing list, *econ-business-educators*, which is exclusively for teachers of economics and business.

Investment simulation

The *Great Game* is a British share-trading competition. It is one of dozens of simulations you can find on the Web (e.g. through Yahoo!'s subcat-alogue *Recreation:Gambling:Interactive Web Games:Financial Markets*). Your objective is to out-trade the other players. You have an imaginary £10 000 to invest. You can buy, hold and sell any of the stocks listed in the TGG-400 share listing. The value of your portfolio is calculated on the prices posted on the TGG-400 listing. Prizes are awarded for the best performance. The Great Game is currently free, although a pay-for play version is being considered.

Edustock is an American educational web page designed to teach what the stock market is, and how it works. It includes tutorials on the stock market and tells you how to pick good stocks. It also provides infor-mation on selected companies to help you start your research into what stock is going to make your fortune. The site has a 20-minute delayed stock market simulation on the World Wide Web which lets you create your own portfolio and follow its progress without actually spending any money.

⟫ *Communication studies*

Communication or media studies is a popular subject for colleges although it is not generally taught at school. This is a subject which has a great deal to gain from the use of the Internet. The course combines the study of human and mass communication, and that is just what the Internet is all about.

The Internet is not only a source of current up-to the-minute news, but also an archive of old news. It is possible to follow the development of an event from when the news first breaks until the coverage peters out. If you have access to RM's *EduWeb* you can browse through a newspaper archive where you can search for articles about any topic in the *Mirror* and the *Sunday Mirror*, the *Independent* and the *Independent on Sunday* since 1992. Otherwise you can simply visit newspapers' own sites – the *Electronic Telegraph*, for example, has a fully searchable archive of articles going back to 1994. The *Times* too has a searchable database of articles in certain areas such as sport, education and politics. The *Guardian* is currently developing its archive.

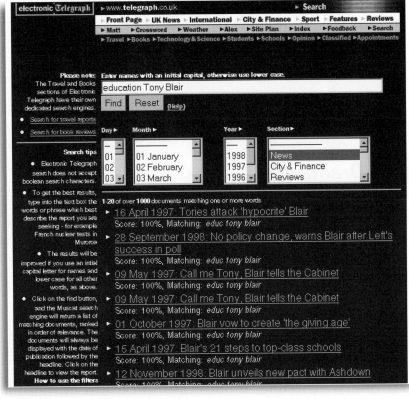

 The Electronic Telegraph archives

An interesting project in Merseyside involves Year 10 and 11 pupils at three schools and a local free newspaper, *Netherton and Litherland NOW*, which also has a web edition. At Bootle High, media project pupils work voluntarily during break and lunch times and come in groups of four for at least eight hours from their media studies lessons to work on an assignment with project staff. The assignment is published in the paper and counts towards the pupils' GCSE. At St Ambrose Barlow pupils spend two 50-minute lessons on the project and get hands-on experience working with project staff on the newspaper. At Litherland High, media studies pupils write stories for the newspaper as course-work for their RSA Initial Award in media studies.

The BBC *News* site also has a facility whereby you can search for arti-cles on a particular subject using key words. When you find your article you can get background information and follow leads to earlier connected stories.

The beauty of the combination of the news media and the Web is that an article on a web site can be linked both to previous articles on the same topic and to other external sources of information. This gives pupils the chance to compare different ways of presenting the same news stories.

The whole field of interpersonal communication can be illustrated by the Web and the Internet's other communication channels. Pupils may find it useful to analyse the effect created by different kinds of web pages and to study the language of e-mail, chat and newsgroups.

 # Drama

The Web is a good source of information in the area of drama. Yahoo! UK & Ireland, for example, will lead you to links to almost 100 British theatre companies, from the Royal Shakespeare Company to tiny village pantomime companies. The largest of these sites have detailed infor-mation about the company's repertoire with a synopsis of the plot of each play, a cast list and press reviews.

UK Theatre Web

The UK *Theatre Web* (UKTW) calls itself 'the definitive WWW guide to professional and amateur performing arts in the UK'. It has a fully current What's On database, a collection of noticeboard discussions on several theatre topics, a database with information about the authors and synopses of 7000 plays, operas, pantomimes, etc., more than 1200 venues, 6400 productions and 740 companies.

Dramatic Exchange

Dramatic Exchange is a web resource which can be valuable for those who are looking for a play to perform. This site is essentially a data-base of over 300 plays by both amateur and professional playwrights.

Most of the plays are not free, but many of the playwrights may be willing to waive fees for plays used in an educational setting.

» English language

The study of English language is enriched by all kinds of reading and writing. The Internet offers ample opportunity to do both. One of the most basic activities is to set together two classes from different countries and pair them off as keypals, the electronic equivalent of penpals. The problem is that this kind of letter writing tends to peter out after a few exchanges unless there is a genuine communicative need which motivates the pupils. This can be arranged as a kind of project or activity where pupils are given a particular topic to compare notes on, such as 'the view from my bedroom window' or 'what I spend my pocket money on'.

Spoken and written language

The difference between the language of speech and the language of writing is always interesting. Internet communication in chats and various kinds of discussion forums is an intermediate form. Pupils might find it worthwhile to analyse the language of e-mail or chat to see just how it compares with other written and spoken language.

Creative writing

As we have already seen, the Web can be used to display pupils' work. For some pupils the knowledge that their work might be read by many people can be very motivating. It is also fully possible to have pupils work together on a story with a partner who need not be in the same class or even in the same country. If the class has contact with another class somewhere else this can be a good way to practise cooperation as well as e-mail skills.

Sites such as the Global SchoolHouse will sometimes have room to publish pupils' writing, but the class web page will usually do just as well.

Web page

A web page can be used for many purposes, but the most meaningful pages communicate information which is needed by the persons accessing the page. Pupils can use their writing and other skills to create a document which others can use. Examples of suitable projects are:

- ❏ a school prospectus or a guide for new pupils
- ❏ a guide to a local tourist attraction

❑   a guide for visitors to the local community (shops, library, banks, post office, etc., with opening times and information).

These guides can include photos, drawings and maps and can involve considerations of layout and style. Pupils might want to visit similar pages produced by others. They will need to consider what kind of information the readers will want, and what format to use to get the message across. These projects can be expanded with interviews with pupils (or shopkeepers etc.) and can be adapted for different levels. Appendix 3 describes the making and publishing of a simple web page in detail.

Newspaper studies

Newspapers are well represented on the Web and they are often generous with web access to old material which they have archived. This means that there is a tremendous amount of absolutely current English available in the web sites of the press of the English-speaking world. Any number of potential uses for this come to mind; for example:

❑   comparison between different newspapers' styles, e.g. the *Mirror* and the *Times* when reporting on the same event

❑   a study of the language of opinion in editorials from newspapers with different political orientation, e.g. the *Daily Telegraph* and the *Guardian*

❑   a comparison of different sections of the papers – for example, how does the sports section differ from the business section?

❑   a study of dialectal differences between English as it is written in the UK, Ireland, the USA, Canada, South Africa, Australia, New Zealand, India, Kenya, China, etc.

❑   a study of how different features of language such as in-words and slang expressions, technical and other jargon, are used by different papers. What does this tell us about the intended readers of the papers?

⏩ English literature

The Internet is attractive to students of literature. Literature is about the communication of ideas from the writer to the reader. So is the Internet, except that a lot of Internet communication is two-way. The Internet can be used in the teaching of English Literature in several ways:

❑   as a source of texts

❑   as a source of critical commentary

❑   as a forum for discussing texts

❑ as a source of information about authors and poets and their lives and works

❑ as a forum to present the results of class work.

Texts

The law of copyright is different in different countries, but it generally expires a certain number of years after an author's or painter's death. In addition there are texts which are not copyright, and are said to be in the public domain. Several web sites are devoted to collecting these documents and making them available electronically. There is no charge associated with visiting these sites, and they are easy to use. Some of the sites also contain works that are under copyright, and these are not always freely accessible. The sites mentioned here are not the only ones that exist, and there are similar collections of online texts for other languages.

Project Gutenberg was begun in 1971. It is an electronic collection of literary works which includes both Cicero's orations and the complete works of Shakespeare.

The *University of Virginia Electronic Text Center* is a very large collection of electronic texts. Most of the texts are in English, but there are also some in French, German, Japanese and Latin. The *Modern English Collection* (AD 1500–present) is a site which has a selection of texts from the University of Virginia Electronic Text Center. The Modern English Collection contains some 1400 titles including over 4000 manuscript and book illustrations.

The *Internet Poetry Archive* is maintained by the University of North Carolina. It has selected poems from contemporary poets from around the world, including Philip Levine, Seamus Heaney and Czeslaw Milosz. The goal of the project is to make poetry accessible to new audiences and to give teachers and students of poetry new ways of presenting and studying these poets and their texts.

Commentary

The Web has dozens of Shakespeare resources of all kinds. Some of them deal with biographical data, others with annotated texts and critical commentary or a combination of these. They generally link to each other, so if you find one you have found most of them. There are also some collections of Shakespeare resources on the Internet, such as *Shakespeare resources on the Internet* from Palomar College.

Other sites have information and analyses concerning texts of a certain period, such as *18th Century Studies*, which is an archive of novels, plays, memoirs, treatises and poems of the eighteenth century along with modern criticism. If you spend a little time in a catalogue such as Yahoo! you will see the vast range of sites available in the subject of English literature.

The English Server at the English Department at Carnegie Mellon University will probably be able to lead you and your pupils to what you are looking for. This site has many functions – it distributes over 18 000 works, including classics and new writing. Visitors can read texts or send in their own writing and discuss with others on electronic noticeboards or in mailing lists, including one on eighteenth-century literature.

Authors

Poets in Person is a web site which provides brief biographies for a selection of contemporary poets. The best part of this site is that it includes audio recordings of the poets reading their own work.

You can search for any author in Yahoo! and in seconds be given a list of links to relevant texts, criticism and biographical resources. Keats, Austen, Woolfe, Dickens, Hardy – they are all well represented in sites created by the world's enthusiasts.

Regional variants

CampusWorld (AngliaCampus) has an interesting component especially for subscribers in Northern Ireland – an area devoted to the English spoken and written in Northern Ireland in accordance with the requirements of the Northern Ireland Curriculum. There is a section on dialect and accent, one on fiction written by women in Northern Ireland, one on modern poetry and one on prejudice.

Foreign languages

Many of the activities suggested for teaching English language and literature with the Internet can be adapted for use in the foreign-language classroom.

Key pals

Key pals are popular, and the basic principle of exchanging letters with speakers or fellow learners of the target language can be adapted to suit the needs of the class. Rather than having the pupils write individual letters to pupils in a class in France or Germany or wherever, the whole class can write a letter together with the teacher helping as much as is necessary. One problem with this kind of exchange is that there must be something in it for both sides. If a class in Germany is going to make the effort of reading letters from a class in England they may well want the English class to read letters they write in English. The alternative is to team up with a class who are learning the same language and exchange letters in the target language. This solution is preferred by classes whose own language, for example Dutch, Finnish or Greek, is not generally taught as a foreign language in other countries. The European Schoolnet helps teachers find keypals for their pupils.

Virtual exchanges

Virtual class visits can be a lot of fun for all concerned although they do tend to need a good deal of preparation. A class visit can be arranged relatively simply, for example using IRC chat in a private room. This is simply a matter of both classes being online at the same time and somebody opening a room with a previously agreed name. Once everybody is present in the chat room the teachers can lead the chat with their pupils. If there is only one computer available at each location the pupils can take turns to be the one at the keyboard. Ideally in such a situation there should be some way for everyone to see the screen. This kind of activity will generally be most successful when there is a planned activity for the two classes to carry out while they are online together.

If the participating classes have access to a web camera and a computer with sound and video facilities they can conduct a video conference using Microsoft NetMeeting, for example. This will let them see and hear each other. Of course, while this is exciting stuff for the pupils, the fast pace of live chat might mean that younger pupils have a hard time keeping up and making themselves understood, especially if the class at the other end are native speakers of French, German, etc.

Surf the Web in Spanish (French, German . . .)

Although English is clearly the dominant language on the Internet, languages like French, German and Spanish have a large and growing presence. For instance, Yahoo! exists in Spanish, Italian, German and French (as well as other languages which are not usually taught in British schools). It is fully possible to find web resources about the countries where the language is spoken, links to online newspapers and magazines, TV companies, radio stations, etc. A visit to, for example, El Diario, a Bolivian daily newspaper, is likely to raise a lot of questions in an A-level Spanish class!

8.7 *The Bolivian newspaper El Diario*
Source: Redacción EL DIARIO (www.eldiario.net)

 # Geography

Geography is one of the best provided for of school subjects on the Internet. This is reflected, for example, in the National Grid for Learning's Virtual Teacher Centre where geography was one of the first subjects to get a well-filled selection of Internet resources on its pages. Other collections of geography resources tell the same story: BT's Campus World and RM's EduNet, for example, both have high-quality material of their own and plenty of links to other material on the Web.

Places

Because of the international nature of the Net there is material available from all over the world. Many governments and national tourist organisations have put copious amounts of time and money into presenting every aspect of their country on the Web. If a class is studying the geography of, say, Italy or Argentina they will find a good deal of web information produced in those countries to complement what they have in their textbooks. Yahoo! is probably the best source of information about a particular country. Its subcatalogue *Regional:Countries* will lead you to a list of names of countries.

The UK *schools forum* has accumulated links to information in English about many countries. This is also a good place to start when researching an individual country.

There are also compilations of facts and figures about the countries of the world. The best known of these is the CIA *World Fact Book*, which has information about the size, population, politics and economy of all the world's nations. These are illustrated with maps, pictures and flags.

Maps and atlases

The nice thing about web atlases is that they can be interactive, which means that you can decide whether you want to see a whole continent or zoom into a particular region, or focus on a single town and the surrounding area, or even go in for a street map. There are a few such resources, such as *MapQuest* and *Pathfinder*. Unfortunately there do not, at present, seem to be any online resources for large-scale maps.

Weather

Nottingham University provides the Internet community with access to the regularly updated weather satellite images transmitted by the Meteosat satellite. You can also see the view from different satellites. If you visit the BBC weather page you will see the same satellite picture

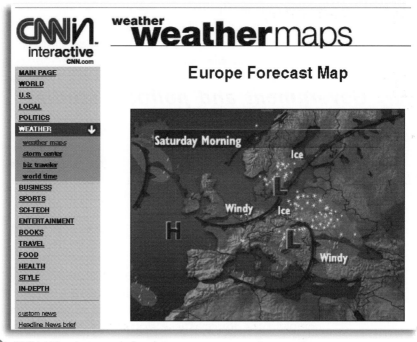

8.8 *CNN Weather*

of the British Isles along with an interpretation of the picture in the form of a weather forecast. The BBC site has a lot of relevant details about how weather forecasts are made and about weather. There is also information about specific weather phenomena such as thunderstorms and tornados.

For up-to-date weather forecasts for other parts of the world you can visit *Yahoo! Weather* or the CNN *Weather* page. The Yahoo! weather catalogues will lead you to sites dealing with all kinds of weather phenomena, from lightening to blizzards.

Volcano World

Volcanoes are for some reason extremely well covered on the Web. The combination of illustrated accounts of the theory behind volcanoes along with the Web's intuitive way of linking further information to a text using hyperlinks makes the Web an attractive medium for this kind of information. In addition, the Internet's immediacy means that active volcanoes can be monitored and eruptions followed step by step with live pictures and contact with the people who are on the spot.

Earthquake watching

The San Andreas Fault is the focus of a large number of web sites. One of the more interesting ones is D*iscovery Channel*, which has a varied site with sound and pictures as well as personal accounts of earthquake experiences and the like. U*nderstanding Earthquakes* is a very useful site with animations showing how earthquakes happen. Yahoo! is a good source of other sites which deal with plate tectonics and seismology.

Government and political studies

Government

Whether you are looking for the B*edford Borough Council* or 10 *Downing Street* on the Web you will find a link to the relevant pages from the Central Computing and Telecommunications Agency (CCTA) *Government Information Service*. This is a complete directory of public-sector web sites. You can browse lists of organisations or lists of functions (such as *forestry* or *museums*).

The D*irect Access Government* site exists to provide information about a wide range of government regulations. It also contains many of the forms commonly needed by businesses as well as guidance on how to complete the forms. These documents can be downloaded from the Web and are generally in *pdf* format, which means that you will need an

Acrobat Reader, which you can download at no charge from the manufacturer *Adobe*'s web site.

The official *British Monarchy* site is well worth a visit. Here you can read about the doings and history of the Royal Family and their properties.

In the 10 *Downing Street* site you can browse through the cabinet committees, follow the news as it affects members of the government, view live and recorded broadcasts involving the Prime Minister and members of the Cabinet. There are also noticeboard-based open discussions on subjects like education or welfare.

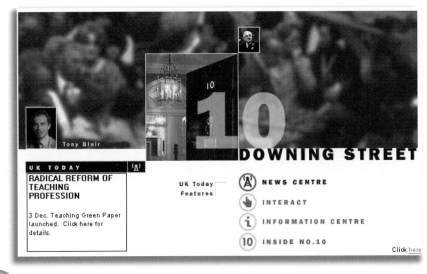

8.9 *10 Downing Street*

Parliament and politics

The *House of Commons* web site has plenty of information for pupils wanting to know more about the parliamentary process. Pupils can follow daily debates and questions with their answers, public bills and their progress through the system. The site also has a number of fact sheets available for downloading about subjects such as *Women in Parliament* and *Northern Ireland Legislation*. You can find a complete list of MPs here with their names, constituencies and parties. A few of them have e-mail links, although there will probably be more who make use of this excellent way to make themselves accessible to voters as time goes on. A very small number of MPs have personal web pages at present.

The political parties, on the other hand, have quickly realised that they have nothing to lose by being where the voters are. Yahoo! UK &

Ireland has a subcatalogue for political parties and groups and you will find them all there.

The *Conservative Party*, for example, lets you watch a party political broadcast on its pages. You can subscribe to an e-mail newsletter and join in the discussion. The *Labour Party* page is currently less flash and appears to be more interested in delivering clear information than in the latest web design. The *Liberal Democrats* describe themselves as Britain's 'most wired Party'. On their site you can read the party policy and party news. The *Green Party of England and Wales* has an earnest page where it accounts for campaigns it has fought, for example for 'decent school meals in Oxfordshire'.

When we visited the sites of *Scottish Conservative and Unionist Party* and the *Scottish Liberal Democrats* they were busy with their campaigns for the Scottish Parliamentary elections in May 1999. The *Ulster Unionist Party* and SDLP, on the other hand, were still celebrating their 1998 Nobel Peace Prize.

Current affairs

With Internet access there is no excuse for not being well informed about what is going on. There are dozens of newspapers, TV and radio sites in Britain and elsewhere. All of them are eager to provide you with the news. Other sites, such as Netscape and Microsoft, Yahoo! and Excite, want to be your start page and provide the news as a service among several others.

History

Even an ultra-modern environment such as the Web is well suited to supplying information about history. The Internet has information from many different sources, and this is very clear in accounts of history. Every conflict has at least two sides and the Internet may sometimes give us the opportunity to hear both sides of a story. At times this may be a problem for the classroom use of the Web, for example if the source of information is not clear.

History discussions

One of the most attractive features of BT's educational content service CampusWorld (AngliaCampus) is that provision is made for teachers and pupils to discuss the subjects they are studying with each other and with subject leaders. The History section of CampusWorld has a lively history discussion noticeboard. This is likely to meet with competition from the European Schoolnet, which also plans subject discussions led by resident subject teachers. Given the European perspective of the European Schoolnet there might be some truly interesting discussions.

Another collaborative effort to represent history is the *International Internet Encyclopedia of the First World War*. This is the initiative of a teacher at Sackville Comprehensive in Sussex, but it includes contributions from Germany, Greece and Ireland, with schools in France, Sweden, the USA and Australia preparing to contribute. Each school is to research a topic such as politicians, weapons, battles, from a local perspective.

World War II material

The BBC *Education Modern History* site covers the main events of the period from the Treaty of Versailles to the Allied Victory in a series of interconnected articles with question, quizzes and discussion subjects. It is intended for GCSE teachers and pupils. The material can be used in various ways: in class, as homework, for pupils' research, to test pupils' knowledge in the quizzes, and so on. The questions posed in the articles can be the basis of class discussions or homework.

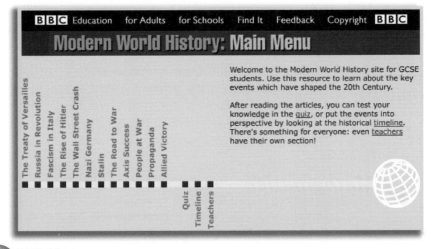

8.10 *BBC History*

We have already mentioned the need to teach pupils to be suspicious of information from unknown sources. This is never more true than when the Internet is consulted for material on the Holocaust. Revisionists have been known to produce credible sites that question the events of the Holocaust. Here teachers need to make the decision whether they can demonstrate how misinformation is spread with the help of the Internet or whether they would rather not draw the pupils' attention to this kind of material. The *United States Holocaust Memorial Museum* is a genuine site with great quantities of information, pictures and other material as well as extensive advice about how to teach the Holocaust and why it is important. Its mission is to promote education about the history of the Holocaust and its implications for our lives today.

Yahoo! has special subcategories with collected resources concerning World War I, World War II and other momentous periods in recent history as well as catalogues dealing with earlier eras. There are links to some 360 sites which deal with World War II from many perspectives. There are other collections of history links on the Web, notably *Horus' Web Links to History Resources* from the Department of History, University of California, Riverside, which has 1700 links in 55 categories. Here you can search for material about particular periods in the history of particular countries, among other things. The Horus site claims that the World Wide Web can give pupils unique insights into the way that historical events affect thousands of people. Because the Web is created from the bottom up by individuals, its resources cannot be sorted into neat categories the way directories like Yahoo! would suggest. Each individual who contributes historical information to the Web is helping to piece together a picture of the events described from slightly different viewpoints. The links of the Web chain lead from one document to another until the reader has built up an impression of the events of history which would have been impossible with a single source.

The CampusWorld (AngliaCampus) History section has classroom-ready material on many different historical topics for its subscribers. The Vikings, the Romans, the Tudors and the Victorians are presented for primary schools, while other topics such as the Cold War are presented in a way suitable for older pupils.

Mathematics

Maths is not one of the biggest subjects on the Web. Computers and IT have traditionally had plenty of other applications in the field of mathematics. But there are a few areas of interest.

*Math*DEN is an American site which works on the principle of learner autonomy. It provides self-paced mathematics units for 12–18 year olds. The idea is that the pupil gets immediate interactive feedback to their work so they can immediately see whether they understand the concepts. It is suitable as extra practice for pupils who are having difficulty as well as for able pupils who need extra challenges. MathDEN gives pupils the opportunity to train mental calculating skills or word problems. There are dozens of sets of problems at each of four levels. New problems are added to the site weekly.

The English mathematician John Conway has written a book of games which teach important mathematical concepts, for example by map-colouring exercises. Some of his games, and many others, are presented in the site *Projects and Investigations in Math*. The site also includes a set of classroom-ready mathematical activities called Mega-math.

The *University of Exeter Centre for Innovation in Mathematics Teaching* has a collection of mathematics resources such as games and advice on their use, and worksheets dealing with topics like how to work out how much more slowly hill walkers proceed uphill than on the level and how to calculate the probability of two individuals having their birthday on the same day of the week.

MathsNet is a must-see place for maths teachers and their pupils. It has been developed by a teacher in Norwich and it has plenty of information about using Logo, spreadsheets (including embedded spreadsheets in web pages) and graphs. There are a multitude of puzzles and games, software to download and articles about maths education and much more.

Algebra Online is an American site which offers personal tutoring via a noticeboard-type discussion. Pupils can write in with something they are having difficulty understanding and get an explanation. The Microsoft newsgroup *msn.uk.homeworkhelp* offers the same kind of service with the difference that questions in all school subjects are welcomed and they

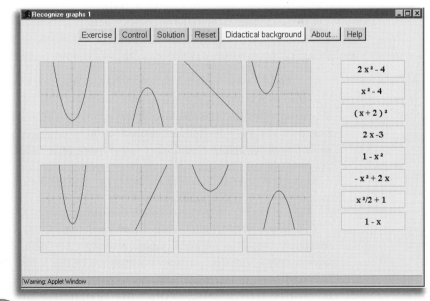

8.11 *Maths Online*

are answered by British teachers in this newsgroup environment. The BBC *Bitesize* site for GCSE revision offers a similar service where teachers answer questions in a range of subjects.

The Austrian site *Maths Online* has a number of multimedia presentations which show various mathematical principles, such as the calculation of sines and cosines and the solving of quadratic equations.

The *Dictionary of Measures, Units and Conversion* has descriptions of most of the units of measurement that are used in the world today and a few that are no longer used. The site has also the information needed to convert the units to the corresponding SI units. There is a presentation of the SI system in its entirety.

Music

Generally music in school includes the three components: listening, composing and performing. The Internet can be useful in several ways, especially for listening to music.

Listening to music

The Web may have information about local concerts and musical performances that the pupils might be able to attend. Concert halls and other venues might have their own web pages with details of current and coming performances.

OperaData is an online database of opera information with opera news and information about current opera productions in 25–30 countries including production details, cast members and booking information.

The *Royal Opera House* in London has a large and useful site with a current programme, several useful noticeboard-based discussions, including one for educators, and an extensive educational site which has a mass of information aimed at schoolchildren and activities including a 'Write an Opera' scheme. There is a newsletter with news about ballet and opera in education, information about current activities for schools and an ideas file with ways you might incorporate opera and ballet into your teaching.

The Web's sound capabilities mean that pupils can listen to live and recorded music from web pages, although the sound quality is not always very good. This is likely to improve in the future as fast connections to the Internet become the standard. Multimedia is becoming more common on the Net and the opportunity to combine music, pictures and text on the Web is very appealing.

There are also quite a few web sites with information about musical works and composers. Yahoo! is a good place to find such pages. You can find your way to pages about individual composers and their works. There are, for example, plenty of Gilbert and Sullivan pages including the *Doyly Carte Opera Company* and the *Gilbert and Sullivan Archive*. The Gilbert and Sullivan Archive has six operas with all the music as midi files and the full lyrics and dialogue. Midi files are a series of instructions to the computer as to how it should play the music. This might be useful for casual listening, but is not to be compared to listening to an ordinary recording. You do not need to be online when listening since you can download the entire operas in text and music as compressed zip files. The main purpose of these files is to let singers practise or enthusiasts sing along using the computer as accompaniment.

Classical Net provides access to over 3400 informational files about classical music and over 2400 links to other classical music web sites. You will find composer timelines dating from 1100 to the present along with links to all you ever wanted to know about any composer.

Classical Music has classical music news, a directory of musicians, a UK concert database and a 'Classical Music Connoisseur Community' mailing list.

The *Guildford Cathedral Choir* has its own page with much choral music available to listen to via Real Audio which gives quite acceptable sound quality (about equivalent to FM radio quality). It has new sound samples every week.

The *Philharmonia Orchestra* has a large site which has all the kind of information you would expect to find (about current concerts etc.) as well as pages intended for schools.

The *Associated Board of the Royal Schools of Music* web site has, among other things, a noticeboard-based discussion for music teachers and their pupils as well as most of the Board's ordinary information material.

The *International Songwriters Association* page will help budding songwriters to find out about competitions and other relevant events. There are tips on getting songs recorded and advice on mixing and composition.

Traditional music is well covered on the Web, for example in the CampusWorld (AngliaCampus) material, which is aimed at teaching the appreciation and analysis of Irish music, song and dance.

PE

Sport in all shapes and forms is one of the major themes on the Web. All the **web communities,** such as MSN UK, Yahoo!, Excite, etc. have liberal amounts of space devoted to sport. Web catalogues such as Yahoo! have subcategories for each sport, from bobsledding to camel racing, with dozens of further classifications for major sports like football. Sports news and sports articles appear here and in many online newspapers.

There are sites dedicated to the rules of various sports and sites which celebrate the successes of a particular team. Some sites cover the sports facilities in a particular area, others are devoted to school sports.

The site PE *Central* is an American site for PE teachers, pupils and anyone else who is interested. The site provides information about PE programmes with a collection of lesson plans, and invites visitors to contribute their own lesson ideas. There are also ideas on how you can best assess your pupils' theoretical knowledge, weekly activity ideas and professional information. There are several mailing lists and discussions which can be reached from PE Central. Live chats are also available but American chats are generally in the evening in the USA, which is the wee small hours on this side of the Atlantic.

The STEM project, The Power and the Glory

The purpose of the STEM project (Students' and Teachers' Educational Materials) is to encourage the development and sharing, through the Web, of educational resources relating to the Science Museum, which have been written by teachers and students. The prize-winning site *The Power and the Glory* from Buttershaw Upper School was created by an individual science teacher as a pre-visit activity for the National Science Museums Sports Gallery Exhibition. It can, however, equally well be used as a stand-alone set of activities in PE and sports studies. You can print out the activities to use in the classroom, but if it is possible to work online, the site has online calculating tools. You can measure your reaction time, measure personal fitness using recovery times or use a staircase to measure your energy expenditure, calculated as the number of peanuts needed to replace the energy used.

 Religion

In the study of religion, as in many other subjects, the international nature of the Internet is a major advantage. Via the Net you can be informed about world religions from the inside. You can get in touch with the faithful and with their leaders to ask questions about their beliefs and traditions, and will generally find that people are very willing to share their religion with others.

The Net is also used for small sects and small churches to spread their view of the world and to attract new members. There may at times be a need for caution if representatives of small churches seem eager to meet young people without parents and/or teachers being present.

Gathering inside information about religions

The Internet's strength (and at the same time its weakness) is that the information it contains is produced by millions of individuals from different cultural backgrounds. This makes the information gleaned from much of the Web fundamentally different from information obtained from schoolbooks or 'official' sources such as the BBC or the government. Exciting as this may be, it does place the responsibility for vetting and evaluating the information firmly in the hands of the teacher and pupils.

Yahoo! has a whole subcategory devoted to the Scientologists and their opponents. There is some very interesting reading there for older pupils and their teachers. You can even listen in to IRC chats or read the newsgroup *alt.religion.scientology*.

Islam 101 is an American online course in Islam from the American Islamic Community. It has an educational site on Islam, its civilisation and culture. It includes an introductory course on Islam and presents Islamic views on contemporary issues. The section on comparative religious studies has articles on the similarities and differences between Islam and other religions which are well worth reading. The site also has a lesson outline for a talk which teachers might be able to ask a Muslim parent to give to a class, as well as other teaching resources.

The UK Buddhist site for children, *Virtuous Reality*, is entertaining and informative. There is a mixture of silliness and serious information, for example about the how and why of meditation, about the Four Noble Truths and the Eight-fold Path to Enlightenment.

The *Hell's Buddhas* site tells the story of a five-month motorcycle pilgrimage across India in 1996. A similar pilgrimage is planned for 1999. The 1996 pilgrimage group had approximately 15 members, and was highly diverse, including citizens of Australia, Austria, Germany, India, Israel, Italy, Japan, New Zealand and the USA. They all rode classic motorcycles, for the stated purpose of 'promoting peace, communal harmony, love and understanding'. This site describes the 1996 pilgrimage in detail.

195

Faith in Today's World from the Christian Union at Queen's University in Belfast has basic information about not only Buddhism but also Judaism, Christianity, Islam, Hinduism and Confucianism. The *Buddhism explained* area of this site has an interesting comparison of Christianity and Buddhism. Here it is important to consider the Christian origin of the material when reading what the site says about other religions.

The Religion area of CampusWorld (AngliaCampus) has material for primary and secondary schools on Buddhism, Hinduism and Sikh festivals as well as on many different aspects of Christianity, such as Celtic crosses and pilgrimages.

Contact with churches and religious people

Individual parish churches have sometimes their own web presence. *St David's Parish Church* in Glasgow, for example, has a collection of articles and publications from the minister, a guide to What's On in the parish, a children's page and the local Boy's Brigade activities.

The *Parish Church of St Mary the Virgin* in Wellingborough also has an ambitious site, with a parish magazine and a Sunday church bulletin for information to parishioners.

You can get in touch with many religious people interested in discussing their beliefs through the UK USENET newsgroups *uk.religion.hindu*, *uk.religion.christian*, *uk.religion.buddhist*, *uk.religion.interfaith*, *uk.religion.islam*, *uk.religion.jewish*, *uk.religion.misc* and *uk.religion.other-faiths*.

Yahoo! has lists of web chats and other chats where you can join in or listen in on live discussions with active members of various religions.

Bible studies

The *Bible Gateway* is a wonderful resource for all bible work. It is in effect an interactive bible. You can search for passages where a word or topic occurs or search for a particular character or event. This resource makes it easy to find biblical events and to set them in their context. This is an invaluable tool for bible studies. You can even use it to link to biblical quotations in your own web pages.

Ethics

Ethics Updates is a full collection of resources pertaining to the study of ethics, from animal rights to world hunger. It is designed primarily to be used by ethics instructors and their students. Its main function is to provide updates on current literature relating to ethics, both popular and professional. It has many directly useful areas such as a collection

The Bible Gateway(TM) is a service of <u>The Gospel Communications Network (GCN)</u> A ministry of <u>Gospel Films, Inc</u>

BIBLE GATEWAY

A Service of the Gospel Communications Network

Other Languages:
<u>GERMAN</u>
<u>SWEDISH</u>
<u>LATIN</u>
<u>FRENCH</u>
<u>SPANISH</u>
<u>PORTUGUESE</u>
<u>ITALIAN</u>
<u>TAGALOG</u>
<u>NORWEGIAN</u>

More Information:
<u>ABOUT THE GATEWAY</u>

<u>SEARCHING INSTRUCTIONS</u>

<u>BIBLE GATEWAY FAQ</u>

<u>WHO USES THE BIBLE GATEWAY</u>

Version: NIV

Passage:

Search word(s):
teacher

Restrict search: (assumes whole Bible)

If your search turns up more than 10 verses, then the results will be shown as references only.

Lookup   Återställ

☑ Show cross references (NASB)
☑ Show footnotes (NIV/NASB)

8.12 *Bible Gateway*
Source: Bible Gateway (http://bible.gospelcom.net)

of discussion questions concerning religion and ethics. The best part of this site is the collections of noticeboard discussion touching on all aspects of ethics. E*thics at the Movies*, for example, has discussion about the ethical issues raised by a dozen films. There are 12 noticeboards concerning ethical theory and 12 dealing with topics in applied ethics.

Science

The Web can be a good complement to traditional textbooks in the sciences. You can find everything from I*nteractive Frog Dissection* sites which let pupils dissect frogs on the computer, to the N*atural History Museum in London* which invites pupils to take part in scientific detective work such as establishing which species a mysterious skull found on Bodmin Moor belongs to. You will find hundreds of links to various fields of biology using a web catalogue like Yahoo! or you can start your exploration of the Web with the following resources.

The *Electronic Zoo* from the American Veterinary Medicine Association is a good general site to start with for a full collection of links to Internet information about any particular species of domestic, wild or zoo animal.

Online courses

There are a number of courses on the Web which are intended for varying kinds of students and pupils. One interesting course which is aimed at non-scientists is *Fundamentals of Microbiology* 101 from the Washington State University. It covers genetics, bacteria and viruses nicely and raises a number of ethical dilemmas which would be suitable for discussion in class.

The Biology Place

The Biology Place is a commercial resource (along with *The Chemistry Place* and *The Psychology Place*) from the American Educational publisher Peregrine. They offer their subscribers selected links and content which is created by educators. This kind of resource is generally useful to the curriculum and includes news of the latest research developments. The site offers learning activities for central parts of the (American) curriculum.

Ecology/environment

The environment is very well represented on the Web. We have already mentioned a few schools projects involving the environment, and there are more. This is a very good subject for international projects. Our views of the environment and of what constitutes an environmental problem are very different depending on where and how we live. British schoolchildren may be concerned about the pollution of rivers by chemical effluents and about the level of lead they are likely to have in their blood. In Sweden the emphasis may be on making the forests accessible for the large predators (such as bears, wolves, lynx and wolverines) to return from the north and on preserving the slow-growing high-altitude forests. In Morocco or Arizona the main area of involvement may be in preventing the desert from encroaching on arable land. In Australia, Spain and Greece the annual drought with the ensuing risk of forest fires might be the principal environmental interest. An international project could involve local work towards sustainable development or simply account for a local environmental problem and what, if anything, is being done to solve it.

There are at least two sites where you can pose ecology questions and have them answered. One is a Swedish site, although it is open for questions from all over the world; the other is American. In both, a team of expert ecologists will answer your questions and you can read previous questions and answers. These resources can be very useful for project work where the contact with active researchers will often be valuable both for ensuring highly relevant answers and in motivating pupils.

Experiments and demonstrations

Many of the chemistry sites on the Web are run by university departments. *Chemistry Teaching Resources* is a collection at the Department of Analytical Chemistry at the university of Umeå in Sweden of every Internet resource even remotely connected with the teaching of chemistry. There are online courses, chemical curiosities, curriculum material, demonstrations and experiments, graphics and visualisations, information about the history of chemistry, chemistry in current affairs, periodic tables, as well as information about mailing lists and newsgroups in chemistry.

Following some of these links will lead to experiments you can perform with your pupils, such as extracting caffeine from tea as described by the Department of Chemistry at Okanagan University College in Canada. You can also find your way to a discussion of caffeine in coffee and the chemistry of other Jamaican products (including rum from sugar cane) from the Chemistry Department of the University of the West Indies.

The *Science Quest* site is a product of the 1996 ThinkQuest competition where schools are invited to produce sites which are useful for other schools. This site has a number of illustrated demonstrations and experiments in physics, chemistry and biology. This is a good example of the kinds of resources which pupils can produce themselves.

The *Chemistry Animation Project* is a collection of animations from the California Institute of Technology (CalTech) illustrating, for example, crystal formation and atomic orbitals. These animations are very old in Internet terms (1995) but still useful.

On the *University of Wisconsin*'s site we found a nice collection of descriptions of physics demonstrations. These 70-odd demonstrations illustrate the principles of motion, heat, sound, electricity, magnetism and light.

The *Visible Embryo* teaches the first four weeks of human development from fertilisation to somite development. This site makes use of animated pictures to show the processes which take place in the weeks after conception.

Technology

Technology education is well provided for on the Web. There are a number of sites which have content intended specifically for schools. These are mainly useful as a source of ideas for projects and activities, although they also offer a forum for discussion and contact between teachers.

The Technology Index has a discussion of the nature of technology and the philosophy of technology as well as a history of technology as a school subject. This British site has a multitude of project ideas including, in the case of electronics projects, a circuit diagram. There are a number of suggestions for simple robotics projects. There is even a design project involving ancient Egyptian graphics. The materials necessary for many of the projects can be ordered directly from the site. Many other resources can be found by following links from this site, for example to the excellent Australian kite design page, *Anthony's Kite Workshop*.

The Technology Resource Center has material for both pupils and teachers. Here too there are circuit diagrams, computer control activities and other project ideas, as well as an interesting list of technology teachers from various countries. The project ideas are divided into Key Stages 3 and 4 and A level and vary from a flashing light for joggers to wear to a coin-operated tablet dispenser. This site even offers guidelines for setting up a school technology department.

The NASA *Spacelink* page has both *Hot Topics*, where current events related to NASA technology and science are highlighted, and *Cool Picks*, a selection of links to NASA's educational sites. Both of these sections have dozens of activities relevant to technology education.

The Canadian site, *Scotty's Center for Technology Education*, has a teacher's section with information about general technology matters and a pupil's section. There is, among other things, an account of a student simulation of a space station.

The Technology Education Lab is an American site with the stated aim of supporting technological literacy for all students and staff. Their slogan is 'Preparing Minds for the 21st Century'. This site is a rich source of ideas and resources for technology education.

The *European Schools Technology Network* is an unusual site. It is hosted by the South Eastern Education and Library Board in Northern Ireland (the local equivalent to an English LEA) to link schools with the EU Comenius project. This is intended as a place for teachers to meet and interact using the Net. There is an annual INSET course organised as a part of the Comenius project to provide teachers with an opportunity to develop a range of skills in the use of computer applications relating to design and control.

≫ *Summary*

❑ The resources and ideas for activities mentioned here do not cover every school subject, and they are but a fraction of all the educational resources there are on the Internet. Think of them as places to start, follow the links you find there and use the catalogues and search tools that exist.

❑ The Internet has much more to offer. When you start exploring on your own you will find plenty of material and contacts you can use.

❑ In time you may want to add your own material for others to use. There is much left to do, and the best resources have not yet been created.

Vocational subjects

Many vocational subjects cover the same kinds of topics as were discussed in the previous chapter. This chapter will discuss the more practical aspects of these subjects. The Internet also opens up channels for young people preparing for a career in a particular field to come into contact with both other young people and adults in the field in the UK and beyond. We refer to General National Vocational Qualification (GNVQ) courses here, but we hope that the tips and ideas here will be relevant and useful for tutors and students in both intermediate and advanced GNVQ and other vocational courses.

Art and design

Students of art and design acquire skills in a variety of media, such as sculpture, ceramics, painting and drawing. Eventually they begin to work on their own projects and build up a portfolio of evidence to show that they have completed each part of the course. Students are taught that presentation of work is important and they are encouraged to present their work as professionally as possible.

Web portfolio

The Web is an excellent setting for a student portfolio. Students can photograph their work (using either a digital camera or ordinary colour prints which they scan in to the computer) and include the photographs on a collection of web pages organised into a site with an entry page (with a menu of some kind). The idea is that a visitor can visit the main page and follow a link to, say, *Sculpture*. That takes the visitor to a page with links to individual sculptures. On each sculpture's page there will then be one or more pictures and a descriptive text.

The advantages of having an online portfolio are many. The student can simply e-mail the URL of the portfolio to any one they want to show their work to. That person can then browse through the student's work at their leisure and return to it later if they wish. The student can show

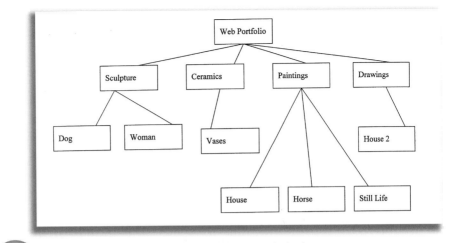

9.1 *A web portfolio for a student of art and design*

their work to people in other countries far more easily than if they had to send photographs by post. A far wider public than otherwise can potentially see the student's work.

You can find artists' portfolios on the Web, for example Laury Dizengremel's pages on the *Artists for a Better World* site. Be warned however that this appears to be a Scientologist site. There are more activities relating to art and design in the previous chapter.

 # Business

Here we present some practical activities aimed at students of business. These are, of course, in addition to the resources and activities discussed in the previous chapter in the section on business studies and economics.

Young Enterprise

The idea behind *Young Enterprise*, a business education charity, is to enable students and business people to engage in practical business projects. The scheme involves a UK-wide network of over 280 voluntary boards and over 11 000 business volunteers. More than 56 500 students in 2300 schools and colleges participate each year.

There are three Young Enterprise programmes all of which claim to help students 'Learn by doing'. The programmes involve business volunteers who act as role models. The *Company Programme* involves students (age 15–19) setting up and running their own company. They work as a team taking all decisions, electing a board, raising share capital, marketing and financing a product or service of their own choice. It is possible to give this programme an international trading link where students can import from and export to a Young Enterprise company in another country. This means that the students can use e-mail and other communication links to contact and work with a Young Enterprise company in another country. (Almost a hundred countries are involved in Young Enterprise, also known as Junior Achievement.

The advantages of this kind of project are many. Students learn about communication as they are required to communicate and form trade links via the Internet, e-mail, fax, video conferencing, telephone, mail and freight carrier. In addition, they will become part of an international network with many contacts abroad through the scheme. The project involves students in real business activities while they are still at school. Young Enterprise also has programmes for younger pupils and special needs students (15–19).

Virtual Factory

The *Virtual Factory* site is part of the Biz/ed scheme discussed in the last chapter. This is an excellent way to study the workings of a real factory. The site has been developed in partnership with Cameron (Hot Air) Balloons. It lets students see the factory's entire business operation including accounts, marketing, production and management. Specially written worksheets enhance the real-life data.

On the *Factory floor* section of the site you will find worksheets, photos, relevant business studies theories and explanations of each main business function. Other features are a section with general information about the company, including its history and product range and a cost breakdown where you can find out how much each bit of a balloon will cost. There is also a glossary of ballooning jargon and a photographic tour of the factory.

The site includes a teachers' guide which shows how to make the most of the resource. It is possible to download a copy of the entire Virtual Factory, which makes it easier to use offline in class.

 # Construction and the built environment

The Web offers all kinds of manufacturers an excellent forum to describe their products. They can produce richly illustrated full-colour catalogues and brochures at relatively little expense. They can use hypertext to give the site visitors the option of clicking on a hypertext link to get further or technical information about a product. Much of this kind of information can be useful for school use. You can easily locate these companies with the help of Yahoo! For example, the following brick and tile companies are in the subcatalogue *Regional:Countries:United Kingdom: Business and Economy:Companies:Construction: Masonry:Materials and Supplies.*

Redland Tile and Brick is a useful site for construction students. They have general and detailed technical information about their bricks and roofing, including different kinds of Dry Tech Roofing systems. A suitable activity with this kind of site might be to set students to find out about different dimensions and qualities of bricks from the Web. They might send an e-mail to the manufacturer asking for further information about a particular product.

Redland Roofing Systems goes a step further. Their site has a collection of Technical Solutions which includes access to technical specialists who will find solutions to roofing queries. There is also a library of over 1800 CAD drawings with roof details for all Redland tiles and accessories, a free, guaranteed tile-fixing specification service and access to free, guaranteed roof specifications to ensure the Redland tiles and fittings you choose are compatible and technically suitable. The site also has an FAQ with answers to nearly 70 frequently asked questions, from Abutments and Appearance to Ventilation and Valleys.

Ideal Electrical Supplies are wholesale electrical and lighting distributors for many UK manufacturers and products. They have a full online catalogue which can be useful for classwork involving electrical installation materials and lamps and lighting, for example costing and simulated ordering. You can order what you need directly from the site and have it delivered.

Granges Building Systems Limited are another example of a supplier with product information on the Web. They supply Glostal and Monarch products, and there is a lot of information on the site about their aluminium systems (from curtain walling systems and shop fronts to doors and windows).

All these sites are from individual manufacturers and suppliers. There are, however, some general resource sites, such as *Construction Materials* – an American site with catalogues of dozens of suppliers and links to their web material.

Homebuilding and Renovating Magazine is a UK-based magazine aimed at the competent do-it-yourself builder, but there can be interesting material in it for students. When we visited their online edition, current articles dealt with the merits of using reclaimed stone rather than newly quarried stone, an article about houses which fit into their surroundings well, and a case study about a barn conversion. The magazine site has also a mailing list where problems associated with building your own home are discussed.

The American trade magazine *Builder* has a useful site, although much of the material is not relevant to British conditions. It has news, archives of past issues and online housing statistics, notices about new products, a database of the 100 biggest builders (in the USA) and an online guide to building events. When we visited their site it had an article with trade secrets and an 'Ask the architect' section. Builder has a database with nearly 1500 house plans from various designers. You can browse through the plans and views of completed houses before sending off an order for blueprints.

The *Department of the Environment, Transport and the Regions* (DETR) site has a lot of British construction information. The papers from the *Construction Directorate* deal with matters such as 'Combating Cowboy Builders'. There is also an official newsletter here, the *Construction Monitor*, which takes up matters such as the trend for timber construction. This newsletter also contains news of amendments and refinements to building regulations.

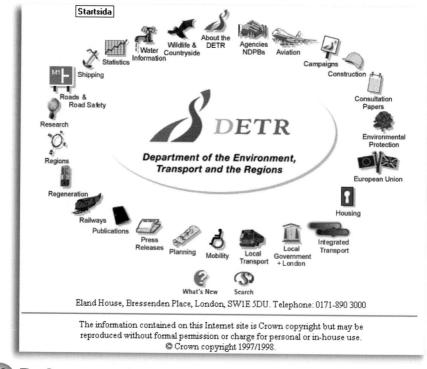

The information contained on this Internet site is Crown copyright but may be reproduced without formal permission or charge for personal or in-house use.
© Crown copyright 1997/1998.

9.2 *The Department of the Environment, Transport and the Regions (DETR)*

Engineering

A wide range of jobs come under the heading of engineering, for example fitter and turner, car mechanic, plumber and technical artist. We will look at a few of the web sites which contain relevant information for GNVQ students.

Technical drawing

Autodesk, who make AutoCAD, have a web site packed with information and useful features. You can download updates to your version of AutoCAD and see a vast collection of tips and tricks. There is even a news group especially for students where they can talk to other CAD (computer-aided design) and related industry students from all over the world about common issues, schools, classes, training, educational software, or anything else that might be on the mind of a student.

Plumbing

Plumbers.uk is a site which describes itself as being for plumbers and people who need plumbers. Over 7500 plumbers have registered with the site, which aims to make it easier for clients to find a plumber. There are tips for people with plumbing problems and a members' area for plumbers. Registered plumbers can have their own web page on the site and an e-mail address. Plumbers.uk undertakes to forward incoming e-mails by fax to plumbers who do not have Internet access themselves. The intention is to negotiate with suppliers to try and get special deals for members and to incorporate technical and legislative information. Plumbers.uk also plans a members' discussion forum.

The web page of the *Institute of Plumbers* is the place to go to find out about the Institute, choose a local registered plumber from their Member Directory (12 000 members) or learn more about the professional and legal requirements which registered plumbers must observe.

On the *World Plumbing Council*'s page you can join in a global noticeboard-based discussion (which you can also choose to receive as a mailing list) with plumbers from all over the world, and a database of accredited training courses. When we visited there was a discussion about gas-heater installation in Hong Kong.

Engineering Council

The *Young Engineers for Britain* site is part of the *Engineering Council*'s site. *Young Engineers for Britain* is an annual competition that enables young people aged 11–25 years to demonstrate their ingenuity and inventiveness. It is described as 'the biggest event of its kind in Europe' and it 'offers a showcase to education and industry of the wealth of innovation and creativity amongst young people in UK schools and colleges'. Projects forming part of an examination syllabus and/or club activity which are broadly based on any aspect of engineering can be entered for this competition. The projects should identify a need and provide an engineering solution to solve 'real-life problems'. The Engineering Council's site has information about European cooperation schemes for young engineers.

The Engineering Council is also behind the notion of the *Neighbourhood Engineer*. This is a scheme which aims to put engineers and technicians in touch with local schools. The idea is that they can work in partnership with teachers, particularly in maths, science and technology, and make young people more aware of the role engineers play in society. The contact between schools and their neighbourhood engineers is an example of a perfect application for e-mail. E-mail is ideal for communicating with busy people since your message lies unobtrusively until its recipient has time to deal with it.

Robots

Those interested in robotics will find plenty to interest them in the online magazine *Robot Science and Technology*. This paper has plenty of articles relevant to robot builders, on all aspects of the subject, such as battery power and collapsible wheels.

There are a number of web pages where you can control robots. For a current listing consult Yahoo! in the subcatalogue *Computers and Internet: Internet: Interesting Devices Connected to the* Net: *Robots*. If you are interested in teaching basic robotic skills you might like to have a look at some of the sites which describe the building of robots with Lego bricks, such as the *Shadow Lego Hand*.

Vehicles

There is a British news group for discussions of car maintenance, *uk.rec.cars.maintenance*. You can ask for advice there or offer advice if you can answer someone else's questions.

On the online edition of *AutoExpress* you will find a used cars buyers' guide and motoring news from around the world as well as road tests and articles about cars. AutoExpress has links to the web sites of over ninety car manufacturers.

Visit some car manufacturers and read about the latest advances in vehicle technology. *Mercedes Benz*, for example, present their dynamic handling systems; *Volvo* are proud of their safety details. Both offer full technical specifications of all their cars.

Top Gear Magazine is Britain's bestselling monthly car magazine, by the same people that do the popular BBC TV show. Their web site has plenty for anyone interested in vehicle technology. There are car tests and a noticeboard discussion on the BBC's *Beeb* site.

The *British School of Motoring* has a very interesting site with plenty of information for learner drivers and people interested in the advanced drivers' test. There is a description of an actual driving test by a retired driving examiner and the opportunity to sit the theory exam.

Health and social care

Students of health and social care will usually be interested in equal opportunities and individuals' rights. The *Equal Opportunities Sites on the WWW* is a site which collects all kinds of web resources which deal with the equal rights of men and women, the disabled, different ethnic groups and sexual orientation.

The *Commission for Racial Equality* (CRE) site has information about the Race Relations Act 1976 which makes racial discrimination unlawful in employment, training, housing, education and the provision of goods, facilities and services. The Act makes it unlawful for organisations in the private and public sectors which provide services to treat their customers or users differently on racial grounds.

Physical aspects of health are also relevant. The *Virtual Body* is a novel educational site which is intended for students of anatomy. Particular attention is paid to the heart, brain, skeleton and digestive system. This site will give you a talk on the skeletal system illustrated by animated pictures. You can use the site to become familiar with the skeleton and all its bones. There is a narrated tour of the heart, an animation showing blood flowing through the heart, and many more features.

Medical and nursing sites

The aim of *HealthIndex* UK is to make it easier and quicker for people to find healthcare sites and resources. The target audience is people with a specific health query, or with a general healthcare interest, or who perhaps work in a healthcare company or organisation.

Healthline is an online version of a magazine. It is a site with articles about many medical topics, such as skin care, nutrition and allergies. Some of the topics have a professional area and a patient area, with relevant information for each group.

WorldWide Nurse is, as its name implies, an international nursing site. There you can meet nurses in the many discussion boards (including one for student nurses), and read about training and every kind of nursing. The USENET news group *sci.med.nursing* has a lot of discussion which might be interesting for students.

The *Health Centre* is a British site run by a doctor in rural Yorkshire. Its aim is to guide you through the huge amount of medical and health information that is available on the Internet. The links are mainly to UK sites, but where no UK alternative exists, some international sites are included.

Official sites

The *Department of Health* has a functional site with online access to many of its reports and documents, including the Chief Medical Officer's updates. The *National Health Service* site has everything that you could wish, including a description of how it works and an account of its history since its start in 1948. There is a lot of information about the different categories of NHS workers and helpful career information.

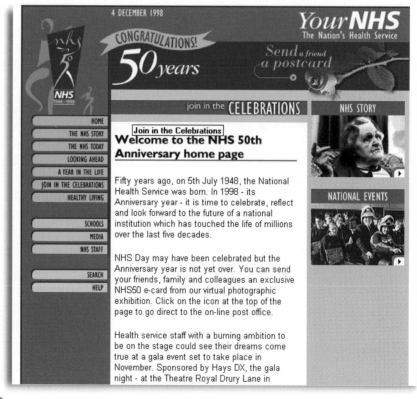

9.3 *The National Health Service (NHS)*

The *International Committee of the Red Cross* site has information about its activities in each of the 50 countries where it is active. There is news and updates on every kind of Red Cross activity.

The *World Health Organisation* site has access to news and articles on dozens of topics, such as AIDS, BSE and immunisation, and everything else that comes under the WHO sphere of activity.

Hospitality and catering

Hotels and restaurants are well represented on the Web, as are food and wine in all forms. There are countless sites with recipes and food discussions, and a few for the catering industry. Yahoo! is, as always, a good source of leads. The sites described here relate to hospitality and catering more directly.

Students might like to study the way hotels and restaurants market themselves on the Web. Compare the sites of luxury hotels to those of small family hotels. What does a web page tell about the establishment it represents? What information should a hotel or restaurant web page contain?

Food and beverages

Leith's School of Food and Wine has details of its long and short courses and demonstrations. There are sample menu selections.

The Institute of Brewers' site is hosted by *breWorld*, which has plenty of technical information about beer hops, malt and brewing. You will find a guide to hops terminology from *English Hops* as well as brewing news.

The *British Beer and Real Ale Database* is a collection of information about individual beers and breweries. *The Campaign for Real Ale* (CAMRA) has a site which explains what real ale is and the difference between real ale and other beers. The CAMRA site has an inventory of historic pub interiors.

The newsgroups *alt.restaurants.professionals*, *alt.business.hospitality* and *uk.food+drink.restaurants* may have discussions which are of interest to students, but they were very quiet when we visited.

Catering

Catering UK claims to be the most popular catering web site in Europe. It offers web space to catering companies and suppliers, as well as news, articles and recipes of interest to caterers.

At the *Culinary Resource Centre* you can receive menus from top London restaurants by e-mail, or Ask the Chef questions, read Catering News from the *Catering Net* and read about restaurants and suppliers. There is a directory of menus and recipes intended for the working chef 'who can see what the rest of the culinary world is doing and so enhance their own imagination'. There are tips here for menu design and costing. This site also has a web chat for chefs.

Hospitality

Yahoo! Accommodation is a resource which travellers can use to find accommodation in a specific city, but if you want information about a specific hotel or hotel chain, you will find them in Yahoo! in the subcatalogue *Business and Economy:Companies:Travel:Lodging:Hotels*. We visited the *Sheraton* site and could choose from a list of hotels and browse their conferencing facilities.

Hotelier describes itself as a global hotel and catering magazine. Its online edition has links to resources, jobs, property, suppliers and promotions. You will find a hotel guide with links to hotels' own web pages.

Other hotels with their own pages can be found on the Web, for example through the pages of the *Cannes Hoteliers Association*. Visit, for example the pages of the *Auberge de la Vignette Haute* to see what individual hotels can do with a very simple web brochure, picturesque English and all.

Information technology

The notion of IT has been replaced by that of information and communications technology (ICT) in many contexts. This is a more accurate term since much of what we call IT has to do with communication in one way or another. Much of the schoolwork in this subject has more to do with basic computer use than with the Internet, but this might change in time as Internet connections become more commonplace in schools.

In the early days of the Internet most of the material there was written by and for the technically inclined. This has changed as web pages have become easier to write and publish and computers have become commonplace. But still there is a tremendous amount of material about computers and the Internet. USENET newsgroups in the *comp* hierarchies (e.g. *uk.comp.misc*) cover many areas.

Yahoo! has a subcategory *Computers and Internet*, which shows the diversity of the material on this subject: from *Art* to the *Year 2000 problem*, with categories dealing with, for example, *Cyberculture*, *Desktop Publishing*, *Hardware*, *Multimedia*, *Music*, *Programming Languages*, *Software*, *Telecommunications*, and many more.

Students are required to prepare, process and present information in the course of their studies. Web publishing is a good way to do this. Multimedia is becoming easier to use and incorporate into web pages. Modern integrated program suites make it easy to incorporate PowerPoint presentations or graphs from Excel spreadsheets into web pages. Students might usefully spend time studying different kinds of web pages and analysing the information they contain and how well they convey it.

Some teachers, for example a teacher of Advanced GNVQ Information Technology in *Aberdare College* in Wales, publish their worksheets and tests on the college web site for the benefit of their students and incidentally the rest of the Internet community. This is a growing trend and means that there will be more and more useful material for teachers and students generally available. The problem is that this kind of material is spread around the Web, and it is difficult to form any kind of course around it. There is a clear need for more cooperation so that teachers in different parts of the country can agree to produce material about different parts of the same courses to share on the Web. The *Virtual Teachers Centre* in the NGfL site will be a natural place for this kind of discussion between teachers.

Land and environment

In the USENET news group *uk.environment* the discussion is about all aspects of concern for the environment. This is a good forum for teachers and students of land and environment to monitor and even participate in. Habitat management and conservation were among the topics being discussed when we listened in.

Yahoo! has a subcatalogue which deals with the environment and nature. You will find further subdivisions there leading to many sites which are relevant to this subject. *Ecology*, *Recycling* and *Wildlife* have their own subcategories, to name but a few.

Organisations

The UK *Agriculture Internet Resources* is simply a link list, but it is a good starting point for all kinds of resources which are related in some way to agriculture.

The *Department of the Environment* site has information about wildlife and the countryside, including documents such as *Access to the Open*

Countryside in England and Wales (a consultation paper issued jointly by the Department of the Environment, Transport and the Regions and the Welsh Office). The *Global Wildlife Division* is part of the Department. In their web pages you can read about, for example, the Dangerous Animals Act, which regulates the keeping of dangerous animals, including ostriches, as pets (apparently ostriches are capable of disembowelling lions). The Department is also responsible for environmental legislation and produces documents about all sorts of related topics, such as energy efficiency and sustainable development.

Sustainable agriculture and biological diversity

There are a number of farms online; many of them have sustainable methods as their niche. *Pond Hill Farm* overlooking Lake Michigan in the USA is well worth a virtual visit just to read about the novel methods that they use to solve what are really quite exotic problems. They have, for example, had problems with deer, coyotes and porcupines damaging the crops. The solution was to have the farm dog patrol the planted areas. The crops were fenced in with radio fencing to confine the dog to specific areas. When the dog approached the radio fence a device in its collar would administer a mild electric shock. This meant that the dog stayed within the area assigned to it and the wild animals stayed out, being understandably reluctant to approach the dog, a pit bull.

The *Forestry Commission* has the basis for a lot of project work on its site, with sections on forests for recreation, on the forestry industry and woodland management. Forestry news is also provided. When we visited the most recent news was the impending release of six pigs into an area of the New Forest to fight unwanted undergrowth without the need for chemicals. The site was not ready when we visited, but it seems that several pages are to be dedicated to education about trees, forestry and wildlife, and visitors are invited. You can take a virtual walk in the woods by visiting forestry properties, such as *Westonbirt Arboretum* with its 18 000 trees of some 3590 taxa.

The Internet is a useful vehicle for campaigns, such as the efforts by the hamlet of Wiggonholt on the South Downs to prevent the excavation of sand from the area. You can read the arguments they present for not turning a part of West Sussex into a sandpit.

Agenda 21

The Council in Moray in the north of Scotland have set up a web page with the details of their *Agenda* 21 work. Agenda 21, adopted by the United Nations in Rio during the summer of 1992, is a comprehensive programme of action to be implemented from now and into the twenty-first century, covering issues such as poverty, consumption, population trends, health, environmental degradation, gender and equity. Among the local Agenda 21 priorities are a sustainability check on the Moray Development Plan and the development of an energy conservation initiative.

Hackney in London also has an Agenda 21 page on the Web. Hackney's vision includes local needs being met locally and the diversity of nature being valued and protected.

The *Four Seasons* project is sponsored by the National Grid (for electricity, not for learning!). On the Four Seasons web site there are three school-based projects and a range of environmental education resources for schools. The projects are related to the weather and make use of data collected from automatic weather stations at a series of sites in England. These sites are at some of the environmental education centres supported by the *National Grid Company* (NGC). Data from the sites is available on the Web. The site has information about environmental events and resources, tips for how schools can become involved in local Agenda 21 work, an action plan for sustainability, seasonal reminders for school grounds maintenance and development, and details of the NGC environment centres.

You can also read about Agenda 21 work in other countries on the Web. The *Estonian Sustainable Development Network* page tells about sustainable forest management among other things. Agenda 21 can form the basis of contact projects where pupils in different countries compare notes on local environmental issues. The pollution problems of eastern Europe make an interesting contrast to the problems associated with the welcome growth of the wolf population in Norway or the conservation of the slow-growing high-altitude forests in Sweden.

Eco-tourism

The *Eco-Source* site is an impressive collection of stories and articles about, for example, how to be an eco-tourist and biological diversity loss in Vietnam. Visit *Chaa Creek Inland Expeditions* for a detailed presentation of an eco-tourism venture in Belize.

There are quite a few sites which inform about environmentally appropriate ways to explore Britain, such as the Peak District National Park site or the Pembrokeshire coast National Park. In the *Council of British Archaeology*'s site *Save Stonehenge* you can read of the efforts being made to protect Stonehenge from being destroyed by the visitors who flock to see it.

» *Leisure and tourism*

The subject of eco-tourism leads on naturally to the GNVQ subject Leisure and tourism. This is an area in which the Internet has a lot of material. The Web resources that exist will be helpful when you and your pupils are investigating the leisure and tourism industry in the UK and beyond. A judicious study of material available on the Internet can greatly enhance a visit to a new place. Students of Leisure and tourism need to know what kind of material the Web and other Internet services contain at present and how to optimally present this kind of information.

Travel and tourism

Travel and tourism involves travel agents, airlines and tourist attractions. Many travel agents, airlines and tour companies have a presence on the Web. Often visitors can browse the company's catalogue or timetable and even book trips directly on the web page. Tourist attractions often use their web site like a glossy brochure to attract visitors and give information about opening times and prices.

Thomson Holidays use the Web to give much of the information that they otherwise have in brochures: descriptions of resorts, activities and flight-only offers with timetable information. They do not have details of individual hotels, but they let visitors order traditional brochures from the site. Thomson's also use their web site to recruit new guides to work in their destinations.

British Airways Global Internet Venue has a lot of information about their latest image change. More useful are the online timetable and a facility whereby passengers can check fares and availability or book and pay for tickets. The BA site has details of their own package holidays and of their business travellers' service. You can read about the comfort of First Class travel and the speed of the flagship Concorde across the Atlantic. For UK domestic travel there is information about the shuttle service from Heathrow including a virtual tour of the self-service electronic ticketing machine.

Stena Line runs ferries between Northern Ireland and Scotland as well as between the east coast of England and the Continent and Scandinavia. You can book crossings online and study a route map as well as look at pictures and technical specifications of the craft. For each route the site gives details of sailing times and the craft used.

The *Giant's Causeway* on the north coast of Northern Ireland is a World Heritage Site. As such it has many web pages devoted to it. Students might find it instructive to do a search for "Giant's Causeway" using

9.4 *Online booking with British Airways*

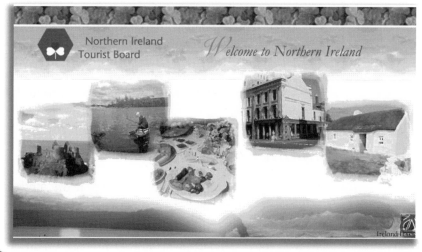

9.5 *The Northern Ireland Tourist Board*

AltaVista or Excite and comparing the kinds of sites they find. The most official-looking page we found was the Infosites page which is part of a *Complete Guide to Irish Tourism*. This site links to the *Northern Ireland Tourist Board*, which has its own Giant's Causeway page.

More commercial tourist attractions such as *Madame Tussaud's*, for example, often have a single site with basic information about what there is to see, opening times and details of exactly how to get there. The Tussaud's site has a mini-movie showing some of the exhibits (slow to load if you have a modem connection), but nothing about entrance fees, etc.

Leisure and recreation

Leisure and recreation includes, for example, leisure centres, fitness centres, theatres, arts centres and museums. Many municipal sites will have details of the local leisure centres on their pages. Islington Council in London, for example, has a site dedicated to its *Aquaterra Leisure Centres*. The visitor can find out about all sorts of activities, from swimming lessons to ice-skating.

The *Theatre Royal* in Bath has an unofficial page apparently written by a regular theatregoer, but with no direct connection to the theatre. Nonetheless the site has full information about the theatre's programme and restaurant, and booking information. This page stands in contrast to the sophisticated *Liverpool Playhouse* site with the latest web multimedia effects.

Many museums have used the Web to make some of their material accessible to people who live too far away to make a physical visit. The British Museum has already been presented in the previous chapter, but the best-known virtual museum is the *Smithsonian* in New York. You can choose between a dozen different tours in the National Museum of Natural History, the National Museum of American History and the National Air and Space Museum, including one for children and one about mammals.

Management studies

The Internet's potential is considerable in the study of organisations. Large companies typically have material on their web pages describing the organisation and its relationship to the wider community.

Students of management studies are often introduced to business statistics and their use. There are several places on the Net where you can get access to up-to-date statistics. Many companies have their own reports and other documents available from their web sites. Biz/ed has this kind of information for a number of companies, as well as other material to aid students and teacher.

Companies often have intranets where web and other Internet technologies are used. You can peek in on internal intranets through the examples on the Microsoft site. Intranets can be used for sharing internal documents, internal e-mail and discussion in a secure environment. Intranets are often connected to the Internet but are typically protected from it by a *firewall* (software which denies access to outsiders while letting outgoing and some incoming data through).

Manufacturing

The *Business Information Zone* (BIZ) has been developed for users seeking UK-relevant business information, products and services on the Internet. The BIZ also has companies which do not yet have an Internet presence in their database. The BIZ Production and Manufacturing page enables you to track manufacturers, suppliers and information sources across the whole spectrum of industry. The BIZ pages are certainly a good place to start when planning visits to manufacturers. You get not only contact information but also links to company web pages. These usually have some details of the kinds of products produced. In many cases it will be possible to study the manufacturing process in a particular producer via their web material.

Budehaven School in Cornwall have been kind enough to make their entire intranet accessible to the Internet community. Their GNVQ manufacturing section is particularly well endowed with material for handouts and the like. This is presumably the work of a single enthusiastic teacher.

Media: communication and production

Not only is the Internet an important medium in its own right, it also devotes a lot of space to other media. When students are investigating the content of media products they will find the Web helpful. Newspapers and magazines have much of their material available to read on the Web, and many newspapers have easily searched article archives. Television and radio companies have information about current and coming broadcasts as well as often having a lot of background information on their web pages.

Students' experience of producing their own print products might be enhanced if they could show their work to a larger group of people.

The Web can provide a forum and even some feedback from readers if contact information is included. Even audio and moving picture products can be included as files on web pages if the students have access to appropriate equipment and software. Those students who are interested in photography will be able to have their own exhibition on the Web.

Media students will often be interested in the new media and motivated to try their hand at web design and at creating web pages with all the latest bells and whistles. Animation and multimedia are a natural progression from this.

Many web pages are designed with the aim of projecting a suitable company image, as is obvious from, for example, *CocaCola's* or *McDonald's* pages. The study of this kind of advertising could be the basis of project work. Students might like to consider the effects of web advertising aimed at children and young people. What effects are achieved and how?

The screens for moving pictures on the Web are still very small, and the Web is not an ideal place to view films, although this is likely to change soon. But there is a tremendous amount of information about films on the Web, with links to production companies as well as to promotional sites for particular films. The film companies pull out all the stops in their efforts to create the right atmosphere in their film sites with animation, multimedia and sound.

The Internet Movie Database has freely available information about over 150 000 movies with over two million filmography entries, and is expanding continuously. You will be able to find soundtrack samples, cast details, plot synopses, reviews and much more.

Yahoo! Movies is a special section dealing with film. You can be linked to the film's own site if it has one, and join in live chat about films or participate in a noticeboard-based discussion.

⏵ *Performing arts and entertainment*

Performing arts and entertainment is by its very nature a practical kind of subject, so the Internet is not much use for the creation of work for performance or for performing, but it does have a function when it comes to promotion. All kinds of performers have found the Net to be useful, from the *Comberbach Swilltub Mummers* to *English National Ballet*.

Those interested in stagecraft, for example lighting and costuming, will find some material on the Web, including the *Costumers Guild* UK site and sites for lighting companies such as the Scottish *Northern Lights*.

The site *Dramaturgical Resources* from the University of Puget Sound in the USA has tips for budding playwrights, especially on how they might use the Web in their research. The page *Script Portfolios* is part of a Canadian Playwrights' site and tells the story of how four Canadian plays make it into production, complete with director's notes and reviews.

The Web can be useful in other ways for these students by enabling them to keep up to date in what is going on in the field of entertainment and by informing them of local theatre activity.

Musical Stages Online is the online edition of *Musical Stages*, which describes itself as 'the only British glossy magazine dedicated to international musical theatre'. You can download snatches of songs from musicals and read all the latest news and gossip from the musical theatre world.

Retail and distributive services

One way that the Web can help students on this course is in their investigation of the retail sector. They can study the web pages of, say, *Tesco*, which has embraced the new technologies so far as to act as an Internet Service Provider. Tesco has home shopping and an ambitious schools' programme, *Tesco SchoolNet* 2000. Compare this with the *Sainsbury's* site. Sainsbury's has a lot of pointers to information about its food – it claims to have expanded its selection of organic, vegetarian and low-fat foods. Sainsbury's, like Tesco, has a scheme for donating equipment

 Sainsbury's

to schools, but it did not offer any educational content on its site when we visited. Sainsbury's slogan is 'Fresh food Fresh ideas'. The emphasis is clearly on the quality of its food and its willingness to provide what customers ask for rather than technology.

Retailers in other branches often have web pages too. Compare the web material from different kinds of multiple outlet retailers. What kind of image do they want to project? How much emphasis do they place on customer service, quality and prices? Some retailers use the Web for promotional material aimed at customers while others have mostly corporate information. Does this reflect a difference in the company's customer base?

The *Hammersmith and West London College* web site has a lot of material for the retail and distributive services course. This is primarily a pack intended to help students through their work placement. The site covers the Retailing and Sales unit in the elements 'Investigating the retail sector', 'Investigating the retail environment' and 'Examine personal selling'. The web pages include assignments and mock element tests.

The Web can provide the basis for international comparisons. Have a look at the pages of, say, IKEA and compare the national sites in different countries. Although they have a common profile there is a difference between them which reflects the interests and concerns of their customers. The Hong Kong site, for example, is eager to show customers how much space they can save by optimal furnishing – important indeed in a city where living space is at a premium.

 ## *Science*

GNVQs in science are about what scientists and engineers actually do in their jobs. The Internet can help students get in touch with scientists to take part in real research projects using real data. An example of this kind of activity is *CoVis – Learning through Collaborative Visualisation*. The idea is that students work with other classes and research scientists in the earth sciences. The students are given access to the scientists' data and methods. The *Weather World* 2010 (WW2010) meteorology project is part of the CoVis scheme. WW2010 aims to integrate real time and archived data with instructional resources using new and innovative technologies. Students learn how to interpret weather data and to make forecasts.

NASA's *Moonlink* project has the slogan 'Bringing Space Down to Earth'. It is based around the Lunar Prospector Mission and it gives students the opportunity to become actively involved in the mission. The Lunar Prospector spacecraft worked throughout 1998 to conduct a mapping mission from lunar orbit, gathering data on the Moon's surface composition, outgassing events, and gravity and magnetic fields. This will lead to greater understanding of the origin, evolution, current state and resources of the Moon. The idea is that students will learn about the lunar environment and make discoveries right along with the Prospector science team as they seek answers to questions asked nearly 25 years ago during the Apollo missions. Even if this mission is over, there will certainly be others from NASA that you and your students can join.

The *Science Online* site is part of *Schools Online* which was funded by the Department of Trade and Industry. The site has apparently run out of funding, but there is a lot of material online to inspire budding scientists. There are suggestions for experiments involving computers and sensors: for example, does coffee keep warmer if you add milk before or after making a phone call? Sensors of various kinds can be connected to a web server and data can be broadcast to the world on the Web. There are quite a number of 'Interesting devices connected to the Web' as the Yahoo! subcategory puts it. Look at the *Buzbee Bat House Temperature Plot*, for example, generated by a digital thermometer connected to a PC.

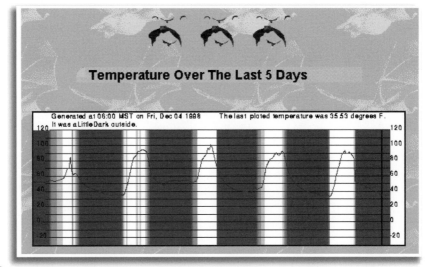

 Buzbee Bat House Temperature Plot

Summary

❑ As you begin to explore the Web on your own it will not matter that the web sites mentioned here have changed or disappeared since we visited them. You will find web resources that are relevant to your subject and the interests of your pupils. You will probably find ways to use the Web that we have not thought of.

❑ As more work places and trade organisations are going online and starting to use e-mail for their correspondence you may find that the Net is an excellent place for your students to come into contact with both students elsewhere and adults working in the field they are aiming for.

❑ You yourself will likely be able to easily get in touch with your colleagues in other schools and colleges, and even in other countries. You are not alone!

Where is the **Internet** headed?

When computers were new in the 1940s it was believed that no more than a handful of computers would ever be needed. The Chairman of IBM in 1943, Thomas Watson, is quoted as having said, 'I think there is a world market for maybe five computers.' Everyone who uses computers and the Internet must at some time be awed be the staggering speed of the technological progress which has brought us to where we are today. If you read predictions from a few years ago regarding the shape of things to come the striking thing is just how cautious the estimates of progress were.

Technological advances

It is quite impossible to predict what we will be using computer technology for in ten or even five years. If we look back five years we can see that the state of computer technology available to schools and people at home was very primitive compared to what we have now. A few years ago there was no Internet outside the universities, computers did not use CDs or have sound capability. Their ability to render graphics was rudimentary compared to what we have now, and a hard disk with 500 Mb was considered large.

Given that we know very little about the equipment and services that will be available in a few years, it is very difficult to foresee how we will use computers in the future. Often new uses for existing technology can send us off at a tangent to the original direction. This has happened with telephone wires, which were originally developed to send speech, although they are now used for sending pictures (fax) and data as well. This demands so much of the phone lines that they are, in turn, being developed for greater capacity. The circle is complete in that this new cable technology benefits voice telephony as well. The buzz of innovation and cutting-edge activity around wireless communication, mobile telephony, satellite and cable television systems and even the electricity distribution net will very likely lead to new ways of working in the near future.

Governmental taxation and incentive policies can allow these new systems to become widespread and even commonplace in the space of a few months. In fact this kind of political factor can alter the direction of the evolution of ICT. Free local telephone calls, for example, might be enough to keep us tied to our modems regardless of the new alternatives.

Putting new technology to work in education

As we have seen, there is an overwhelming political and popular will to make extensive use of the Internet in education. This is variously attributed to considerations of democracy, concern for educational standards in a national and international perspective, and anxiety lest the education provided in school fail to prepare pupils adequately for adult life. The challenge is to teach pupils how to use the Internet and then to use it together with them to enhance the teaching and learning of other subjects in ways which are meaningful to pupils now rather than in the future.

It seems likely that the massive governmental investments of time and money into programmes such as the National Grid for Learning mean that the government is committed to this course for some time to come. It remains to be seen how the next series of technological innovations will be incorporated into our education system.

⊗ *Visions of the future*

We have made a study of statements issued by a number of governmental and commercial bodies in an effort to divine how their vision of the future looks. In some cases we have asked them for their comments.

The DfEE

The government's consultation paper on the National Grid for Learning's *Connecting the Learning Society* appeared in October 1997. The following was an answer to the question 'What will the Grid offer that we don't have already?'

> *Learning through ICT not only offers the chance to become proficient in the skills needed in the world of work. It enhances and enriches the curriculum, raising standards and making learning more attractive. The best educational software is not an alternative to books or class teachers – it is a new chapter of opportunity. The Grid will mean that:*

> *teachers will be able to share and discuss best practice with each other and with experts while remaining in their schools;*

materials and advice will be available on-line – when learners want them – to help develop their literacy and numeracy skills, including in their own time;

children in isolated schools will be able to link up with their counterparts' curriculum, to help them to work together and gain the stimulus they need;

language learners will be able to communicate directly with speakers of the target language;

learners at home or in libraries will be able to access a wider range of quality learning programmes, materials and software.

The paper goes on to state the following noble aim:

[The Grid] will also send a clear message, both here and internationally, that the UK intends to be among the world leaders to harness new technologies to raise educational standards, improving quality of life and the UK's international competitiveness.

Stirring words indeed!

BECTa

In a live chat in July 1998 about the National Grid for Learning on *Teacher Grid* UK (BT, Microsoft and RM's joint Teacher site), Owen Lynch, the Chief Executive of BECTa, gave the following vision of the future of the Internet in education:

The value of the technology must be judged in terms of its ability to enhance the quality of teaching and learning. There are many examples, now well researched, of the direct relationship between the use of ICT and improved quality of education. But given the nature of today, it is worth noting the potential impact of the communications element of ICT. Clearly, for teachers, this technology will provide the opportunity for them to access quality information, advice on best practice, a wider range of resources, research opportunities, professional dialogue with colleagues and wider In-service activities, all of which should hopefully provide them with the capacity to improve their practice. For pupils, they too will be able to access a wider range of resources and enter into electronic dialogue with others. But possibly for them, one of the more significant outcomes will be the opportunity to access wider educational opportunities from home. This could generate a new learning partnership between the home and school which would revolve not only around the concept of the extended learning day, but more importantly, take advantage of the opportunity to ensure continuity of learning between the home and school.

BT

The BT book *Teaching and Learning with the Internet* (1997), which was sent to CampusWorld subscribers, suggests that in the schools of the future we will be able to spend more time developing social skills and learning about learning. We will use community resources – other people as much as technology – and work collaboratively with people all around the world. It will even be possible to be physically at home while at school, according to BTs vision.

BT comments on the difficulty of making accurate predictions about the future:

> Gazing into the technological future is a hazardous activity. We all know that the rate of change in terms of IT development can be plotted as an exponential curve – the further into the future we predict, the steeper the curve. It then becomes more difficult to predict accurate time scales, hence the hazard of making predictions in the light of rigorously evaluated evidence and still ending up with egg on your face.
>
> For example, ten years ago, who would have predicted that the fax machine would be a significant method of business communication? Who would have thought then that small children could publish their own work on a network with potentially millions of users/readers?

BT also comments on the difficulty of accepting that children are often more proficient in the use of ICT than their teachers, and asks:

> Do we have the confidence and willingness to provide structured opportunities to allow them to share their expertise with us and, together, work towards a deeper understanding of how we can use the Internet in teaching and learning?

RM

RM is one of the major educational Internet Service Providers in the UK with its Internet for Learning service and the stand-alone online content services for schools, EduWeb and Living Library. The content of EduWeb has, according to RM's Finbar McGaughey, been developed to help schools address three key needs:

> Communication – with other education professionals and students
>
> Publishing – help and advice in ensuring schools take advantage of the web as both a marketing medium and a showcase for pupils' work
>
> Finding resources – essentially to help enhance teachers' delivery of the curriculum.

RM has a statement of the corporate vision for the four years of the National Grid for Learning's framework (reaching until the year 2002). It sees the role of curriculum ICT resources as being 'to provide solutions which enhance the teaching and learning of subjects, across the whole curriculum'.

RM wants to provide the technical and curriculum solutions 'to ensure that schools can easily and transparently connect their pupils and staff to the information and communication resources that will become available'.

In RM's vision the National Grid for Learning will ultimately extend beyond supporting teaching, learning, training and administration in schools. It believes that the Grid will connect a whole range of facilities in 'one coherent communications network'.

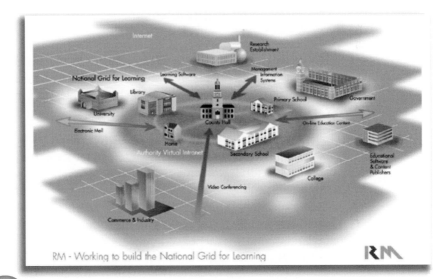

10.1 *RM's vision of the National Grid for Learning*

RM sees its role as allowing schools to create their local component of the National Grid, with appropriate facilities within the schools, and with the appropriate resources available to pupils and teachers. Its statement of vision concludes that 'in the future we can integrate with, or even help you to create, the wider Grid which is at the heart of the Government's vision'.

Microsoft

Microsoft has seized for itself a position where it is able to shape the future in any direction it pleases, both in the field of education and in every other sector where the computer has a role. Microsoft always has a comment to make and its own vision of how the world might be in a few years. Bill Gates, Chairman and Chief Executive of the Microsoft Corporation, is quoted in Microsoft's material as saying:

> *We at Microsoft strongly believe that the single most important use of information technology is to improve education.*

Microsoft has introduced the concept of the *Connected Learning Community*. It states that an 'enriched learning environment' is now realisable in which:

> *All students have access to a PC and information online.*
>
> *Each student is empowered to pursue the individual path of learning best suited to his or her needs.*
>
> *Learning results not from access alone but from continuous, dynamic interaction between students, teachers, parents and the extended community.*

The idea behind the notion of the Connected Learning Community is that there the Internet is available and used for communication 'within and between schools, between schools and homes, and between schools and the larger community of learning resources'.

In the school world, connections within and between schools are used to allow pupils, teachers and administrators to exchange electronic mail, post announcements, coordinate work and share documents. Pupils can produce reports with a classmate or a partner in another school. Teachers and administrators can share resources such as databases, bulletin board services and electronic mail within school buildings and districts. Teachers can collaborate on lesson plans and share student portfolios both within the school and with colleagues in other locations.

> *No single capability excites teachers and parents more than the ability to increase communications between school and home. Connections between schools and home provide teachers and parents with an efficient and interactive way to discuss student progress and school activities.*
>
> *Students and parents can view lesson plans, homework assignments, schedule changes and other information from home on bulletin boards. Students, parents and teachers can exchange work and collaborate on assignments, even when the school isn't necessarily open.*

The Connected Leaning Community includes the connections between schools and the community at large, such as libraries, museums, zoos and 'a host of community resources'. The idea is that 'students, teachers and learners of all ages can make the world their classroom' with 'virtual field trips to faraway places, consultations with experts world-wide and collaborative projects with other learners across the globe'.

> *In the Connected Learning Community, the barriers of time, distance, convenience and access will diminish. Every learner will have access to technology throughout the day and technology tools will be available to help students and teachers find, evaluate, organise and use information effectively. Students will acquire information skills they need to become lifelong learners and develop a passion for exploration and discovery.*

Microsoft's description concludes by saying that the Connected Learning Community is not merely a vision of the future, but that it is already in operation in pilot schemes such as the Highdown Hub in Reading, Berkshire, which involves several primary and secondary schools. Microsoft seem to be committed to the path of involving the entire local community in the doings of the school and vice versa.

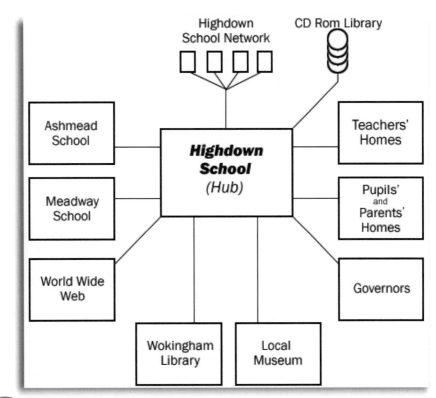

10.2 *Highdown Hub*

ICL

Chris Yapp of ICL, a major IT systems and services company, provided his personal view of learning in the future at a headteachers' conference for the BBC's *Computers Don't Bite: Teachers* campaign, which was launched in May 1998. The full version of his presentation is on the *Computers Don't Bite: Teachers* CD-ROM.

> *I've come to the conclusion very broadly that no country in the world has an education system fit for the future, and that's quite scary at one level, but the reverse side is quite positive because all of sudden teachers aren't to blame.*

> *What we have to get used to is the idea that we have to reinvent education for a new climate for a global world – one in which 7 year olds come across awkward questions, and one in which we are going to have to rethink the nature of what learning is about and the skills that people will need to be able to survive and thrive. The important thing is we've got ourselves over the last few years to talk down our aspirations, talk down our achievements, and I think that's really quite sad. And I think one of the things we really need to do is to actually look at what we are doing and open up some of the good practices inside schools and make them more visible. It is very clear wherever you go in the world, everybody but everybody is saying that we have got real problems thinking through the nature of learning in the next century.*

Yapp goes on to say:

> *The real challenge as I see it is that the lifestyles children in our schools are going to face have changed from that of my parents' generation. If you look at my fathers' life – primary school, secondary school, into the army, to apprenticeship, to work and retirement – by the age of 30 he had the skills to see him through a lifetime, raise a family, pay off the mortgage and build a pension fund. That world has gone. What we now face is a world where you work or you don't, and where people in work are finding them- selves needing to be trained more and more often, and actually having to go back into education to top up their employability.*

The solution he proposes is:

> *We must move towards learning on demand, and that is the basis if you like of the education purpose, and the education society of the future. One of the important things is that this is not about a PC for every child, it's not about internet into every school or every class- room. It may be necessary but it is certainly not as efficient. The his-*

tory of fifty years of information technology now tells us that technology does not improve organisational efficiency in the long run.

The important thing is that what it does do is offer the opportunity to rethink what you are trying to do and how you are trying to do it. It raises and increases capacity for effectiveness, that is, doing things differently rather than doing things better. But if you're talking about schools' effectiveness rather than schools' efficiency, you're talking about organisational change, you're talking about thinking about different models for organising the teaching profession, different staffing routes, different school buildings, different sizes of schools, different patterns, different role models. And that's inevitably the 'people first, technology second', change that we're going to have to think through and therefore the role of the education profession in this is one that has to be addressed up front.

It seems that ICL is propagating for a learning revolution. Yapp wants us to examine the way we do things and be prepared to change completely to let schools become more effective. He claims that our education system, and that of every other country, is not fit for the future. The move towards learning on demand may well be inevitable, and is not questioned when it comes to adult education.

While the seven-year-old child who comes across material which leads him to ask awkward questions must be answered, we cannot leave the planning of the basic curriculum to be steered by considerations of responding to whatever comes up in the children's own experience, even if their experience is indeed much wider now than it has been in the past. This is too haphazard a way to provide children with the basic skills they need now and in their future. There is a need for caution here. We already have a situation where some children do not have the basic skills which enable them to go on to relatively independent learning situations. But if we can concentrate on basic information-processing skills (e.g. reading and writing, listening and speaking) in the early years then the pupils will be well able to benefit from a learning-on-demand system as they grow older.

What do we want from the new technologies?

Well, we have seen what the individuals and companies who shape the Internet in education want. But there is no reason to assume that they want what is best for the pupils or for society. They are influenced by considerations of politics and economy rather than humanism and pedagogy. Many teachers are disturbed by what they perceive as change for its own sake and the spending of vast sums of money on ICT in schools which might be better spent in other ways.

A recurring theme in the above visions of the shape of things to come is the possibility for parents to become more involved in what is going on at school. But this does require that the pupils' homes are equipped with computers and Internet access. This means that the level of connected homes will have to rise dramatically from the 10 per cent that currently have Internet access (1998). Of course, politics and economy can be used to influence the public if government incentives are arranged to encourage parents to acquire equipment and to support low-income families in this matter.

Teachers' reaction to the above visions

In mailing lists such as UK-SCHOOLS, newsgroups like the Microsoft *Teachers' Staffroom* (*msn.uk.education.teaching*) and in the educational press teachers and administrators express their excitement over the possibilities of ICT and their concern about how to pay for it.

Some of those who express concern are enthusiasts who have been struggling, often for years, to involve other teachers in using computers and the Internet in their teaching. Major concerns are:

❑ The problem of motivating teachers to use ICT at all ('Teachers are trained to teach!' – a comment from the UK-SCHOOLS mailing list).

❑ How to get teachers to progress beyond the stage of needing intensive help from the ICT teacher or a technician at every turn. One solution proposed by a newly qualified teacher is to persuade staff to buy a PC to use at home. Government incentives will most likely support this kind of tactic.

❑ The 'problem' of the pupils often knowing more about the technology than the teachers ('It is only those pupils of ability (namely the pupils who use PCs at home) who can use the technology' – again, a comment from the UK-SCHOOLS mailing list). This suggests alarming correlations between family economy and how well children do at school.

Headteachers are faced with the headache of fitting all the demands for equipment and training into a very tight budget. They express concern about the low standard of computer equipment they have. The National Grid for Learning creates enormous pressure for schools to go online. Major concerns here are:

❑ how to afford the necessary investment in hardware, software and teacher training

❑ how to justify the time spent by teachers in becoming proficient in using the new equipment and the resources of the Grid

❑ whether the sums involved would not be better spent on more teachers or better library facilities.

Now a good deal of this concern may well be removed by extra governmental funding for struggling schools. The pioneering schools who have been involved in large-scale Internet use involving contact between schools, distance learning and curriculum material available on the Web have returned very favourable reports with satisfied teachers and pupils and higher examination pass rates (e.g. in the Kent Broadband Learning Project and Project ConnectEd in the Education Department's Superhighways Initiative).

Summary

❑ We cannot see into the future. We have no way of knowing what technology we will have in five, or even three years. Nonetheless, the Internet appears to be firmly established as a necessary classroom tool. Pupils who do not currently have Internet access at school will probably get it soon.

❑ If this improves the dialogue between teachers so that they can exchange ideas and experiences of successful methods then we have everything to win. If parents and schools can use technology to dramatically increase the communication between them, as in the Highdown Information Hub Project, then nothing can stop us!

❑ Technological development provides the means for change. It is up to us to see the potential for applying the technology to improve our schools.

Appendix 1
The **Internet** at school

» *A two-day in-service training course for teachers*

This book aims to provide the information teachers need to get started using the Internet. We have tried to help teachers become aware of what the Internet has to offer in the subjects they teach. Nonetheless, a book is no substitute for actually being shown what to do and having the opportunity to ask for help. Many schools are taking the time to provide teachers with a structured course on the Internet.

We propose the following structure for a course based on this book. Ideally each teacher will receive a copy of the book to read before the course and keep as reference after the course.

Preparation

Participants should read this book in its entirety before the course. It can be a good idea to make notes while reading, particularly if something sparks off an idea about how the participant might use the Net in his own teaching.

It is notoriously difficult to learn to use computers or new programs on your own. The learning process would be made much easier if each participant were assigned a mentor (a colleague or student who is well versed in the use of the Internet). The mentor can assist the participant in a few first sessions at the computer as he learns to get online, use the browser and send and receive e-mail.

Teachers who have no experience at all of using computers will probably need extra help before they start learning about the Internet.

Course

First morning
After an introduction, the tutor might address the question 'What is the Internet?' After a brief visual presentation of the various areas of the Net (e-mail, the Web, news, IRC, etc.), there should be time for a

practical hands-on session with online computers (no more than two to a computer). This is an opportunity to make sure all the participants can start the browser, surf to a given address, follow a link, use the back-button, send e-mails to themselves and receive them.

The next topic is searching. After a presentation of different kinds of searching tools and simple ways of refining searches, participants can try themselves to find specified information using AltaVista, Excite and/ or Yahoo!

First afternoon
This period is set aside to show the participants what there is for teachers and pupils on the Web. All available computers should show downloaded sites relevant to teachers and pupils. Participants can circulate from computer to computer and explore all the sites. Particular attention can be paid to sites which bring teachers and pupils together in collaborative projects.

Second morning
The theme this time is 'Working with the Internet'. This should include an introductory summary of how to get involved in project work and what it involves, followed by a discussion of how participants can use project work in their own teaching.

Following this, participants divide into broad subject groups, such as English and languages, sciences, practical subjects, vocational subjects. (Participants should be divided into reasonably sized groups before the course.) The idea is to brainstorm for ideas about how the Internet can be used as a source of contacts and information in the classroom and also for communication between teachers, between teachers and pupils (and parents), and between pupils. Have each participant write down five concrete ways they might use the Net in their own classrooms. Results and ideas can be reported to the rest of the participants.

Second afternoon
Panel debate: 'Does the Internet belong in our school?' This will be most interesting if different kinds of interests are represented, for example teachers (for and against), parents, local politicians, pupils and governors. Follow up this with a discussion of the school policy on regulating pupils' access to the Net.

Finally the participants need to know what to do next. Where do we go from here? There is usually a need for a follow-up to this kind of course. Perhaps participants could meet back in a couple of months to compare notes and give each other inspiration and feedback.

Appendix 2
Teaching pupils to use
the **Internet**

The following curriculum outline is intended to be used for teaching basic Internet skills to 11–18-year-olds in a series of five lessons. If it suits the school's Internet policy, satisfactory completion of the course can lead to some kind of 'certification', giving pupils certain rights as Internet users.

The time required for each lesson will depend on the class's level of familiarity with computers and the Internet. Each lesson can be spread over several meetings if it is difficult to see the pupils for long enough at a time. The course includes basic how-to as well as appropriate use and safety considerations.

1 What is the Internet, what is the Web?

This lesson will be theoretical and explore the pupils' prior knowledge of and attitude to the Net as well as presenting the Net and the part of it known as the Web using diagrams and examples. They will learn:

❑ how the Internet is built up
❑ about the Web and about how hypertext works
❑ how to use the browser program and its main functions.

2 Getting on-line, using a browser to get an address, searching

In this lesson the pupils will need access to an online computer. They need to know how to get online, what their username and password are and how to start the browser. Then they should be given time to explore the browser. They need to know what the button row can do and how to enter an URL they want to visit. An initial unrestricted (but supervised) surf session can be useful.

Often pupils can already do the above or learn to do it very quickly. They may have more difficulty with searching. There are tips on teaching searching in chapter 5.

The main things here are to be able:

❑ to get to a given web address

❏   to follow links

❏   to search for information using suitable search tools.

3 E-mail and news

Your pupils may not have their own e-mail address. Opinions vary as to what age is appropriate for this kind of responsibility. Whether or not they have their own address, they can acquaint themselves with the e-mail program and send themselves a mail.

Newsgroups, as we have seen, are more of a problem. Many schools decide to dispense with news access altogether, preferring to steer their pupils to web-based forums. You might compromise by showing them how to read newsgroups from the Web via, for example, *Deja News*.

They need to learn:

❏   to use the e-mail program

❏   to write, send and receive e-mail

❏   to attach files to e-mail

❏   to join, participate in and leave a mailing list

❏   to read newsgroups, if available.

4 Netiquette, safe and responsible behaviour, conditions of acceptable use

This is a very important section of the course. You might like to collect examples of failed netiquette from your own surfing and mailing lists. You may need to go through what the pupils are allowed to do with the school computers, and what they may not do.

Pupils need to learn:

❏   about the written and unwritten rules of the Internet

❏   about the school computer policy

❏   to be aware that not everyone they meet has the same linguistic, cultural and social background as themselves.

5 Practising skills and directed work

At this stage pupils should be ready to go on their own, but may find it helpful to have the support of a tutor while becoming more familiar with what the Net has to offer. Activities such as a treasure hunt or web orienteering can be useful here. See chapter 5 for further details. Pupils may be keen to make their own web pages, and they can be encouraged to make simple pages with the web editor which comes with the browser, for example *FrontPage Express*.

Appendix 3
Making a web page

Making a simple web page need be no more difficult than writing a document in your favourite word processor. In fact you can even use your word processor if it is fairly new (e.g. Word 97 or later). But not everybody has access to a modern word processor, so we will show you how to make a page using FrontPage Express, the web editor which comes free with the free web browser Microsoft Internet Explorer. (Netscape's browser also has a free editor).

A web page will typically be made up of any or all of the following components:

❑ *Text*, with headline and subheadings where appropriate. You can choose any size, colour and font you please.

❑ *Pictures*: not too many or too big though, otherwise your page will take a long time to download for those on slow connections.

❑ *Links* so that you can send visitors on to other pages on your own or other sites.

❑ *Graphic enhancements*, such as a coloured and/or patterned background, buttons used as links and lines to divide off sections of the page.

Step 1: Planning your page(s)

Whether you are planning to publish an entire web site or a single page you will need to know what kind of effect you want to achieve. The Web is a visual medium and there are many ways to present the same information. If you want your page to link to other pages you will need to know the web addresses of those pages before you start (unless they are part of the same web site). You may have seen a page you admire, but try to keep your first efforts simple. It is easy to remove pages you have published, so don't be afraid to experiment. You can always start afresh.

One way to plan your page is to make a sketch of it on paper. Think about where you want to place headlines, pictures and text. Do you want a menu of other pages your visitors can choose to visit? If so, do you want a simple list of hypertext words or a row of buttons? What about colour? Do you want coloured text? A background colour or pattern? What kind of image do you want to project? Zany? Sober?

One of the most often used ways of controlling exactly where on the page the various elements are to be placed is to use a table. Then you can place text and pictures in the table cells. If you want you can let the leftmost column be a menu of links to other pages on the site.

⊘ Case study

Mary's new page design

Mary Smith is making a new front page for the English Department at her school. She wants a discreet page with easy-to read text. She does not want a background pattern, since that interferes with the page's legibility. It should have the title *St Eric's Secondary School English Department* and the heading *English Department*. She wants a bar with links to other pages describing the activities of the English Department. She decides to make the link bar by giving certain cells in the table she is using to place the elements of the page another background colour from that of the rest of the page. Mary wants some kind of picture off to the left of the page, and an e-mail link at the bottom. Above the picture she wants to have the school name as a link back to the school's main page.

Step 2: Graphics

It is fully possible to design your own backgrounds and other graphics in a program such as Paint (which comes along with Windows), but you will probably prefer to use ready-made graphics until you have made a few pages. You can choose a background colour in FrontPage Express, but if you want a background pattern, or other buttons or pictures, you will have to have an image file ready. There are freely available graphics called ClipArt which come along with certain programs such as Word and the full, commercial version of FrontPage. If you do not have access to any of these you can visit a web site which offers this kind of free graphical element (just search, for example, for *free button* in Yahoo! and you will find what you are looking for). Many of these buttons and images are animated, such as a twinkling star or a letterbox which opens and closes. We suggest that you make some pages without this kind of embellishment first, then you can choose the kind of graphics that suit the style of your page.

Right-click on the picture while the web page is in the browser and save the picture to use later.

Web pages often have pictures of some kind. You can **use pictures** from other web pages (if you have permission to do so), or pictures you have taken yourself with a digital camera, or printed pictures you have scanned in with a scanner, or computer-generated pictures from a ClipArt collection or a drawing program.

⊚ Case study

Putting in the graphics

Choose *New* from the *File* menu.

Choose *Background* from the *Format* menu.

Choose *Insert Table* from the *Table* menu.

Choose *Combine Cells* from the *Table* menu.

Mary **opens** a new FrontPage Express document and chooses a dark red **background** for the page. While she is in the background panel she also changes the text colour and the link colour to the same pale yellow, since the standard black text and blue links colour is not easy to read against the red background. Mary inserts a three-row by four-column **table** one line from the top of the document. She marks the leftmost column and makes it into a **single row**. She then marks the first and last rows in the rest of the table and combines each row into a single cell.

Mary has found a suitable ClipArt picture, which came along with another program. She inserts it into the prepared leftmost column of the table. It is a bit too big, so she clicks on the picture and takes hold of one of the corner handles which she then moves diagonally inwards until the picture is the size she wants.

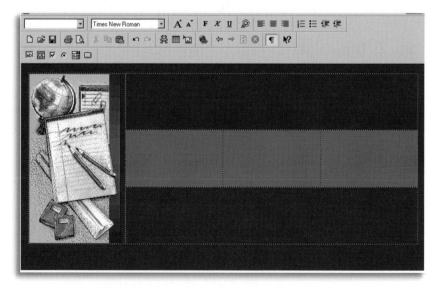

Tables in FrontPage Express

Choose *Cell*
Properties from
the *Table* menu.

Next Mary marks the middle row, which still has three columns, and gives it a dark turquoise **background**. This panel appears to be too wide, but it will be narrower when the page is viewed in a browser.

Step 3: Text

It is generally not a good idea to put a lot of closely written text on a web page. Many people find it tiring to read too much text from the screen. It can also be irritating to have to scroll down the screen if the page is very long. On the other hand, if your readers have a slow connection to the Internet, they may resent having to load in too many pages each with just a few lines on. Obviously you will have to use your judgement as to how much text you can have on your page, but as a rule of thumb a page should not be longer than one or two screens.

Most pages have a title and a main headline, which need not be the same, but often are. The headline should tell the visitor what the page is about, or whose page it is. Make sure your text is easy to read against the background you have chosen.

⊗ *Case study*

Choosing a font

Mary chooses an easy-to-read font (VAG Rounded) from the fonts available to her. She writes the headline and the text she wants in the top row of the table. She then adjusts the size of the text using the *Text Size* buttons at the top of the screen, and centres all the text using the *Centre* button. She writes the words that she will later make into links in the coloured panels she has prepared in the table. She then centres these words too. In the bottom row of the table she writes when the page was last updated (the day's date since the page is new) and her name. In the line above the table she writes the name of the school in the fancy font the school has chosen (Viner Hand ITC) as a kind of logotype.

Step 4: Hypertext

FrontPage Express will let you link to another web page in your own computer, another page that has been published, or an e-mail address. The two most important links on a page are the link back to the site's main page, which helps your visitors to find their way around, and the link to the e-mail address of the person behind the page. Web pages are an excellent way to meet people who share your interests.

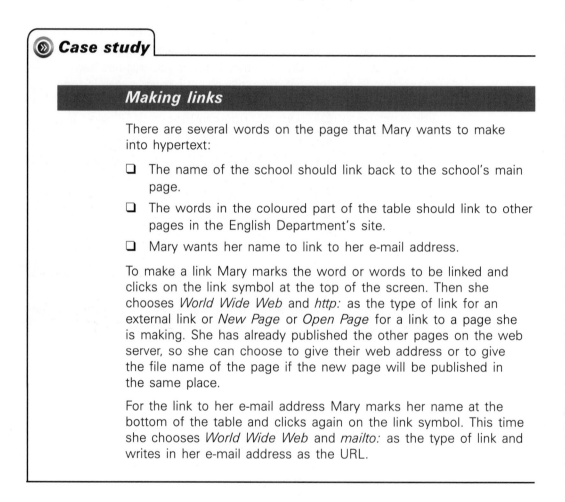

⊗ Case study

Making links

There are several words on the page that Mary wants to make into hypertext:

❑ The name of the school should link back to the school's main page.

❑ The words in the coloured part of the table should link to other pages in the English Department's site.

❑ Mary wants her name to link to her e-mail address.

To make a link Mary marks the word or words to be linked and clicks on the link symbol at the top of the screen. Then she chooses *World Wide Web* and *http:* as the type of link for an external link or *New Page* or *Open Page* for a link to a page she is making. She has already published the other pages on the web server, so she can choose to give their web address or to give the file name of the page if the new page will be published in the same place.

For the link to her e-mail address Mary marks her name at the bottom of the table and clicks again on the link symbol. This time she chooses *World Wide Web* and *mailto:* as the type of link and writes in her e-mail address as the URL.

Step 5: Test your page

When you are satisfied with your page you can save it and then open the page in your browser. It might not look the way you expected it to. Check all the links. If you go online you can even check the external links. Mary saves her page as *index.htm* since it is the main page in the subdirectory *english* on the web server.

⊗ *Case study*

In the browser

Mary is relieved to see that the coloured panel in the table is much narrower in the browser than it was in FrontPage Express. The links to the other site pages do not work since they are not in the same directory as the current page in Mary's computer (although they will be in the web server). The other links appear to work.

The English Department web page viewed in Explorer

Step 6: Publish your page

Exactly how and where you can publish your page will depend on the terms of your Internet connection. You will need to know the address of the web server you will be using, as well as your password. You should have got this information from your ISP.

It is possible to publish single pages using a web-publishing wizard function in FrontPage Express, but a much simpler method which lets you see what you are doing on the web server is to use a special FTP program (freely available from the Net or the cover CD of almost any computer magazine). You simply fill in the information about the web server's address and your password when presented with a form, and then the program will connect to the server. You can then freely copy files from your hard disk to the directory on the web server which you have been given access to. You can create subdirectories if you want to keep several sites separate or if you have a large hierarchically organised site. You can rename or delete files if you wish, or move them from one directory to another. You will need to copy the following files to the web server:

❏ The web page itself (which has a file name ending in *htm*). If your page is the entrance page to a site (and the main page in a subdirectory) it should be called *index.htm*.

❏ Any pictures you are including on the page. These should usually be in *gif* or *jpeg* format (i.e. have names ending in *.gif* or *.jpg*). FrontPage Express will have converted any other formats for you or refused to let you use the picture if it could not convert the format.

❏ Any other graphic files, such as a background pattern or any buttons, logotypes or symbols you are using.

After your files are in place you can visit them with your usual browser and check that everything works.

⊗ *Case study*

FTP

Mary has used the FTP program WS-FTP before. She starts the program and is greeted by a screen where she has previously entered the address of the web server and her user name and password. When she clicks on *OK* the program connects to the Internet in the usual way and then presents Mary with a screen with two windows. The left window shows files in her own computer and the right window shows the subdirectory *english*, which is the only one Mary has access to in the web server. Mary chooses the files she needs for her page and marks them in the left window, just the page itself, *index.htm*, and the picture file, which is called *school.gif*. She clicks on the right arrow between the windows to send a copy of the files to her directory. The old front page was also called *index.htm* so it is overwritten by the new page.

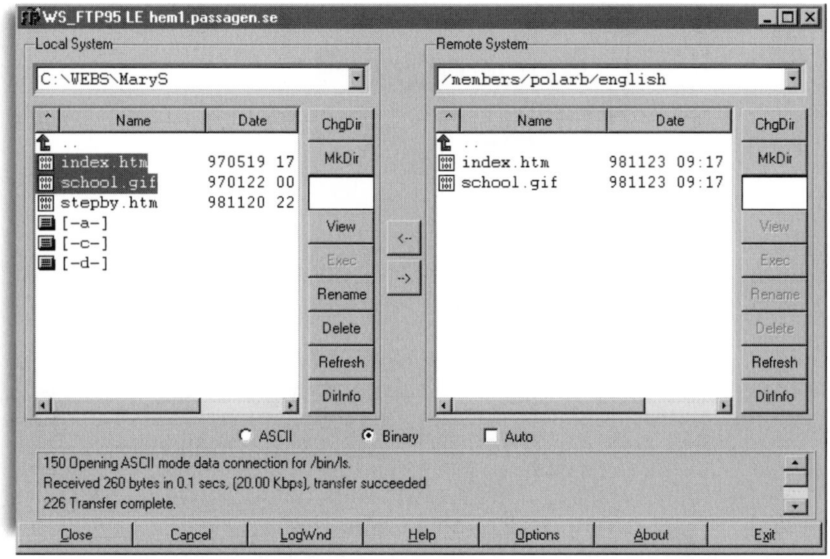

Publishing with FTP

Appendix 4
Links

10 Downing Street	http://www.number-10.gov.uk/public/home/homepage.html
18th Century Studies	http://english-www.hss.cmu.edu/18th/
Aberdare College	http://mhs.aberdare.ac.uk/F/F2-2.HTM
AfricaQuest	http://africaquest.classroom.com/
Alexa	http://www.alexa.com/
Algebra Online	http://www.algebra-online.com/
All Souls School, London	http://www.rmplc.co.uk/eduweb/sites/allsouls/index.html
AltaVista	http://www.altavista.com/
AncientSites	http://www.ancientsites.com/index.rage
Anglia Interactive	http://www.angliainteractive.com
AngliaCampus	http://www.angliacampus.com/
Anthony's Kites	http://www.sct.gu.edu.au/~anthony/kites/
AOL	http://www.aol.com/
Aquaterra Leisure Centres	http://www.ilc.co.uk/
Archaeology on the Net	http://www.serve.com/archaeology/
Artists for a better world	http://www.aestheticart.com/
ArtsEdNet	http://www.artsednet.getty.edu/
Ask an Ecologist (Sweden)	http://fisher.teorekol.lu.se/query_an_ecologist/
Ask an Ecologist (USA)	http://www.nceas.ucsb.edu/nceas-web/kids/center/ask.html
Associated Board of the Royal Schools of Music	http://www.abrsm.ac.uk/
Aussie SchoolHouse	http://www.ash.org.au/
Autodesk	http://www.autodesk.com/
AutoExpress	http://www.autoexpress.co.uk/
Ballad of an E-mail Terrorist	http://www.gsn.org/teach/articles/email.ballad.html
BBC Bitesize GCSE	http://www.bbc.co.uk/education/bitesize/Revisionaskteach.htm
BBC Education	http://www.bbc.co.uk/education/
BBC Education Modern History	http://www.bbc.co.uk/education/modern/mainmenu/mainfla.htm

BBC News	http://news.bbc.co.uk/
BBC Weather	http://www.bbc.co.uk/weather/
BECTa	http://www.becta.org.uk/
Beeb.com	http://www.beeb.com/
Bible Gateway	http://bible.gospelcom.net/
Biology Place	http://www.biology.com/
Birka	http://www.rashm.se/birka/eng/index.htm
Biz/ed	http://bized.ac.uk/
Boston Museum of Fine Arts	http://www.boston.com/mfa/
British Airways	http://www.british-airways.com/
British Beer and Real Ale Database	http://www.personal.u-net.com/~thepub/beers/ /
British Council	www.britcoun.org
British Monarchy	http://www.royal.gov.uk/
British Museum	http://www.british-museum.ac.uk
British School of Motoring	http://www.driving.co.uk/
BT Internet	http://guest.btinternet.com/
Budehaven School	http://www.budehaven.cornwall.sch.uk/intranet/departs/gnvq/gnvq.htm
Builder	http://www.builderonline.com/
Business Information Zone	http://www.thebiz.co.uk/default.htm
Busy Teacher	http://www.ceismc.gatech.edu/busyt/
Buzbee Bat House Temperature Plot	http://www.nyx.net/~jbuzbee/bat_house.html
Campaign for Real Ale	http://www.camra.org.uk/
CampusWorld	http://www.campus.bt.com/CampusWorld/
Canadian Schoolnet	http://www.schoolnet.ca/
Cannes Hoteliers Association	http://www.cannes-hotels.com/index.shtml
Catering UK	http://www.catering-uk.co.uk/catering-uk/
Chatback	http://www.rmplc.co.uk/eduweb/sites/chatback/index.html
Chemistry Animation Project	http://bond.caltech.edu/
Chemistry Place	http://www.chemplace.com/
Chemistry Teaching Resources	http://www.anachem.umu.se/eks/pointers.htm
Children's BBC	http://www.bbc.co.uk/cbbc/
CIA World Fact Book	http://www.odci.gov/cia/publications/factbook/index.html
City of York	http://www.york.gov.uk
Classical Music	http://www.classicalmusic.co.uk/
Classical Net	http://www.classical.net/
Classroom Connect	http://www.classroom.net/
Club Yahooligans	http://www.yahooligans.com/docs/club/index.html

CNN Weather   http://cnn.com/WEATHER/cities/europe.html
Coca-Cola   http://www.coca-cola.com/
Comberbach Swilltub   http://www.silverd.demon.co.uk/comberba.htm
  Mummers
Commission for Racial   http://www.open.gov.uk/cre/crehome.htm
  Equality
Computers Don't Bite: http://www.bbc.co.uk/education/cdb/teachers/
  Teachers
Conservative Party   http://www.conservative-party.org.uk/
Construction Materials   http://www.constructionmaterials.com/index.htm
Coollist   http://www.coollist.com/
Costumers' Guild UK   http://www.ireadh.demon.co.uk/cguk
Council of British   http://britac3.britac.ac.uk/cba/
  Archaeology
CoVis   http://www.covis.nwu.edu/
Culinary Resource Centre   http://www.culinary-resource.co.uk
Cyber Patrol   http://www.cyberpatrol.com/

Dead Romans   http://www.iei.net/~tryan/deadroma.htm
Deja News   http://www.dejanews.com/
Department of Health   http://www.doh.gov.uk/dhhome.htm
Department of the   http://www.detr.gov.uk/
  Environment
DETR   http://www.detr.gov.uk/
DfEE   http://www.dfee.gov.uk/
Dictionary of Measures,   http://www.ex.ac.uk/cimt/dictunit/dictunit.htm
  Units and Conversion
Direct Access Government   http://tap.ccta.gov.uk/dagii/welcome.nsf
Discovery   http://www.discovery.com/
Discovery Channel   http://www.discovery.com/online.html
Download.com   http://www.download.com/
Doyly Carte Opera Company   http://www.geocities.com/Broadway/Stage/
                                   4618/company.html
Dramatic Exchange   http://www.dramex.org/
Dramaturgical Resources   http://www.dramaturgy.net/dramaturgy/Resources.html

Eco-Source   http://www.podi.com/ecosource/
Education   http://vtc.ngfl.gov.uk/reference/edsi/
  Department's
  Superhighways
  Initiative
Edustock   http://tqd.advanced.org/3088/welcome/welcome.html
Eduweb   http://www.eduweb.co.uk/home.html
El Diario   http://www.eldiario.net/

Electronic Telegraph	http://www.telegraph.co.uk
Electronic Zoo	http://netvet.wustl.edu/e-zoo.htm
Engineering Council	http://www.engc.org.uk/mainpage.htm
English National Ballet	http://www.ballet.org.uk/
English Server	http://english-www.hss.cmu.edu/
Equal Opportunities Sites	http://www.bilston.ac.uk/bcc/resource/equal_op.htm
ERIC	http://www.accesseric.org:81/
Estonian Sustainable Development	http://www.agenda21.ee/pages/forestry.htm
Ethics Updates	http://ethics.acusd.edu/index.html
Eudora	http://www.eudora.com/
European Schoolnet	http://www.eun.org/
European Schools Technology Network	http://www.seelb-eurotecnet.demon.co.uk/
European Schools Project	http://www.esp.educ.uva.nl/
European Studies Programme	http://ireland.iol.ie/esp/
European Union	http://europa.eu.int/
Evaluweb	http://calvin.ptloma.edu/~spectre/evaluweb/
Excite	http://www.excite.co.uk/
Faith in Today's World	http://quis.qub.ac.uk/qubcu/
Forestry Commission	http://www.forestry.gov.uk
Four Seasons	http://www.4seasons.org.uk/
Fundamentals of Microbiology 101	http://www.wsu.edu:8080/~hurlbert/pages/101hmpg.html
Giant's Causeway	http://www.infosites.net/tourism/topten/causeway.html
Gilbert and Sullivan Archive	http://diamond.idbsu.edu/GaS/GaS.html
Global SchoolHouse	http://www.gsh.org/
Global SchoolNet	http://www.gsn.org/
Government Information Service	http://www.open.gov.uk/
Granges Building Systems	http://www.granges.co.uk/
Greek Mythology	http://www.maicar.com/
Green Party	http://www.greenparty.org.uk/
Guardian	http://www.guardian.co.uk/
Guildford Cathedral Choir	http://www.peterson.demon.nl/gcc.html
Hackney Agenda 21	http://www.hackney.gov.uk/agenda21/contents.htm
Hammersmith and West London College	http://www.hwlc.ac.uk/college/learnr/randtrade/rdu3rsf.htm
Headbone Zone	http://www.headbone.com/
Health Centre	http://www.healthcentre.org.uk/

HealthIndex UK	http://www.healthindex.co.uk/
Healthline	http://www.healthline.com/
Hell's Buddhas	http://www.hellsbuddhas.com/
Hellenic Ministry of Culture	http://www.culture.gr/home/welcome.html
Homebuilding and Renovating Magazine	http://www.ihomes.co.uk/
Horus' Web Links to History Resources	http://www.ucr.edu/h-gig/welcome.html
Hotelier	http://www.hotelier.co.uk/
Houses of Parliament	http://www.parliament.uk/
I*M Europe	http://www.echo.lu/
Ideal Electrical Supplies	http://www.idealelectrical.co.uk/
IKEA	http://www.ikea.com/
Infoseek	http://www.infoseek.co.uk/
Institute of Brewers	http://www.breworld.com/iob/
Institute of Plumbers	http://www.plumbers.org.uk/
Interactive Frog Dissection	http://curry.edschool.virginia.edu/go/frog/
International Committee of the Red Cross	http://www.icrc.ch
International Internet Encyclopedia of the First World War	http://www.spartacus.schoolnet.co.uk/FWW.htm
International Song-Writers Association	http://www.songwriter.co.uk/
Internet Classics Archive	http://classics.mit.edu/index.html
Internet Movie Database	http://www.imdb.com/
Internet Poetry Archive	http://metalab.unc.edu/ipa/
Irish Education Web	http://kola.dcu.ie/~iednet/welcome.htm
Islam 101	http://www.islam101.com/
JASON	http://www.jason.org/
Jorvik Viking Centre	http://www.jorvik-viking-centre.co.uk/
Jumbo.com	http://www.jumbo.com/
Kidlink	http://www.kidlink.org/
Labour Party	http://www.labour.org.uk/
Leith's School of Food and Wine	http://www.leiths.co.uk/
Liberal Democrats	http://www.libdems.org.uk/
List of Lists	http://catalog.com/vivian/interest-group-search.html
Liszt Search	http://www.liszt.com
Liverpool Playhouse	http://www.playhouse.org/first.html

Louvre	http://mistral.culture.fr/louvre/
Madame Tussaud's	http://www.a-london-guide.co.uk/beta/ attractions/madamet.html
Mailbase	http://www.mailbase.ac.uk/
MapQuest	http://www.mapquest.com/
MathDEN	http://www.actden.com/
Maths Online	http://www.univie.ac.at/future.media/moe/galerie.html
MathsNet	http://www.anglia.co.uk/education/mathsnet/intro.html
McDonald's	http://www.mcdonalds.com/
Memories	http://www.rmplc.co.uk/eduweb/sites/chatback/ memories.html
Mercedes Benz	http://www.mercedes-benz.co.uk/
Meteosat Images	http://www.nottingham.ac.uk/meteosat/
Michael Jackson	http://www.histeria.com/
Microsoft	http://www.eu.microsoft.com/uk/
Microsoft Education	http://www.microsoft.com/uk/education
Microsoft Games	http://zone.msn.com/msn_home.asp
Microsoft Homework help	news://publicnews.msn.com/msn.uk. education.homeworkhelp
Microsoft Kids	http://msn.co.uk/
Mirabilis	http://www.mirabilis.com
mIRC	http://www.mirc.com/
Modern English Collection	http://etext.lib.virginia.edu/modeng/ modeng0.browse.html
Moray Council Agenda 21	http://www.moray.org/agenda21/
MPs	http://www.parliament.uk/commons/lib/almsad.htm
MUD (Yahoo!)	http://www.yahoo.co.uk/Recreation/Games/ Internet_Games/MUDs__MUSHes__MOOs__etc_/
Musical Stages Online	http://members.aol.com/spiper007/ MusicalStages/mshome.htm
NASA	http://www.nasa.gov/
NASA Moonlink	http://www.moonlink.com/
NASA Spacelink	http://spacelink.nasa.gov/
National Grid Company	http://www.ngc.co.uk/
National Health Service	http://www.nhs50.nhs.uk/home.htm
Natural History Museum	http://www.nhm.ac.uk/
Net Nanny	http://www.netnanny.com/
Net Shepherd	http://www.netshepherd.com/
Netherton and Litherland Now	http://fox.rmplc.co.uk/eduweb/sites/medproj/ indexL.html
Netscape	http://www.netscape.com/uk/
NGfL	http://www.ngfl.gov.uk/

NickNacks	http://www1.minn.net/~schubert/NickNacks.html
Nine Planets	http://www.seds.org/billa/tnp/
Northern Ireland Tourist Board	http://www.ni-tourism.com/index.asp
Northern Lights	http://www.northernlight.co.uk/
Nottingham Forest	http://www.nottinghamforest.co.uk/team/ registed.htm
Open.gov	http://www.open.gov.uk/
OperaData	http://www.operadata.co.uk/
Parental Controls	http://www.aol.com/info/parentcontrol.html
Parish Church of St Mary the Virgin	http://www.parish.oaktree.co.uk/pageb.htm
Pathfinder	http://www.pathfinder.com/travel/
PE Central	http://pe.central.vt.edu/
Philharmonia Orchestra	http://www.philharmonia.co.uk/
Plumbers.uk	http://www.plumbers.uk.com/
Poets in Person	http://www.wilmington.org/poets/
Pompeii Forum Project	http://jefferson.village.virginia.edu/pompeii/page-1.html
Pond Hill Farm	http://www.pondhill.com/phf/home.htm
Power and the Glory	http://schoolsite.edex.net.uk/323/stem.html
Project Gutenberg	http://www.prairienet.org/pg/pg_home.html
Projects and Investigations in Math	http://www.cs.uidaho.edu/~casey931/ nc_math/index.html
Psychology Place	http://www.psychplace.com/
RCHME	http://www.rchme.gov.uk/
Redland Roofing Systems	http://www.redlandroof.co.uk/
Redland Tile and Brick	http://www.redland-tile-brick.co.uk/index.html
RM	http://www.rmplc.net/
Robot Science and Technology	http://www.robotmag.com
ROMARCH	http://www.sys.uea.ac.uk/Research/ researchareas/JWMP/ostia/brit.html
Royal Opera House	http://www.royalopera.org/
Runeberg	http://www.lysator.liu.se/runeberg/
Sainsbury's	http://www.sainsburys.co.uk/
Science Online	http://www.shu.ac.uk/schools/sci/sol/ contents.htm
Science Quest	http://library.advanced.org/3542/main1.html
Scottish Conservative and Unionist Party	http://www.conservative-party.org.uk/scottish/
Scottish Liberal Democrats	http://www.scotlibdems.org.uk/
Scottish National Party	http://www.snp.org.uk/

Scotty's Center for Technology Education	http://www.igs.net/~mascott/
Script Portfolios	http://www.playwrightsworkshop.org/portfolio.html
SDLP	http://www.indigo.ie/sdlp/
Shadow Lego Hand	http://www.shadow.org.uk/projectsPast/hand.stm
Shakespeare resources on the Internet	http://daphne.palomar.edu/shakespeare/
	http://www.rdg.ac.uk./globe/Links.html
Shareware.com	http://www.shareware.com/
Smithsonian	http://www.si.edu/
St David's Parish Church	http://ourworld.compuserve.com/homepages/ Howard_Taylor/
Stena Line	http://www.stenaline.com/
SurfWatch	http://www1.surfwatch.com/
Teacher Grid UK	http://www.vtcentre.com/index.html
Teachers Helping Teachers	http://www.pacificnet.net/~mandel/
Teachers, Pupils and the Internet	http://www.thornes.co.uk/internet_add
Teaching and Learning with the Internet	http://www.campus.bt.com/CampusWorld/ services/databases/Teachandlearn/index.html
Technology Education Lab	http://www.techedlab.com/
Technology Index	http://www.technologyindex.com/
Technology Resource Center	http://www.boff1.demon.co.uk/
Tesco	http://www.tesco.co.uk
THAIS	http://www.thais.it
Theatre Royal, Bath	http://www.rcs1.demon.co.uk/trb/trbhome.htm
ThinkQuest	http://www.advanced.org/thinkquest/
Thomson Holidays	http://www.thomson-holidays.com/
Tile Net	http://www.tile.net
Time for Kids	http://www.pathfinder.com/TFK/
Times	http://www.the-times.co.uk
Top Gear Magazine	http://www.topgear.com/
UK Agriculture Internet Resources	http://www.agriworld.net/uk-agriculture/
UK schools forum	http://members.aol.com/uksforum/ uk-schools/international/
UK Theatre Web	http://www.uktw.co.uk/main.html
UKplus	http://uk.infoseek.com/dynamic/index.html
Ulster Unionist Party	http://www.uup.org/
Understanding Earthquakes	http://www.crustal.ucsb.edu/ics/ understanding/
United States Holocaust Memorial Museum	http://www.ushmm.org/

University of Exeter Centre for Innovation in Mathematics Teaching	http://www.ex.ac.uk/cimt/games/gameindx.htm
University of Virginia Electronic Text Center	http://etext.lib.virginia.edu/
University of Wisconsin	http://www.wsu.edu/
Viking Project	http://viking.no/
Virtual Body	http://www.medtropolis.com/vbody/
Virtual Factory	http://bized.ac.uk/virtual/cb/
Virtual Teachers Centre	http://vtc.ngfl.gov.uk/vtc/
Virtuous Reality	http://www-ipg.umds.ac.uk/~crr/ virtuous-reality/home3.htm
Visible Embryo	http://www.visembryo.com/
Volcano World	http://volcano.und.edu
Volvo	http://www.volvocars.volvo.co.uk/
Ward Freman School	http://members.aol.com/wardfreman/
Web66	http://web66.coled.umn.edu/
WebWhacker	http://www.bluesquirrel.com/whacker/
West Virginia prison project	http://168.216.210.13/mjhs/pproject/pproject.htm
White House	http://www.whitehouse.gov/
WhoWhere?	http://www.whowhere.lycos.com/
Why Files	http://whyfiles.news.wisc.edu
Wiggonholt	http://freespace.virgin.net/alex.holmes/ Wiggon.htm
World Health Organisation	http://www.who.org/
World Heritage Sites	http://www.unesco.org/whc/
World Magazine Online	http://www.nationalgeographic.com/media/world
World Plumbing Council	http://www.worldplumbing.org/
WorldWide Nurse	http://www.wwnurse.com/
Xpedition Hall	http://www.nationalgeographic.com/xpeditions/
Yahoo!	http://www.yahoo.co.uk/
Yahoo! Accommodation	http://www.yahoo.co.uk/travel/accommodation/
Yahoo! Games	http://games.yahoo.com/
Yahoo! Movies	http://movies.yahoo.com/movies/
Yahoo! Weather	http://weather.yahoo.co.uk/
Yahooligans!	http://www.yahooligans.com/
Young Enterprise	http://www.young-enterprise.org.uk

Glossary

Acceptable Use Policy (AUP)
an agreement between, for example, a school and its pupils to regulate the use of the Internet

account
An Internet account is an arrangement whereby subscribers pay an ISP for access to the Internet.

address book
Many e-mail programs will let users save the e-mail addresses they use regularly in an address book.

ARPANET
the military network from which the Internet developed

attached file
a file that is sent along with an e-mail message

bandwidth
the range of frequencies used to transmit data, which is reflected in the amount of data which can be sent or received every second through a connection

bps
bits per second, a measure of how fast data is transferred, e.g. via a modem

BECTa
British Educational Communications and Technology Agency, formerly NCET (the National Council for Educational Technology)

beta version
a test version of a program, released to the public to let the
developers see how the program works on different kinds of computers

bookmarks
a list of addresses of sites or pages that the user wants to be able to find again. Netscape uses the term 'bookmark' but Microsoft Internet Explorer uses the term 'favorites'.

browser
a program used to view web pages, e.g. Netscape and Microsoft Internet Explorer

cache
temporary memory used to store web pages so that they can be reloaded quickly from the memory instead of from the Internet

CD-ROM
Compact Disc – Read Only Memory, a disc on which programs and/or data can be stored and distributed

channel
a special kind of web site which is automatically updated and available for offline browsing. In Internet Relay Chat (IRC) a channel is one of thousands of virtual room, where a single discussion is going on.

cheat codes
can be used in adventure games, for example to make a player invisible or immortal. They are readily available from enthusiasts' web pages.

client
a program that communicates with a server

compression
makes files smaller by removing unnecessary information

computer-mediated conferences
mailing lists or noticeboard-type web discussions

crash
A computer which crashes stops working and will need to be restarted. Valuable data can be lost in a crash.

cursor
usually an arrow or other symbol on the screen showing the point reached. In web browsers, when the cursor moves over a hyperlink it usually changes into a hand.

cyberspace
the imaginary (virtual) place where Internet activity takes place

demo
a demonstration version of a program

domain names
registered names which refer to an individual's or company's address on the Web

download
To download a file is to copy it from one computer to another,
e.g. from the Internet to the user's own computer.

electronic mail (e-mail)
electronic messages sent from one computer to another

favorites
see bookmarks

FAQ
a list of Frequently Asked Questions and answers to them. The idea is that newcomers to a newsgroup, mailing list or web site should read the FAQ rather than asking the same basic questions.

firewall
protects an intranet from intruders from the Internet while allowing specified traffic access to and from the Internet

flame
a personal attack on an individual in the course of an Internet discussion

flame-war
an Internet discussion that turns nasty and gets personal

freeware
programs which can be copied and shared at no cost

FTP

File Transfer Protocol, a protocol which lets different types of computers exchange files

FTP site

a directory on an FTP server connected to the Internet. Files can be downloaded using a web browser.

GIF

Graphics Interchange Format, a graphics file format often used on web pages

home page

either the web page shown by a browser when it is started up or the main page in a web site

HTML

Hypertext Mark-up Language, the formatting language used by web editors to construct HTML documents. When a browser interprets the HTML document it shows it as a web page.

HTTP

Hypertext Transfer Protocol, the protocol used to send web pages from web servers to users' clients (web browsers)

hypertext

a (usually marked) word or phrase which users can click on to be shown another document

ICQ

'I seek you', a handy little program which lets users chat with other registered users

ICT

Information and Communications Technology. The term ICT is generally used to refer to computers and their use. ICT has almost completely replaced the term IT to better reflect the role of both information and communication in the new technologies.

Internet

a global network of computers which can communicate with each other

intranet

an internal network of computers (within a school or a company) which can communicate with each other, e.g. via e-mail or web pages

IRC

Internet Relay Chat, a part of the Internet where real-time written conversations take place in thousands of separate channels

ISDN

Integrated Services Digital Network, a system for sending any kind of data over the telephone network more quickly than with ordinary telephone wires

ISP

Internet Service Provider, a company which sells access to the Internet and other services

IT

Information Technology. This term, generally used to refer to computers and their use, has almost completely been replaced by the term ICT.

Java

a programming language used, among other things, for programs which are started from within a web page

LAN

Local Area Network, a network of computers within a building or school

left-clicking

pressing the left mouse button while the cursor is pointing to the link on the screen

links

web addresses or e-mail addresses associated with text or images in a web page

list

see mailing list

list server

a program which administers a mailing list. Every time a message is posted to the list, the list server sends a copy of the message to all the subscribers.

mailing list

a group discussion via e-mail

Mb

megabyte, a measure of the amount of data or data storage available, e.g. on a diskette or computer memory

modem

a device which allows computers to communicate via the telephone system

modem pool

a group of modems connected to an ISP's server

MUCK, MUD, MUSH (etc.)

Multi-User Character Kingdom, Multi-User Dungeon, Multi-User Shared Hallucination (etc.), text-based role-play games or conversations in a virtual (imaginary) setting, often accessed via TELNET

Net

When written with a capital N, Net is another name for the Internet. Otherwise it can be used to refer to a computer network.

netiquette

Net etiquette or netiquette is the way to behave when interacting with others on the Internet. There have been attempts to define netiquette as a set of written rules.

network

a system of computers and programs which are connected to each other

newbie

a person who is new to the Net

newsgroup

one of thousands of open discussion forums on set topics in an area of the Internet known as USENET

newsreader

a program for reading and posting contributions (posts) to a USENET newsgroup

news server

a program which relays the latest contributions to news groups to computers elsewhere on the Net when requested to do so by a newsreader program

NGfL

National Grid for Learning, a large-scale government scheme to encourage schools to adopt the new technologies. The aim is to
give all British schools access to the Internet and to establish a series of web sites on the Internet which guide schools to useful material.

offline

A computer that is not connected to a computer network can be said to be offline.

online

A computer that is connected to a computer network, e.g. by modem, can be said to be online.

PICS

Platform for Internet Content Selection, a method for classifying the contents of web pages

post

a contribution to a USENET newsgroup or a mailing list

protocol

Protocols control the format and timing of the exchange of
information between systems on a network.

RAM

Random Access Memory, the internal memory a computer uses while working. The contents of RAM are lost when the computer is switched off.

robot

Search engines have robots which make automatic visits to all web pages they can access. The robot stores the words of the page in the search engine's massive database for later retrieval by a searcher.

screen savers

programs which start up when the computer has not been used for a specified time. They put a moving picture on the screen to avoid damage.

search engine

a program, e.g. Alta Vista or Excite, which scans the Web, organising words which occur on web pages into a database for later retrieval by users

server

a computer that provides files to other computers, for example in a computer network. A web server provides web pages to computers accessed by individual users; a mail server makes sure that e-mail reaches the right address.

shareware

programs that can be copied freely, and used for a test period. Longer use involves paying the programmer a small sum for the program.

site
a group of associated web pages, usually on a single computer

subscribe
A site that a user subscribes to will be updated as often as they specify and be available for offline browsing.

surfing
moving via links from one web page to another, especially with no particular aim

SVGA
Super Video Graphics Array, a standard system for colour display on computer screens

TELNET
a primitive way of communicating directly with another computer that is connected to the Internet

thread
a discussion thread is all the contributions to a newsgroup or mailing list discussion on a single subject

topic
Contributions to a discussion are either on-topic (relevant to the forum's general topic) or off-topic (a sidetrack).

upload
to copy a file to another computer, for example when publishing a web page

URL
Uniform Resource Locator. A web address is an example of an URL.

USENET
a part of the Internet occupied by over 70 000 discussion groups (newsgroups)

video conferences
a communication system whereby two or more people can communicate using sound and images. Video conferences can be arranged by a direct video link or via the Internet.

virus
a computer virus is a computer program that spreads by copying itself to other computer programs. A computer can be infected via diskettes from other computers or by downloading a virus attached to, for example, a shareware program from the Internet. A virus may destroy files on the computer it infects.

virus protection program
a program that detects when a computer has been infected by a virus, removes the virus and repairs the damage caused by it

VTC
Virtual Teachers Centre, part of the NGfL web site

web
(World Wide Web, WWW) The part of the Internet which supports web pages.

web communities
web sites offering contact and activities (financed by advertising). They aim to be chosen as users' start page and thus attract so many visitors that they can charge high fees for advertising space.

web page

an HTML document as displayed by a browser. A web page can contain text and pictures and will generally have links to other pages.

webchats

live two-way communication via a web page

Index

Index